A SHORT HISTORY OF
AUSTRALIA

A SHORT HISTORY OF
AUSTRALIA

Illustrated Edition

MANNING CLARK

PENGUIN BOOKS

For Sebastian and Elizabeth
and in memory of Katy Clark

By the same author
Select Documents in Australian History 1788-1850
Select Documents in Australian History 1851-1900
A History of Australia, volumes I-VI
In Search of Henry Lawson
Occasional Writings and Speeches
Collected Short Stories
The Puzzles of Childhood
The Quest for Grace

Penguin Books Australia Ltd
487 Maroondah Highway, PO Box 257
Ringwood, Victoria 3134, Australia
Penguin Books Ltd
Harmondsworth, Middlesex, England
Viking Penguin, A Division of Penguin Books USA Inc.
375 Hudson Street, New York, New York 10014, USA
Penguin Books Canada Limited
10 Alcorn Avenue, Toronto, Ontario, Canada M4V IE4
Penguin Books (N.Z.) Ltd
182-190 Wairau Road, Auckland 10, New Zealand

First published 1963
This revised illustrated edition published by Penguin Books Australia, 1986
10 9 8 7 6 5 4 3 2 1

Designed by Barbara Beckett
Typeset in Australia by Meredith Trade Lino
Made and printed in Singapore by
Kyodo Printing Co (S'pore) Pty Ltd

National Library of Australia
Cataloguing-in-Publication data:
Clark, Manning, 1915-1991
A short history of Australia.
Rev. illustrated ed.
Bibliography.
Includes index.
ISBN 0 14 016689 0
1. Australia – History. I. Title
994

Cover photo supplied by Dymphna Clark.
All reasonable attempts have been made to contact the owner of the photograph; any reasonable claim will be honoured in good faith.

Pages 2 and 3: When a French ship put in to Sydney in 1802, an artist on board, Charles Lesueur, recorded this view.

CONTENTS

Praise life while you walk and wake;
It is only lent.
> — David Campbell, 'The Return of Jason'

Out of the past and the books we must have
learned something.
> — Judith Wright, 'Winter'.

AUTHOR'S NOTE

I am very pleased that at long last *A Short History of Australia* is being published by Penguin.

The text now covers the period up to 1986 – two hundred years after the British Government decided to transport the convicts to Botany Bay. Some alterations have been made in the text, and some corrections have been made.

I would like to thank Roslyn Russell, Dymphna Clark, Don Baker, Ian Hancock, Humphrey McQueen, and Pat Dobrez for help and support in a difficult time.

Manning Clark
31 March 1986

Sidney Nolan's painting 'Burning at Glenrowan', from his Ned Kelly series.

CHAPTER ONE

THE COMING OF THE ABORIGINE AND THE WHITE MAN

SO FAR there have been two cultures in Australia—one Aboriginal and the other European. Like the Americas, Australia was probably first colonized by *homo sapiens*, as distinct from his antecedents, during the last ice age. Carbon tests have established the presence of such a man on the mainland of Australia thirty thousand years ago. The same tests have shown that a physically modern man probably was not active in Tasmania until much later.

The reason for this is simple. At the time when the Aborigines first colonized Australia, there was probably an ice barrier—which effectively barred human occupation—across the south-eastern part of the continent where the Snowy Mountains now stand. During the passage of time between the coming of the Aborigine just about thirty thousand years ago and the coming of the white man in 1788, the changes in the appearance of Australia were caused probably more by changes in climate than by human activity. For apart from fire, the stone implements he used for hunting and food gathering, and the rock paintings on which he portrayed his vision of the world, the Aborigine handed on to posterity few other memorials of his encounter with the weird and harsh land his people had occupied since time immemorial.

Some time in the last ice age there was a revolution in climate during which the ice receded from the southern part of the continent, thus making possible man's colonization of the islands in Bass Strait and Tasmania. Those who survived the revolution in climate developed a culture but not a civilization of their own. Their numbers remained few: on the mainland there were approximately three hundred thousand, and in Tasmania between four and seven thousand. While the inhabitants of most of Asia and of the islands from Sumatra to the Moluccas and Timor gradually progressed from barbarism to civilization, the Aborigines retained their primitive Stone Age culture.

The absence of suitable seed-bearing plants and animals suitable for domestication probably were the main causes of this changelessness, though their cosmology also contributed to it. So they lacked the material strength to resist an invader.

Not that they were called upon to defend themselves. As other peoples made the transition from barbarism to civilization, chance protected the Aborigines from such an invader. By the second millennium BC, people who had made the step forward to civilization began to migrate towards the continent. The Malays began their first invasion of the Indonesian Archipelago probably two thousand years before the birth of Christ, but they did not reach Australia. In the first century of the Christian era the Hindu-Buddhist people from southern India began to colonize the islands of Indonesia in search of gold, spices, and converts to their religion. Their expansion farther east or south

Captain Arthur Phillip, Captain-General and Governor-in-Chief of New South Wales from 1788 to 1792. Among the instructions he received was to cultivate the affections of the Aborigines and to encourage amity and kindness between them and the Europeans.

'They may appear to some to be the most wretched people upon the earth; but in reality they are far happier than we Europeans,' wrote Captain James Cook of the Aborigines he encountered during his voyages.

of Lombok was arrested, not by the absence of any incentive, but by the crisis in the mother country caused by the Muslims, who invaded northern India in the fifteenth century and destroyed the Hindu states in Indonesia during the fifteenth and sixteenth centuries. Similar causes interrupted Chinese settlement of the islands, which began in the ninth century. By the early fifteenth century Chinese were trading with Sumatra, Java, Timor, and Macassar in the Celebes. The Chinese interest in the trepang and the bird of paradise, which commanded high prices in Peking, had caused them to use the Bugis seamen from Macassar as carriers. The exhaustion of the trepang fishing-beds close to Macassar sent the Bugis in time as far afield as the northern coast of Australia, to which they gave the name Marega, or 'land of the trepang'.

In 1432 a palace revolution in Peking brought to power a group opposed to foreign trade and discovery. This ended Chinese expansion in the South Seas till the nineteenth century. For a time Muslim merchants from the western coast of India and from the Persian port of Ormuz inherited the trade—and with it the role of civilizer formerly exercised by the Hindu and the Chinese—till their expansion to the east and the unknown south was halted by the arrival of the European at the beginning of the sixteenth century.

In this way the expansion of all three—Hindu, Chinese, and Muslim—petered out just as they came to that invisible line on the map between Timor and the Moluccas where civilization ended and barbarism began. So chance probably prevented the coming of civilization to Australia two or three centuries before the arrival of the European. The history of Asian colonization in the area, however, influenced the European. The Hindus invented the story of islands of gold to the south and east of Java; it was while searching for these islands of gold that the European bumped into the north coast of Australia. The material weakness of the Hindu, Chinese, and Muslim kingdoms in Indonesia made possible the coming of the European. All three invented stories to deter their seamen from sailing into the unknown seas to the south and south-east of Java because their ships, their navigation instruments and their ideas on the shape of the world confined their sailors to the role of coast-huggers. Improvements in shipbuilding, aids to navigation and cartography at the end of the fifteenth and the beginning of the sixteenth centuries enabled the European to scoff at such stories as the products of superstition, ignorance, and material weakness. While the Hindu had been deterred by the fear of being sucked into the maelstrom of Pausengi, the Chinese by stories of the kingdom of women and great holes in the ocean, and the Muslims by reports of the kingdom of anti-Christ, the European was driven on by an overwhelming confidence in his powers as well as the same greed for material gain and the same religious zeal that had motivated the Hindu, the Chinese and the Muslim.

Like the Asian, the European was attracted by the wealth of the Spice Islands, as well as by that promise of 'infinite merit' for those who converted infidels and pagans to the true religion. From the beginning, too, the European was influenced by the hope of finding the unknown southland that beguiled geographers and seamen from the time of the Greeks until the eighteenth century, with a brief interval during the early Christian period when the apologists for the church took their ideas on the shape of the earth from the accounts in the Old Testament. But the wealth of the Spice Islands was the substance beside which ideas of unknown southlands were but pale shadows. By 1520 the European had discovered two sea routes to this wealth of the east: the first was by the west coast of Africa, around the Cape of Good Hope, up the east coast of Africa to Malindi, east to the Gujarati coast of India, and then to Malacca, Jakarta and the Spice Islands; the second, which was discovered by Magellan and del Cano in their immortal voyage of 1519-21, was across the Atlantic, down the east coast of South America, through the Straits of Magellan, and then by the northern route across the Pacific to the Philippines or the Spice Islands. All those who searched for the unknown southland by attempting to sail west after passing through the Straits of Magellan were driven north by the great swell of the South Seas, prevailing winds, and the absence of islands. So fate, or the nature of things, preserved the east coast of Australia from both the ravages and the gifts of a conqueror for more than two hundred and fifty years after Magellan's black eyes wept when his ship, the *Vittoria*, first swept on to the Pacific.

From 1515 to 1607 the sailors of Catholic Christendom searched spasmodically for the mythical islands of gold to the south or east of Java, and for the unknown southland. The Portuguese sent expeditions from Malacca, Jakarta and the Moluccas in the course of which, according to their national historians, they discovered Australia. But despite the proud boast of the poet Camoens that, if there had been other lands in that area, the Portuguese would have discovered them, there is no conclusive evidence that their sailors saw any part of the Australian coast. In the second half of the sixteenth century several Spaniards in New Spain, spurred by dreams of gold and the missionary high-mindedness that was the finest flower of the Catholic reformation in Spain, dispatched expeditions from Callao, Peru, to search for the unknown southland. Mendaña sailed in 1567 and again in 1595. Quiros, with Torres as his second in command, sailed in 1606 as far as the New Hebrides. From there

Torres sailed for Manila via the Moluccas and passed through the strait that bears his name, but in his letter describing the voyage he made no reference to seeing land to the south. From the people on the south-western coast of New Guinea, who were Mohammedans, he heard that Dutch ships had sailed into the strait. So in 1607 Mohammedans, Catholics and Protestants had come to the northern gateway to Australia. It was, however, the limit of Mohammedan expansion and the limit, at least temporarily, of the Catholic contribution to the quest for the unknown southland. Though their ultimate goal had eluded them, the ideals that had inspired them probably influenced their remotest posterity. In their zeal to stamp out the 'horrid sect of Mafomade' the Portuguese committed actions that gave the Europeans a reputation for perfidy, barbarity and cruelty with the inhabitants of the islands of Indonesia. Quiros, with his ideal of a land dedicated to the Holy Spirit, showed that not all those who were driven to search for a southland were the servants of Mammon. So in time some of the inhabitants of that land looked to him for spiritual comfort and refreshment in an otherwise materialist age. But in the early seventeenth century it looked as though the future of civilization in the South Seas lay with the Protestants.

Like the Portuguese and the Spaniards, the Dutch searched the South Seas for the islands of gold and the unknown southland. The first Dutch ship had arrived in Jakarta in 1596. In 1606 Captain Willem Jansz in the ship *Duyfken* sailed east from Banda to look for the islands of gold, passed along the south coast of New Guinea and across Torres Strait until he reached the west coast of Cape York Peninsula at Cape Keer-weer, and then returned, finding, as a later account put it, that 'there was no good to be done there!' It was probably the first description by a European of his attitude towards Australia. Seventeen years later, in 1623, Dutch seamen again sailed into the Gulf of Carpentaria in search of uncommonly large profits in gold, spices and souls for their Calvinist Jehovah, but found to their chagrin a land of exceedingly black barbarian savages.

In the meantime Dutch sailors had also bumped into the west coast of the continent. While following the new sailing directions for ships on the voyage from the Cape of Good Hope to Java in 1616, Dirk Hartog came on an island off the entrance to Shark's Bay on the west coast of Australia. Between 1616 and 1640 other Dutch sailors touched on parts of the same west coast. One of them, Peter Nuyts, was blown so far off course that he reached the islands of Peter and Paul, at the eastern end of the Great Australian Bight. In 1642 the council of the Dutch East India Company decided that the time was ripe for the discovery of the remaining unknown part of the terrestrial globe situated in the south, especially since they believed that it contained many fertile regions, many rich mines of metals, and other treasures.

As commander of the expedition they chose Abel Tasman, a seasoned seaman in the service of the company, who was not endowed by nature with the talents to fulfil tasks that were probably beyond the reach of even the giants of this world. The company wanted many things, and they wanted them in a hurry. Tasman made two voyages, in 1642-43 and 1644. On the first he discovered what is known now as Tasmania, which he named Van Diemen's Land, and the west coasts of the two islands of New Zealand, which he named Staten Landt. On the second he charted the coast of Australia from Cape York Peninsula west to Willem's River in the centre of the west coast. By the end of Tasman's voyages, then, the Dutch had charts of the coast of Australia from Cape York west and south to the east end of the Great Australian Bight and the southern part of Tasmania. They had hoped to hit upon some silver or gold mines to the solace of the general shareholders and the signal honour of

the first discoverers, but had instead met with naked, beach-roving wretches, destitute of rice, excessively poor, and of a very malignant nature. 'He who makes it his business to find out what the land produces, must walk over it.' Or so the members of the council in Batavia thought in 1644, for it could hardly be supposed, they argued, that no profit of any kind should be obtainable in so vast a country. But that discovery they were prepared to leave to others, while they, impatient as ever for 'uncommonly large profit', began to look elsewhere for a land with some rich mines.

Forty years later, an English vagabond with a perceptive eye and a warm heart, William Dampier, anchored his ship at Shark's Bay. Like the Dutch, he recoiled in horror. The land was dry, sandy and destitute of water, and there were no trees that bore fruit or berries. As for the inhabitants, they were 'the miserablest people in the world', because 'setting aside their humane shape, they differ but little from brutes'. Dampier made these observations after his first voyage in 1688 and after his return visit to the west coast in 1698. He popularized his views of New Holland and the Aborigines in his books, which influenced English literature on primitive people in the South Seas until the myth of the noble savage in the second half of the eighteenth century

A number of superimposed paintings executed over a considerable span of time by Aborigines in the Northern Territory.

When Captain Cook returned to London, the coffee-house wits and the mockers ridiculed his enthusiasm for the noble savage. The metamorphosis of the 'miserablest people in the world' into a people who had discovered the secrets of human happiness began with Cook's voyages.

metamorphosed the 'miserablest people in the world' into a people who had discovered the secrets of human happiness.

This revolution in thinking began with the voyages of Capt. James Cook. In 1768 the English Admiralty instructed Cook to observe the transit of Venus at Tahiti and then search for the unknown southland. During the voyage Cook and his officers discovered the noble savage at Tahiti, circumnavigated the north and south islands of New Zealand, and then, by chance, chose to return to England via the east coast of New Holland, Java, and the Cape of Good Hope. By such throws of chance must the historian explain the coming of the white man to Australia. Cook landed at Botany Bay, near Sydney, in April 1770, and three times more on the east coast before taking possession of the country at Possession Island for George III under the name of New South Wales. This eastern side he found was not that 'barren and Miserable Country that Dampier and others have described the Western Side to be. . . . In this Extensive Country it can never be doubted but what most sorts of Grain, Fruits, Roots &ca of every kind would flourish here . . . and here are Provender for more Cattle at all seasons of the year than can be brought into this Country.'

As for the natives of New Holland, he wrote:

They may appear to some to be the most wretched people upon the earth: but in reality they are far more happier than we Europeans; being wholy unacquainted not only with the superfluous but the necessary Conveniences so much sought after in Europe, they are happy in not knowing the use of them. They live in a Tranquillity which is not disturbed by the Inequality of Condition: The Earth and sea of their own accord furnishes them with all things necessary for life; they covet not Magnificent Houses, Household stuff &ca they live in a warm and fine Climate and enjoy a very wholesome Air: so that they have very little need of Clothing and this they seem to be fully sensible of for many to whome we gave Cloth &ca to, left it carelessly upon the Sea beach and in the woods as a thing they had no manner of use for. In short they seem'd to set not value upon anything we gave them nor would they ever part with any thing of their own for any one article we could offer them this in my opinion argues that they think themselves provided with all the necessarys of Life and that they have no superfluities.

But when Cook returned to London in 1771 the coffee-house wits and the mockers ridiculed his enthusiasm for the noble savage. Dr Johnson pontificated to Boswell on the advantages of civilization over primitive societies. Cook, with more modesty, reported to the Admiralty his failure to find a southland, adding characteristically that perhaps it did not exist. The Admiralty was not so sure. They sent him again in 1774 with two ships, the *Resolution* and the *Adventure*, to renew the search. After enduring incredible hardships in high latitudes in the South Seas, where land and sea were condemned to remain under eternal ice and snow, Cook returned to England in 1776, convinced that the unknown southland of the geographers did not exist. In that year it looked as though the only result of all the human effort and anguish by Hindus, Chinese, Mus-

An Aboriginal sepulchre.

lims, Catholics, Protestants, and men of enlightenment such as Cook had been to prove that the stories of islands of gold were a lie, that the unknown southland did not exist, and that the known southland was either a barren waste or a land that excited the imagination but not the greed of those searching for wealth.

Three years later, in 1779, Sir Joseph Banks, who had travelled with Cook on the *Endeavour* on the first voyage, told a committee of the British House of Commons that the government should found a colony at Botany Bay. Ironically enough, what moved Banks had not crossed the minds of any of the geographers, navigators, seamen, statesmen, or publicists who had dreamt of transplanting civilization to the South Seas. Banks recommended a thief colony as a solution to the problem of what to do with the people sentenced to transportation from the British Isles. From 1717 to 1776 the British government had sold such convicts to shipping contractors, who transported them to the southern colonies in America, where they were sold to the planters as workers. The revolt of the colonies in 1776 ended this method of transportation. The British government, with the arrogance and complacency of most privileged classes, used such temporary expedients as the hulks until, they believed, the Americans would be brought to their knees. But by 1783, with the acknowledged independence of the United States of America, they were looking for a place to send convicts sentenced to transportation.

Compared with the other problems confronting the Pitt government, the convict question was as a gnat is to an elephant. There was the consequence of defeat in America, the problem of the government of the occupied parts of India, the debts of the Prince of Wales, the agitation against slavery, and the ground-swell of that upheaval in Europe that to some contained the promise of better things for mankind and to others represented a cancer at the heart of civilization. Alarming reports of convict riots in the hulks and fears of contagious diseases spreading over the countryside from overcrowded gaols prodded the Pitt government into making a decision on the convict question. Lord Sydney, who held the seals at the Home Office, announced in August 1786 that His Majesty had thought it advisable to fix upon Botany Bay as a place for convicts under sentence of transportation. He instructed the Admiralty to provide a proper number of vessels to convey 750 convicts to Botany Bay together with such provisions, necessaries, and implements for agriculture as might be necessary for their use in the new land.

The wits in London mocked at the idea of a colony of thieves. Members of the government, they argued, had grown giddy by being carried to a great elevation and had conceived the mad scheme of a land of thieves. One man in Scotland, reduced to the deepest woe when told of the expense of the proposal, described it as the most absurd, prodigal, and impracticable vision that ever intoxicated the mind of man. Some convicts groaned at the prospect of perpetual exile and arbitrary government in a barbarous country where their lives would be made bitter with hard labour. A self-styled writer for the sober part of the community believed the Botany Bay settlement would enhance the comforts and add to the lights of polished society and tend to the general happiness of mankind and the glory of that Being who had preserved the discovery for their own generation. Others with more modesty accepted Botany Bay as a solution to overcrowding in the gaols, or contemplated greedily the benefits of increased Asiatic commerce to the British homeland. The more imaginative let their minds wander over a society in which thieves had flourished and become respectable.

As first governor of the colony, the British government appointed Arthur Phillip, a retired naval officer of mixed English and German descent who was living on half pay as a farmer in the south of England. He was just forty-eight when he was commissioned in 1786. He had served with distinction, though not with brilliance, in both the English and the Portuguese navies. He was in many ways a fine flower of the eighteenth century, a common-sense man with a contempt for the consolations of religion but, at the same time, a belief in the established church as a means to promote the subordination of the lower orders in society. The members of the upper classes, he believed, should cultivate the Roman virtues of self-discipline, self-mastery, and endurance. Phillip's face, as it has survived in the portraits, suggests that, like other worshippers at the shrine of 'cool reason'; he was also driven by darker passions, though the dignity of his bearing and the high-mindedness that informed his every action provided eloquent testimony both to the nobility of his mind and to his success in sublimating such passions.

He was appointed Captain-General and Governor-in-Chief in and over the territory called New South Wales, from Cape York to latitude forty-three degrees thirty-nine minutes south and westward as far as the one hundred and thirty-fifth degree of east longitude, including all the islands adjacent in the Pacific Ocean. He was instructed to found the settlement at Botany Bay; to proceed to the cultivation of the land, distributing the convicts for that purpose in such manner as might be best calculated for procuring supplies of grain and ground provisions; to explore the coast; to open an intercourse with the natives, and to cultivate their affections, enjoining all his subjects to live in amity and kindness with them; to enforce a due observance of religion and good order among the inhabitants; to procure women from the islands to offset the great disproportion of female convicts to males; to emancipate and discharge from their servitude any of the convicts who from their good conduct and disposition to industry were deserving of favour, and to grant every such male thirty acres of land, with twenty acres more if married and ten for each of his children resident in the colony, together with victuals from the public stores for twelve months and such tools, seed, cattle, sheep, hogs, and so on as could be spared from the general stock of the settlement. To assist him in the administration of affairs there was to be a criminal court, presided over by a judge advocate and six military officers, and a civil court, consisting of the judge advocate and two officers appointed by the governor. It was a government designed to ensure law and order and subordination by terror, a government designed for men living in servitude rather than for free men.

The other military and civil officers shared in varying degrees the ability and high-mindedness of the governor. They shared his common sense and his disdain for the consolations of religion, while sharing his view that the Protestant religion and British institutions were the finest achievements of the wit of man for the promotion of liberty and a high material civilization. These features distinguished the Protestant states of Europe from the Catholic states, which in their eyes were enslaved by arbitrary despotisms and a superstitious and idolatrous religion. So they mocked their religion in private as a false mythology, while in public they supported it for its social utility.

Understandably enough, this view was not shared by the first chaplain of the colony, the Reverend Richard Johnson, a product of the evangelical revival in England who had been educated at Magdalene College, Cambridge. The unbelievers had scoffed at it as a 'nest of Methodists' and a place that caused tea-leaves rather than the dregs of alcoholic beverages to float on the waters of the river Cam. Johnson was the first of a group of parsons through whose work evangelical Christianity dominated the religious life of Protestant Christianity in Australia throughout the whole of the nineteenth century. It was a religion with an obvious social usefulness in a convict society, for it preached in favour of subordination and against drunkenness, whoring, and gambling.

A caricature of 'hump-backed Maria', an Aboriginal woman well known in Sydney in the early 1800s, typified the approach of some artists.

By such labours the evangelical parson became in the eyes of those in authority the natural moral policeman of society. But the parson also believed in his God, and so spent his life in torment partly because those in power approved of his moral functions but were indifferent to his religious aspirations, partly because of his failure to communicate the Word to his charges. The evangelical parsons spent their days in anguish, publicly attributing the failure of their mission to the depravity of their charges, while in the privacy of their chambers lacerating themselves for their unworthiness to serve the Lord. Their work as moral policemen so identified them in the eyes of the world with a particular social order that their charge to all to receive the gifts of divine love seemed arrant hypocrisy. The price they paid for serving the material interests of the English governing classes was to be branded as civil servants in cassocks by all who did not share their faith.

Seven hundred and fifty-odd convicts embarked in the first fleet for Botany

Bay. They had all been sentenced to transportation for their crimes, a punishment that consisted of exile.for seven years, fourteen years, or life—and forced labour. The aims of the punishment were to deter from crime, to reform the convicts, and to provide labour for the colonies. At the end of the eighteenth century the criminal law in England, Scotland, and Ireland was a draconian and bloody instrument to defend life and property in a society in which extreme inequality and the degrading poverty of the masses caused crime to flourish. Over one hundred and sixty offences were punishable by death. In London, Edinburgh, Glasgow and Dublin a section of the working class obtained its living by crime. The class of thieves in London at the end of the eighteenth century was composed of men and women with an aversion to labour, who, according to an observer, were reduced by their idleness to indulge in gambling and scenes of debauchery and dissipation. In addition, he added, there were 'spendthrifts, rakes, giddy young men . . . in the pursuit of criminal pleasures. Profligate, loose, and dissolute characters, vitiated themselves and in the daily practice of seducing others to intemperance, lewdness, debauchery, gambling and excess . . . strolling minstrels, ballad singers, showmen, trumpeters, and gipsies.' Chaplain Johnson said of the first convicts that they indulged themselves in mere sloth and idleness, engaged in the most profane and unclean conversation, and committed abominations it would defile his pen to describe.

At least one-third of the women were prostitutes who reduced the men they had solicited to a drunken stupor, picked their pockets, and handed over the night's takings to the pimp. 'My Lord,' Sarah Sophia Ann Brown said in her defence in 1788, 'I live in Mrs Foy's house, as a girl, an unfortunate girl . . .' The men at times attributed their fall to drink. When Francis Flexmore was indicted in London in 1788 for stealing two pairs of plated shoe buckles, he pleaded that he was very much in liquor at the time. He was transported for seven years. Some pleaded destitution as their excuse. When Christian Klencke was indicted in London in 1788 for burglariously breaking and entering a dwelling-house, he pleaded he was in great distress and could not get any victuals, and seeing these things he had a temptation to help himself to them. He was transported for seven years. The great majority of the convicts, however, probably were professional criminals or men and women with such a deep aversion to labour that they earned their living by preying on their fellowmen. In addition there was a group of casual criminals—that is, those goaded into crime by want—a group of middle-class criminals sentenced for such crimes as forgery or embezzlement, and a group from the army and navy who were sentenced for offences against their codes.

Early in the new year of 1787 the civil and military officers, the convicts, and a contingent of marines assembled at Portsmouth. To ship them to Botany Bay the Home Office contracted with shipowners to provide transports, while the Admiralty provided store ships and a naval supply ship, the *Sirius*. In the beginning there was indescribable chaos: food supplies were inadequate, there was no clothing for the women convicts, no ammunition for the guns on the ships, no medical supplies, and no grog for the marines. By patience and hard work Phillip and the officers obtained most of the necessaries of life and some of its consolations, including the grog, before sailing day.

Early in the morning of Sunday, 13 May, 1787, the first fleet sailed down the English Channel and out on to the high seas. On that day the shutters of the shops went up for the first time since the convicts had arrived early in the New Year, while a clergyman on shore went down on his knees to ask the forgiveness of God for all of them. On the ships the convicts showed no signs of distress on the occasion of their exile from their native land. The clergyman Johnson wanted to pour his soul out before his Lord, while Phillip fussed and

Some Europeans enjoyed the cruel fun of encouraging intoxicated blacks to murder or mangle each other for the amusement of white spectators.

fretted over his charges. His mind was still sustained by the vision that had first come to him in the dark days at Portsmouth before departure, when he had written that since he would not wish convicts to lay the foundations of an empire, they should remain separated from the garrison and other settlers, because there could be no slavery in a free land and consequently no slaves. Yet, at Rio de Janeiro, which they reached on 7 August, they heard and saw how the labour of convicts could be used to lay the material foundations of a civilization in the New World. On the night they sailed from their next port of call, the serious-minded again pondered over their relationship with civilization; as they saw it they were then leaving behind them the lands of civilization and sailing towards a land of savages, and, as though to imprint the thought more sharply on their minds, they bespoke a ship marked 'London'.

By 20 January, 1788, all the ships were safely anchored in Botany Bay. That day the hopes of even the most sanguine were dashed by the waterless and drought-stricken environment that surrounded them. They looked in vain for those grassy meadows Cook and fellow-travellers had assured them were only awaiting the hand of human industry to bring forth an abundant harvest. Phillip and a small party of officers sailed north in a small boat and found to their delight 'the finest harbour in the world', in which a thousand ships of the line could ride in perfect safety. He christened it Sydney Cove, after happily rejecting another suggestion that it should be called Albion. He decided there and then to move the settlement from Botany Bay to Sydney Cove, in Port Jackson. On 26 January the convict transports moved into their new home as a handful of Aborigines on the shore set up a horrid howl and indicated by angry gestures with sticks and stones that the white man was not wanted. That night, after the convicts were landed, the British flag was unfurled at Sydney Cove, shots were fired, and toasts were drunk. It has been celebrated ever since

as the day on which European civilization in Australia began.

On the night of 6 February the convict women were landed. Extra rations of rum were also issued, and soon there developed a drunken spree that ended only when the revellers were drenched by a violent rainstorm. The next day the convicts were marched to a clearing where, to the accompaniment of a regimental band, they heard Phillip sworn in as Captain-General and Governor-in-Chief in and over the territory of New South Wales, and heard the judge advocate read the long and rather dreary commission to Phillip. They heard him swear on the Bible, in which he did not believe, that he would not attempt to restore Charles Edward Stuart to the throne of Great Britain, not knowing then that a week or so earlier the said Charles Stuart had died of alcoholic poisoning in Rome. Then, as though to add to the sufferings of men with a hang-over during a hot, sticky day in Sydney, Phillip harangued them on the evils of promiscuity, counselled marriage as a fit and proper state for human beings, and threatened to put a charge of buck-shot into the backside of any convict who wandered into the women's quarters during the night.

The men were set to work to till the soil, to build the huts, and put up the tents. The Reverend Richard Johnson gathered all who were willing under a great tree, probably on the first Sunday, to offer up thanks to the Lord for His great mercies. A week later he celebrated Holy Communion in an officer's tent, and another officer, Ralph Clark, whose heart was hot within him, asked to keep the table on which the Lord's Supper was first celebrated in the colony. Within a few weeks convicts had stolen food so shamelessly that Phillip decided to have them flogged as a warning to both European and Aborigine of his determination to defend property. When floggings failed to deter, Phillip agreed to use the last sanction of the law and launched one of the thieves into eternity. The white man had come to Australia.

A man of the Aranda tribe.

CHAPTER TWO

CONVICTS AND SETTLERS 1788—1809

'BUSINESS NOW SAT ON EVERY BROW,' wrote an observer, 'and the scene, to an indifferent spectator, at leisure to contemplate it, would have been highly picturesque and amusing.' In one place a party was cutting down the woods; a second party was setting up a blacksmith's forge; a third was dragging along a load of stones or provisions; a fourth was pitching a marquee with a detachment of troops. Confusion soon gave place to system. Then the real business began: to use the labour of the convicts to provide food for the settlement and punishment for their crimes.

Near Sydney, Governor Phillip named rolling countryside Rose Hill, later Parramatta, and built there Government House, the focus of Sydney's social life.

This proved no easy task. The ground bent the blades of their hoes; the timber twisted the blades of their axes; the summer heat oppressed them; giant ants bit them. The Aborigines did not respond to their gestures of amity and kindness. The Europeans offered the Aborigines the precious gift of their civilization in return for the right to use the wealth of their land. The European hoped that the Aborigine would perceive the benefits of civilization, abandon the life of the savage, and become a labourer on the bottom rung of the ladder of European society. But in the beginning the Aborigine resisted every attempt to approach him. So to produce food and provide shelter the settlement had to rely on the labour of men and women who had taken up a life of crime because of their aversion to labour. Neither the fear of the lash, nor the promise of emancipation, nor special indulgences, overcame this innate aversion to labour.

Not surprisingly, the early food harvests were failures, and the colonists were obliged to fall back on stores imported from England. To add to their difficulties disaster befell their attempts to seek relief from overseas when their one surviving supply ship, the *Sirius*, was wrecked at Norfolk Island in March 1790. The delays in the departure of the second fleet from England and the shipwreck of the *Guardian* off the Cape of Good Hope delayed the arrival of relief from home. By early in 1790 the settlement was threatened with starvation. The weekly allowance of food was reduced in October 1789, and by April 1790 had been cut to four pounds of flour, two and a half pounds of salt pork, and one and a half pounds of rice per week. One old man collapsed and died while waiting to collect his food ration; the surgeon who opened up his body found his stomach completely empty.

On 3 June, 1790, a large ship with English colours flying was seen moving in between the heads at the entrance of the harbour. A small boat was sent down the harbour to escort her, and when the men in that boat read the word 'London' on the stern of the big ship, they cried out '. . . Hurrah for a bellyfull, and news from our friends.' It was the *Lady Juliana*. Her arrival marked the end of the battle for survival. They heard for the first time of the illness of George III and his happy restoration to health; they heard, too, of that momentous event, the French Revolution, which some of them found 'wonderful and unexpected', while others pondered on their great good fortune in living under the blessings of the British constitution.

By that time Phillip had become convinced that the settlement would not progress so long as it depended for the production of its wealth on convicts working in gangs on government farms, roads, or public buildings. He had come to the conclusion that its future depended on the attraction of free settlers to whom convicts could be assigned as workers, the granting of land to officers, the working of that land by convicts, and the granting of land to those ex-convicts who by their industry and good conduct proved themselves worthy of such favour. He had granted land to one ex-convict, James Ruse, who by hard labour and the knowledge of farming he had learnt in England was able to support himself and family free from the public stores within a year of taking up his grant. But Phillip did not remain in the settlement long enough to observe the fruits of his policy. Worn out by the hardships and fatigues of the battle for survival in an alien environment and in a society of whom he believed nine-tenths did not deserve to survive, he finally asked for home leave because a chronic pain in the stomach was not responding to treatment. He sailed out on to the high seas in December 1792 in the sure knowledge that he was beloved and respected by all in the settlement, and that His Majesty was graciously pleased to approve of his conduct in the execution of the arduous and important service that had been committed to his care.

Landing at Botany Bay, which the London wits mocked as a colony of thieves.

After his departure the settlement was administered by the senior army officer, Major Francis Grose, who lacked both the dignity and stature of Phillip. Yet, by one of those ironies in history, when the fortunes of men are influenced

by the little men rather than the giants of this world, Grose made two decisions
that were decisive for the next fifty-odd years. He made land grants to the
officers and persuaded them to work their land with convict labour and sell
their surplus to the government stores. To encourage the convicts to work on
the officers' land after working the regulation hours at government work, he
allowed them to be paid in rum. He also encouraged officers to engage in trade
by buying goods from ships arriving in the colony and retailing them at their
own prices.

The quantity of goods in the settlement increased rapidly. In time the news
circulated that there was profit to be made from the sale of a shipload of goods
at Sydney Cove. Whalers arrived from England and the United States of
America with cargoes of goods they sold to the officers before sailing south
to hunt the whales and seals that abounded off the coast of New South Wales,
the east coast of Van Diemen's Land, on the islands in Bass Strait between New
South Wales and Van Diemen's Land, and as far afield as Dusky Sound at the
southern tip of the south island of New Zealand. Ships from Sydney Cove
sailed to the Pacific islands to collect cargoes of salt pork for sale to the officers
and the government stores at Sydney, or cargoes of sandalwood and trepang
for sale in China. In 1798, Robert Campbell, the representative of the trading
firm of Campbell, Clark & Co., Calcutta, dispatched a trial cargo to Sydney,
but the ship foundered in Bass Strait. He sailed himself with a second ship,
founded the firm of Campbell and Co., merchants, at Sydney Cove, and soon
proved that there was a career open to enterprise in the thieves' colony over
and above its original purpose as a settlement for British convicts.

At the same time a few of the ex-convicts began to rise to a condition of
affluence and even respectability. Simeon Lord, who had been transported for
seven years in 1790 for stealing one hundred yards of muslin valued at sixpence
and one hundred yards of calico valued at fourpence, reached Sydney in 1791,
and had become his own master by 1798. He began to invest his savings in
sealing, whaling, and the salt-pork trade with the Pacific islands. James Larra,
a French Jew who had been picked up by the London police as a receiver of
stolen goods in 1790, took up land after emancipation and then invested in
the profitable business of selling alcohol, which he combined with the more
civilized activity of regaling travellers with French foods at his inn in Parramatta.
A few other ex-convicts took up land grants, too. One, Charles Williams, took
up thirty acres near Parramatta, but after farming it for a few years he fell
into disgrace with his fellow-convicts and ex-convicts for an act of treachery
against one of his class. He began to drink heavily, as did his wife, who was
drowned during one of his drunken sprees in Sydney. Thereafter, he was often
seen pouring one glass of rum down his throat and another over his wife's
grave, explaining to those who passed by that she had enjoyed it so much in
her lifetime, it was just possible she was still able to enjoy it. The passion for
rum became overwhelming with Williams. He sold his land to an officer to
obtain money to gratify his insatiable thirst and became, in the words of the
contemporary chronicler of his story, a hireling for wages on the land he had
owned, and a stranger to all sense of shame.

In this way more and more of the wealth of the settlement of New South
Wales became concentrated in the hands of the military and civil officers. Some
of them accumulated wealth rapidly by the extension of their estates and by
the sale of goods. Before 1800 the officers had established a monopoly in the
sale of goods and were making, according to hostile witnesses, profits of up
to one thousand per cent in the sale of goods purchased from the captains of
ships. According to the apologists for their actions, they established this
monopoly to protect the helpless convicts, ex-convicts, whalers, and fellow-

Sydney, 1804. In 1788 convicts had been building huts and putting up tents, but in a few short years a township was thriving.

officers against the greed of those who were not restrained by a gentleman's code of honour. By 1800 the officers were beginning to develop some of the features of an exclusive caste: they were haughty and arrogant to all outside their class, from whom they expected a doffing of the cap and other visible proofs of obsequiousness. They were ruthless and vindictive towards all those who attempted to interfere with the sources of their wealth. One of those officers was a man of great tenderness and charm in his family life, who had great talent, overweening ambition, and the drive to crush all who stood in his path. He was John Macarthur, who arrived with his wife Elizabeth and infant son in 1791 as an officer in the New South Wales Corps. Macarthur was a man with ideas. While others gossiped or drank themselves into stupefaction, he experimented in ways of improving farming in the settlement. By 1800 his farm at Parramatta, Elizabeth Farm—which consisted of two hundred and fifty acres, one hundred of them under cultivation—was a model for the whole colony, with its vines, fruit trees, vegetables, grain crops, pigs, cattle, and poultry. In 1795 he introduced the first plough into the settlement, and soon was musing on the possibility of growing fine wool in New South Wales. He was also the model employer of convict labour—severe, exacting, upright, and just. The breath of scandal never touched his private life, nor did any whisper of cruelty to convict servants.

But while ambition and talent were leading him along the path of material success, a fatal flaw in his clay began to cheat him of respect and affection from his fellow-men and lead him on to the lonely madness of his later years. Macarthur was driven to crush utterly all who stood in his way. On the convict ship on which he travelled to Australia, for instance, he had fought a duel with a ship's officer over a quarrel that began about the stench from sewage buckets placed outside his wife's cabin. Within seventeen years this same touchiness on questions affecting his interests and his honour led him to quarrel with every governor of New South Wales from Hunter to Bligh.

In the creative period of his life he was able to 'turn the hard rock into a standing water'. When he was sent to England in disgrace by Governor King in 1802 to face court martial, he seized the opportunity to convince the Secretary of State, Earl Camden, of the profitability of growing fine wool in New South Wales. Another man might have been led on to his destruction by such vanity and pride: Macarthur returned to Sydney with an order from Camden to King that he should be granted ten thousand acres of land at the Cow Pastures, later named Camden, which was forty miles to the south-west of Sydney. Macarthur soon proved that the grasses on his land could so feed the merino sheep that its wool could compete in quality and price with the wool from Spain and the German states. Within the next fifteen years he perceived how the convicts could be used to serve both the English interest in their reformation and punishment and the increasing colonial interest in their labour. For Macarthur was one of the pioneers in perceiving how the natural wealth of New South Wales could be exploited in such a way as to harmonize with the economic interests of Great Britain.

Before 1810 the convict system had not been ripe for such a purpose. The convicts were distributed among the government, the military and civil officers, and the settlers, with the government having first choice. Up to 1810 the needs of the government for convict labour were overwhelming. Convicts were needed to work on government farms, to build roads, and to erect public buildings. In both government service and assignment the convict worked nine hours a day for five days of the week and a five-hour day on Saturday, with intervals on the weekdays for breakfast and dinner. After these hours the convict could sell his labour for wages to an employer. Convicts in government work were victualled and clothed by government, while those on assignment were victualled and clothed by their master. The women in government service worked as menders and washers of clothes and in spinning linen. A few were assigned as domestic servants, and after 1798 these were fed, clothed, and

By 1800 John Macarthur's farm at Parramatta, Elizabeth Farm, was a model for the whole colony. He was a model employer of convict labour – severe, exacting, upright and just.

housed by their masters. The convict labour force was supplemented by the free workers—men and women whose terms had expired, the children of convicts, and a few ex-convicts who had taken up land and decided to sell their land grants to satisfy their appetites for liquor, or their disposition to indolence, or in response to chance and circumstance.

Those convicts who by their industry and good conduct proved deserving of favour might receive a ticket of leave that exempted them from forced labour and permitted them to sell their labour in their own police district. They had no legal rights in the courts, where they could neither sue nor be sued, and the law forbade them to own land, thus ensuring their continued subservience for the rest of their servitude. The government could also grant conditional or absolute pardons, which restored a convict to the full legal rights and privileges he had forfeited on becoming a tainted felon, the one restriction being that the holder of a conditional pardon could not return to any part of the British Isles until the time of the original sentence had expired.

Punishment was used to preserve law and order and to deter the convict from further crime. For neglect of work, not obeying orders, being absent without leave, drunkenness, or insolence to a master, whether government overseer or settler, the convict was brought before a magistrate and sentenced to the treadmill, to work in a road party, to a flogging, or transportation to a penal settlement. For some offences a convict might be sentenced to fifty lashes, for others up to one thousand lashes. A few convicts who had survived the ordeal of one thousand lashes could be seen hobbling around the settlement, unable to straighten their backs. Government officers and settlers preferred flogging as a punishment, partly because the loss of labour time was negligible, partly because the convicts dreaded the extreme physical suffering and the consequent loss of self-respect. The unflogged man believed in his future; the flogged man generally surrendered to despair and moved from one wretchedness to another till he ended his days at a 'launching into eternity' ceremony, or took to the bush, where he lived like a savage. The punishments designed to deter tended to deprave and to degrade.

By 1824 Parramatta was a well-established town with all the outward and visible signs of civilization.

The infant town of Sydney was 'agreeable and picturesque', wrote François-Auguste Péron while the French expedition was in port in 1802.

The regulations were designed to prevent abuses in the system: to stop masters being tricked by convicts to permit them to sell their labour; to stop masters making money by letting out their convicts for hire; to stop masters horse-whipping their convicts; and to stop convicts bribing the clerks in the lower ranks of government to alter their terms of servitude from life to shorter periods. The settlers grumbled at the disastrous effects of clemency on convict discipline, and by 1810 they were looking back fondly to the golden days of severity when backs were bloody and men were servile. Some convicts groaned at the degree of suffering and brutality. Out of the anguish, the terror, the suffering and the labour of the convicts the outward and visible signs of civilization began to appear at Sydney Cove and Parramatta: churches, schools, law courts, and government offices arose as a monument to the convicts' agony and labour.

During the same time the settlements at Sydney and Parramatta began to expand. Norfolk Island was occupied within a few weeks of the arrival at Sydney Cove. Some emancipists took up their land grants in the fertile valley of the Hawkesbury at Windsor. Coal was discovered in 1795 at a place first called Coal River, and later Newcastle. A naval surgeon, George Bass, and Matthew Flinders began to examine and chart the coast south from Sydney. In 1798 in the naval sloop *Norfolk* they finally proved that the great sea their predecessors had observed pounding the north-west shores of Van Diemen's Land was part of a strait dividing Van Diemen's Land from New South Wales. On this voyage they circumnavigated Van Diemen's Land and charted its coasts. In 1802-03 Flinders circumnavigated Australia and finally demonstrated that New Holland was not separated from New South Wales by a sea.

Early in the new century both British officials and officials in New South Wales were alarmed by French exploration of the south coast of Australia. To forestall any French attempt to begin a settlement, and to exploit the opportunities for trade in sealskins and whale oil, the British government sent a small expedition in 1803 of convicts, soldiers and settlers under Captain David Collins to occupy Port Phillip. At the same time, and for the same reasons, supplemented by a local desire to get incorrigible convicts out of the settlements of New South Wales, Governor King sent a small expedition of convicts, soldiers and settlers to establish a settlement on the Derwent on the south coast of Van Diemen's Land. A few months later he dispatched a similar expedition under Colonel Paterson to occupy Port Dalrymple on the north coast of Van Diemen's Land. After a few months at Port Phillip, Collins decided early in 1804 to move his party to the Derwent, where he took over the command from John Bowen and chose and named Hobart Town as the site for the settlement. As in the early years at Sydney Cove, food shortages, shoddy tools, refractory convicts and soldiers, and the revenge of the Aborigines against the white man for stealing the land brought great hardship and suffering, though not the tragic grandeur that informed the first struggle for survival. For while the Reverend Richard Johnson consumed himself in his attempt to save the convicts from everlasting damnation, the chaplain at Hobart Town, the Reverend Robert Knopwood, spent his days pleasantly, hunting the kangaroo, drinking wine with the officers, and cheerfully cancelling religious services if the weather was at all unfavourable. While the breath of scandal never touched Phillip at Sydney Cove, Collins spent so much of his time consorting with convict women at Hobart Town that, when he died suddenly in 1810, the righteous believed he had been struck down by God for his sins and wondered why God had spared that other notorious evil-doer, the parson!

In the meantime an event occurred in New South Wales that was to influence profoundly the texture of civilization in Australia. In September 1791 the first Irish convicts arrived on the convict transport *Queen*. By October 1800 there were 1,207 in the settlements at Sydney Cove and Parramatta. They were the occasion of the coming of Catholicism to Australia. In Ireland the priest was attached both by the needs of survival as well as by moral convictions to the side of the peasant in the long and bloody fight against the Anglo-Saxon. In Australia this association between the priests and the lower classes was perpetuated because both bond and free tended to remain on the bottom rungs of the social ladder.

Australia's Catholics, both priests and laity, were steeped in prudery. In addition, except for the few born to and educated in the aristocratic tradition of European society, they were also steeped in a credulity and superstition that nauseated the Protestant majority and that other tiny minority that had been taught by the writers of the Enlightenment that religion barred the path to human progress. What the Protestant was unable to perceive were those affections of the Irish mind and heart that were outside the range of the men of enlightenment, that image of Christ the Irish had kept alive despite the appalling squalor, the superstitious practices encouraged by their priests, and the stupor and ignorance in which they prepared for 'the life of the world to come'. For their religion explained to them why riches did not belong in this world to men of understanding and promised them that, although the Protestant boys had gained the day, they would not gain the night.

The Protestants saw the Irish Catholics in quite a different light. To them the superstition and the squalor provided proof of the commonplace in their view of the world: that the Protestant religion and British institutions protected liberty and a high standard of material civilization, while the Catholic religion encouraged arbitrary despotism and material squalor. So when the Irish convicts began to arrive in large numbers at Sydney Cove, the Protestant establishment began to take alarm, not only at a people who threatened English rule in Ireland and who were in that sense disloyal, but also at a people whose religion and way of life threatened 'higher civilization'. From the beginning the Anglo-Saxon was on his guard against the menace of what he called these 'deluded and infatuated' people.

The Protestant establishment had some reason to be alarmed. In April 1798 an Irish convict who worked in a gang at Toongabbee threw down his hoe and gave three cheers for liberty. He was rushed off to the magistrate, then tied up in the field where his 'delusions' had first overwhelmed him, and flogged so that his fellow-Irishmen might ponder on the consequences of challenging the English supremacy. In September 1800 Governor Hunter, who had taken over from Grose in 1795, believing that the Irish convicts were forming seditious assemblies, held an inquiry. The magistrates sentenced suspected

ringleaders to be flogged till they divulged the plot: one was flogged on the back, and when the skin in that area became too raw, he was flogged on the bottom, till the Protestant magistrate confirmed that an Irishman would die rather than betray a fellow-countryman to enemies of his race and religion.

In March 1804 William Johnston, an Irish convict, gathered his fellow-Irishmen at Castle Hill with a mixture of blarney, threats, and promises of liberation from their Anglo-Saxon oppressor, armed them with sticks, staves, hoes, and a few rifles, and marched them towards the Hawkesbury in preparation for the conquest of Sydney. But an informer warned Governor King, who had taken over from Hunter in late 1800, in time so that before their numbers became formidable they were cut down by a small detachment of troops. In the sequel the leaders were hanged; those close to the leaders were sentenced to floggings of up to one thousand lashes and transported to the penal settlement at Newcastle, where on weekdays they hewed coal and on Sundays heard of the gifts of divine love from the Book of Common Prayer, which was read to them by the military commandant acting on orders from the Captain-General and Governor-in-Chief of New South Wales. The rank and file were pardoned as deluded but not wicked men. In this way the Irish were cowed into subjection, but not at the price of the surrender of their precious faith, for the faith survived as a vision of the world different from that which sustained the minds of the Protestant ascendancy. In this way the wrongs of the Irish in New South Wales began to be added to their melancholy history in Ireland.

In the beginning, however, the dominant note of civilization in New South Wales was sounded by the Protestants. From the pulpit and, after 1803, when an ex-convict began to publish the *Sydney Gazette*, from the press as well, the evangelists presented their view of the world. They painted terrifying pictures of the evils of drunkenness, sexual promiscuity and gambling, which robbed

Armed with sticks, staves, hoes and a few rifles, Irish convicts attempted to gain liberty and conquer Sydney but were confronted by the military.

a man of the prize of respectability in this world and condemned him to everlasting flames and torment in the next. On politics they taught the simple lesson that throne and altar fell together, and they warned all and sundry to beware of that great snare for the wicked—the principles of liberty, equality, and fraternity. They reminded congregations and readers that in the sanctuary of God men learnt the significance of those gradations of rank and wealth that God in His infinite wisdom had created for their own good. From the Holy Bible the poor learnt to raise their eyes to those scenes of bliss that grew brighter and more enchanting as they approached the grave. From the same source the rich could read a stern reminder of how difficult it was for them to reach the promised land.

The clergy and the *Sydney Gazette* never wearied of reminding people of all the blessings Divine Providence had bestowed on the members of the established Church of England. By contrast, the members of all other persuasions wandered in great darkness: the Asians practised disgusting superstitions; Catholics wanted to enslave mankind; Jews belonged to a limbo between the Protestant paradise and Catholic hell; the followers of secular creeds were baited and hounded from pulpit and press; unbelievers were reminded of their handicaps in the law courts, where their testimony was discounted, and of their even greater handicap when they approached the throne of Judgment. The clergy and the *Sydney Gazette* urged the education of the young to rescue them from the evil influences of their parents and to prepare them for their eternal salvation—the purpose of literacy, in their eyes, was to learn the way to eternal glory. Knowledge was to be encouraged as a foe to vice and not first and foremost as the means of learning a trade. Schools had been begun by the Reverend Richard Johnson in the time of Phillip, and as the settlement expanded the clergy and government tried to provide a parish school for each church, where the children were instructed in reading and arithmetic, read the Bible, and studied the catechism according to the Church of England. The schools were both foes to vice and wickedness and, at the same time, centres of proselytism for the Anglican Church. The Catholics grieved; the Presbyterians and dissenters accepted the secular enlightenment.

It was this unqualified and uncritical faith in their Protestant civilization that lent pathos to, and imposed a tragic note on, their relations with the Aborigines. They expected the Aborigines to be grateful for the precious gift of 'higher civilization', and as long as they seemed prepared to receive such a gift the colonists proposed to extend to them that amity and kindness their instructions from England had urged them to use. But when the Aborigine became convinced that the white man proposed to stay, and that the white man was driving him away from all the best food-gathering areas into more barren places and at the same time committing sacrilege against those trees and animals that had been sacrosanct for his people since time immemorial, he began the long, unequal struggle of fighting the white man, spearing his animals, setting fire to his crops and his houses, and murdering him. On 30 May, 1788, two rush cutters were murdered by the Aborigines and their bodies dreadfully mangled and butchered. At the same time the Aborigines began to evince disgust and hatred for some features of the white man's civilization. When a convict was detected stealing tackle from an Aboriginal woman in 1791, Phillip decided to have him flogged in the presence of the Aborigines to prove that the white man's justice benefited blacks as well as whites. All the Aborigines displayed strong abhorrence of the punishment and sympathy with the sufferer. They shed tears, and one of them picked up a stick and menaced the flagellator.

At the same time the idea of amity and kindness waned in the minds of the Europeans as they came to know the Aborigines better. They were disgusted by their personal habits, by the filth, the flies, and the stench that surrounded the Aborigines. They were angered by the indolence of the Aborigine, by his inability and absence of desire to exert himself, to raise himself out of his material squalor. They were appalled too by the vindictive cruelty with which the Aborigines punished their people who lived with the white men. In 1796 an Aboriginal girl who was working as a maidservant in the house of a European was enticed into the woods and hacked to pieces.

The Europeans were also appalled by the disastrous effects of civilization on the natives, many of whom became hopeless drunkards, prepared to fight, dance, indeed to do anything for the temporary gratification to be obtained from a bottle of rum. The noble savage whom Cook had described with such enthusiasm had degenerated in the towns into a cadger of 'booze and baccy'. In the country districts he had become an incendiarist and a murderer. So the white man began to retaliate. When Aborigines burnt some settlers' houses and murdered others on the Hawkesbury, two Aborigines were captured, tied to a tree with a rope used for the dogs, and shot. That was in 1800. By 1806 it was commonplace for the governor to order a party of soldiers to drive Aborigines from any area where outrages had occurred. The settlers in Hobart Town and Port Dalrymple had the same experience of drunkenness and degradation in the towns and murder and pillage in the country districts. With such experience the settlers especially and, to a lesser extent, the officials dropped talk about amity and kindness and spoke more and more of innate racial characteristics. The teaching of the New Testament was replaced by the more primitive Mosaic law of the Old Testament of an eye for an eye and a tooth for a tooth. The former spoke of compassion for all men; the latter said that in acts of revenge men should not look with the eye of pity on those whom they were destroying.

The idea of amity and kindness soon waned and the Europeans, as they came to know the Aborigines better, were disgusted by their habits.

Layers of Northern Territory Aboriginal paintings depict Darwin's wharf in the 1880s with the jetty and two boats, one a paddle-steamer in midstream.

By the end of 1804 the Irish had been squashed, the Aborigines in both New South Wales and Van Diemen's Land had pitted the weapons of the Stone Age against steel, lead and gunpowder, the convicts were in a state of tranquillity, and the French were in no position to menace the future of English civilization in Australia. Then suddenly in January 1808 the tiny settlement at Sydney Cove was convulsed by a civil commotion, and the governor deposed. He was William Bligh, who had taken over the office of Captain-General and Governor-in-Chief from King in 1806. He was a man with his mind on the big things in life who was cheated of his honour and his glory by his own egregious folly.

Some have written of Bligh as the champion of the small farmers, and especially the emancipist farmers on the Hawkesbury, against the larger landowners. Some have written of him as a man who paid a price for his noble and magnanimous attempt to suppress the traffic in rum. But the interests in society were represented on both sides: merchant Robert Campbell plumped for Bligh, and merchant Simeon Lord for the rebels; some landowners plumped for Bligh, some for the rebels; two civil officers remained loyal to Bligh, and the others joined the rebel cause.

The key to the upheaval lay in the personality of Bligh, an English naval officer who had served under Cook on his third voyage from 1776 to 1779. Bligh had commanded the *Bounty* on a voyage to collect breadfruit at Tahiti when a section of the crew, goaded to desperation by his ungovernable rages, mutinied near Tahiti and placed him and several others in a long boat. With that blindness to his own faults that he displayed to the end of his days, Bligh attributed the mutiny to the sensual appetites of those who deposed him. These ungovernable rages were his undoing in New South Wales, where again, as on the *Bounty,* he had the folly to provoke those who never forgave an injury. He raged at Macarthur; he degraded Simeon Lord by sentencing him to revert to the status of a felon, which Lord had devoted all his talents and industry to abandoning for ever; he harangued officers in coarse and obscene language. Within a year of assuming office he was known as Caligula. By then he had behaved sufficiently arrogantly against his opponents for them to talk of tyranny. Between November 1807 and January 1808 he played into the hands of his enemies by threatening to arrest and charge with treason six senior military officers in the settlement.

On 26 January, 1808, a day traditionally spent by the troops in drunken carousals to celebrate the founding of the colony, John Macarthur appealed to the senior military officer, Major George Johnston, to arrest Bligh at Government House. That night not a finger was raised to help Bligh as he raged on as a prisoner in that same Government House in which he had been formerly surrounded by all that pomp and ceremony he so desperately loved. Then by acts of egregious folly he proceeded to alienate one by one all those who might have come to his aid, beginning with the tubby Foveaux, then the gouty Paterson, and finally the Lieutenant-Governor of Van Diemen's Land, David Collins, with whom Bligh's method of ingratiating himself was to have a supporter tied up to the triangle on board the *Porpoise* in the estuary of the Derwent and flogged. The mild punishment of the mutineers by the subsequent court martial in England in 1811—the cashiering of Johnston and the enforced exile of Macarthur—was a hint that even those who were staking their all in Europe, and at home, in defence of established order had perceived the fatal flaw in Bligh that had caused so many to judge a brave and gifted man so harshly.

In the interregnum between the deposition of Bligh and the arrival of Macquarie, the acting administrators—Johnston, Foveaux, and Paterson—quickly revealed that the rebels had no policy. They made some show of rewarding their supporters by appointments to public offices and by grants of land, but in neither did they behave in that lavish and irresponsible manner of which Bligh later accused them. Nor did Bligh have any permanent effect on the society of New South Wales, for apart from his encouragement to agriculture and his cantankerous and rather irrational opposition to trade and to sheep farming, Bligh had not the gifts of the creator. The one result of his rule and the interregnum was the division of the upper ranks of society in Sydney and Parramatta into warring factions. Bligh's successor was instructed to end this division, but factions in New South Wales were beyond the power of any mortal to remove, because they sprang from the dark side of the human heart.

CHAPTER THREE

THE AGE OF MACQUARIE 1810—1821

TO CONCILIATE these factions, to improve the morals of the colonists, to stamp out the evils of the traffic in rum, and to restore the colony to a state of tranquillity, the British government appointed Lachlan Macquarie in 1809 Captain-General and Governor-in-Chief in and over the colony of New South Wales and its dependent territories. He was then forty-eight years old, a lieutenant-colonel in the British army who had served in four continents of the world, where his observations of the Buddhist, Hindu, Islamic, and Catholic civilizations had confirmed his belief in the superiority of British institutions and the Protestant religion. He was endowed by nature with great gifts of heart and mind, and above all he had the gift of making important any position to which he was appointed, as all his creations were monuments to his vanity as well as his industry. For he was born with a passionate heart and a high-mindedness that equipped him admirably to sweep the Augean stables of New South Wales.

After taking the oaths of office in January 1810, Macquarie spoke 'with animation and peculiar energy' of his intention to exercise strict justice and impartiality. He was hopeful that all dissensions and jealousies would terminate for ever. He urged the upper classes to conduct themselves with propriety and rectitude, and the lower classes to remain sober. To all he recommended a strict observance of religious duties and a constant and regular attendance at divine service on Sundays. He urged the magistrates to prevent all forms of vice and immorality and charged all and sundry not to molest the Aborigines. The honest, sober, and industrious inhabitant, he concluded, would ever 'find in him a friend and protector'. The crowd burst into three cheers, and then the band played 'God Save the King'.

Within a few weeks he took his first actions to improve the morals of the people: indecent profanation of the Sabbath was to cease; all public houses were to be closed during divine service; profligacy of manners, dissipation, and idleness were to be reduced by cutting down the number of licensed houses. He published a proclamation against the scandalous and pernicious custom so generally and shamefully adopted throughout the territory of persons of different sexes living together unsanctioned by the legal ties of matrimony. He took steps to reduce the traffic in spirits and to cut down its consumption by the lower orders. To instruct the rising generation in those principles that he believed alone could render them obedient to their parents, honest, faithful, and useful members of society, and good Christians, he opened more schools in Sydney and the outlying settlements.

With the same high moral purpose he began a vigorous campaign of public works. He began work on a new hospital, letting the contract to a group who

Francis Greenway's beautiful St Matthew's Church at Windsor, New South Wales, was completed in 1820. A rival architect had designed a two-storey church but the construction was so poor that Greenway condemned it and produced a new design.

Above: Lachlan Macquarie, Governor of New South Wales from 1810 to 1822, soon began a vigorous campaign of public works.

Above right: Macquarie's wife, Elizabeth, brought with her from England a book of building designs that helped her husband plan the colony.

Above far right: A cricket match near the military barracks.

Far right: Macquarie ordered that townships should be laid out in each district and that each township should have a church, a school and a courthouse.

promised to pay all expenses in return for the exclusive right to import spirits for three years. He put up a new barracks; he improved roads and bridges. He ordered a new town plan for Sydney, partly from a belief in beauty and grandeur, partly from a belief that orderliness and cleanliness would improve the morals of the lower classes. To bring the outward forms of civilization to the outlying settlements, he ordered that townships should be laid out in each district, each township to have a church, a school and a courthouse, to raise the area from barbarism to civilization.

To promote this reformation of manners amongst convicts and ex-convicts he took the earliest opportunity of proving to them that rectitude and long-tried good conduct would lead an emancipist back to the rank in society that he had forfeited. With great delicacy he invited four emancipists to his table at Government House. He appointed an emancipist, Andrew Thompson, a justice of the peace and a magistrate at the Hawkesbury and announced his intention to appoint Simeon Lord, the opulent emancipist merchant, a magistrate as soon as a vacancy occurred. On 31 March he announced in the *Sydney Gazette* the appointment of the Reverend Samuel Marsden, Simeon Lord, and Andrew Thompson as trustees and commissioners for the turnpike road from Sydney to the Hawkesbury. Marsden believed his superiors in England would not approve of such an association with ex-convicts, especially men who lived with convict concubines, as did both Thompson and Lord. In two interviews with Macquarie, Marsden firmly declined to accept the appointment. At the second encounter Macquarie lost his temper and shouted that it was just as well Marsden held a civil commission, as otherwise he would have him court-martialled for disobedience. Marsden believed that on such questions he must obey the commands of God: Macquarie believed every man in the colony should obey him. So Macquarie in the full flush of his high-mindedness revealed the weakness that would bring him to destruction.

All through 1811 and 1812 success seemed to be crowning Macquarie's efforts. In England, press, parliament and government were reporting fav-

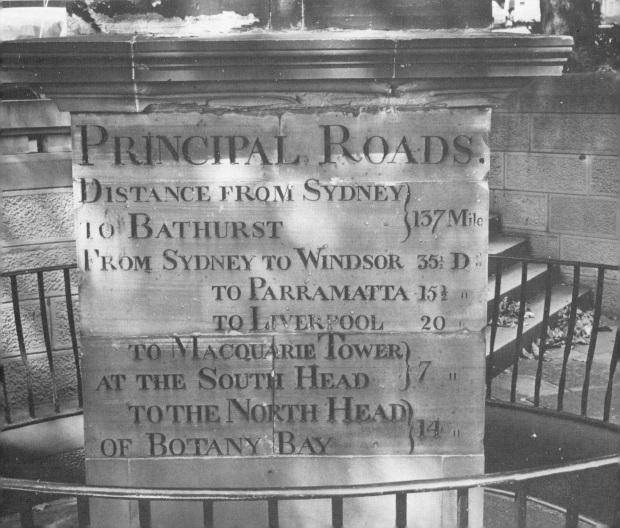

ourably on the improvements in the religious, moral, and educational life of the colony. A committee of the House of Commons on transportation summed up his work in this way: '. . . the colony of New South Wales . . . is, in their opinion, in a train entirely to answer the ends proposed by its establishment.' In the meantime in the colony a similar optimism and enthusiasm prevailed. At a dinner in January 1813 to commemorate the anniversary of the founding of the colony as well as of his assumption of office, a bumper toast was drunk to Governor Macquarie: 'May the anniversary of his assuming the command of the territory be commemorated and reverenced by our latest posterity!' That was the halcyon year of his work in New South Wales.

In the same year, being convinced that new grasslands must be discovered for the ever-increasing numbers of cattle and sheep, Blaxland, Wentworth and Lawson found a way to cross the Blue Mountains, which lay to the west of the settlement of Sydney Cove. Setting out in 1813, they kept to the ridges until they reached the peak of Mount Blaxland, where a boundless champaign burst on their view, opening, as one of them put it, like Canaan on rapt Israel's view. They then returned to Sydney to report on their journey. To examine the possibilities more closely Macquarie sent Evans, the surveyor, over the Blue Mountains at the end of the year; then, in the following year, he began to build a road over the mountains. In May 1815 he visited the new country himself and christened the site for a town: Bathurst, after the Secretary of State for the Colonies in London. He perceived at once that the discovery of this new country furnished an outlet for the increases of population for a century to come, for here was the opportunity for his sober, industrious men from the middling classes to take up one-hundred-acre plots, while gentlemen of the upper classes took up large grants in the fine grazing land.

To find out more about the new country, he dispatched John Oxley in 1817 on a voyage down the Lachlan River, which ended with Oxley despairing of establishing even the rudiments of civilization in such an arid and harsh land, or of ever finding the mouths of those inland rivers that the optimists hoped would flow into an inland sea and so provide wealth for future generations of sober and industrious sons of English civilization. The Lachlan seemed to end in swamps and morasses in a green year and empty riverbeds in a dry. On the way back he found promising grazing territory in the valley of the Macquarie River near Bathurst.

Oxley was off again in 1818 to trace the Macquarie to its mouth, but again the marshes or arid plains mocked his search for an inland sea. On the return journey to the coast the sight of the fertile river valley of the Hastings gladdened

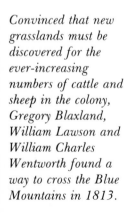

Convinced that new grasslands must be discovered for the ever-increasing numbers of cattle and sheep in the colony, Gregory Blaxland, William Lawson and William Charles Wentworth found a way to cross the Blue Mountains in 1813.

On a voyage down the
Lachlan River in
1817, John Oxley
despaired of the
rudiments of
civilization being
established in such an
arid and harsh land.

his heart, as did the beautiful setting of Port Macquarie, with its tropical vegetation and the deep blue of its waters at journey's end. Between 1817 and 1819
Throsby, Wild, and the young Hamilton Hume, explored the country south-
west from Camden to the Murrumbidgee in the Yass-Canberra district and
Jervis Bay on the coast. By 1819 there were abundant opportunities for the
expansion of settlement at Bathurst, along the valley of the Hunter River to
the Patrick and Wallis Plains, in the Moss Vale, Goulburn, and Canberra districts, and along the coast from Illawarra to Jervis Bay.

In the meantime Macquarie continued to devote his attention to the task of
raising the settlements of New South Wales and Van Diemen's Land from
barbarism to civilization. Towards the end of 1814 and in the beginning of
1815 he devoted much time to the problem of the civilization of the Aborigines.
He aimed not only to protect them against the aggression of the white man
but also to teach them habits of industry and decency so that they might abandon
the indolence and squalor of their own way of life and join the working classes
in both settlements. He decided to open a native institution at Parramatta for
boys and girls and a farm on the shores of Port Jackson for adults. The parents
tried to seduce the six boys and six girls away from the school at Parramatta,
as their repugnance to the ways of the civilized was as strong as ever. Each year
after 1815 Macquarie attended a ceremony at the native school to commemorate its opening, when the children displayed their progress in reading and
writing. There were cheers for Macquarie, much beef, potatoes, and grog for
the Aborigines. The Aboriginal chiefs burst out laughing, leapt in the air, and
made other wild gesticulations that the *Sydney Gazette* called 'the spontaneous
offerings of uncultivated nature'. By 1818 the *Sydney Gazette* in an almost mes-
sianic mood predicted the day would come when the Aborigine would rise
above the role of kitchen boy to the white man. But the facts were against

them. The numbers of the school at Parramatta never rose above twenty. In the towns the Aborigines continued to remain figures of cruel fun for schoolboys and adults. One of the great popular sports in Sydney, Parramatta, and Hobart Town was to encourage intoxicated black people to murder or mangle each other for the amusement of the white spectators. In the country districts the Aborigine exacted what revenge he could for the theft of his land, and the white man in turn continued to exact an eye for an eye and a tooth for a tooth.

Macquarie had more success with his attempts to promote the moral well-being of the European inhabitants of New South Wales and Van Diemen's Land. Between 1811 and 1816 he erected schoolhouses at Liverpool, Windsor, Richmond, and Wilberforce to ensure that religious principles would be implanted in the minds of the rising generation. In 1815 he began to encourage the work of the British and Foreign Bible Society because he shared the conviction of its founders that the sacred teaching of the Bible corrected the most ferocious manners and promoted worldly comfort. For the same reasons he encouraged the work of the Sunday School movement. In this way, under the influence of Macquarie and with the full support of Bathurst as Secretary of State for the Colonies, the evangelicals assumed an ascendancy in the society of New South Wales. The Governor; the principal chaplain, the Reverend Samuel Marsden; the judge advocates, Ellis Bent and John Wylde; and other civil and military officers, were all good evangelicals. Under their influence, and through the talents of Francis Greenway, a convict architect who had absorbed the atmosphere of Regency Bath, churches were built at Liverpool and Windsor that breathed the very spirit of the evangelical Protestant view of the world. Their vast domes, their chastely furnished sanctuaries, and their classical external proportions moved the worshipper to contemplate the grandeur and omnipotence of God freed from all those accessories, those statues,

Francis Greenway had been sentenced to death for forgery and was instead transported to Botany Bay for fourteen years. He flourished as an architect, creating an enduring legacy for New South Wales.

gorgeous vestments, rich music, incense, and gesture the Catholic believed to be proper aids to worship. From the pulpit, in the school, in the press, and in their ecclesiastical architecture the tone of their civilization became more firmly Protestant and evangelical.

Just as the permanent monuments to the work of Macquarie began to take shape, chance and those flaws in his being soured his last years in the colony. The more convinced he became of the righteousness of his own position the more censorious he became with the weak. Lieutenant-Colonel Thomas Davey, the Lieutenant-Governor of Van Diemen's Land after the death of David Collins in 1810, spent much of his energy providing adequate barracks for the troops, a hospital for the rich, or coping with the depredations of bushrangers and Aborigines. But Davey was also an eccentric. 'Mad Tom', the locals called him. He often drank to excess with convicts at the 'Bird in Hand' in Argyle Street, walked the streets in his shirtsleeves, called all and sundry by their Christian names, and cohabited openly with convict women to the great pain of his long-suffering wife and the scandal of the few respectable families in Hobart Town. When Macquarie heard that Davey spent so much time in drinking and other forms of low depravity in company with the basest and meanest of the people, he recommended that he should be dismissed, and he suppressed the achievements of Davey in all correspondence with Bathurst about his future.

When people in high places in Sydney opposed Macquarie's pro-emancipist policy, he found it impossible to concede that they might do so for just as high-minded reasons as the ones that prompted his own defence of the emancipists. More and more he saw himself as a man motivated by righteous indignation and his opponents as men motivated by baseness and infamy. He detected in himself, he said, a spirit of charity that caused him to despise their unjust and illiberal sentiments. He became morbidly aware of the faults of character in all those who opposed the emancipists and was blind to the weaknesses of character amongst his supporters. An emancipist who was a sanctimonious hypocrite and simulated religious piety shamelessly to promote his career in the colony became in Macquarie's eyes proof of the wisdom of restoring men of tried good conduct to the rank in society that they had forefeited by their crimes. This fatal conviction of the righteousness of his own position and the wickedness or malevolence of his opponents caused him to quarrel in a most unseemly way with the senior civil and military officers in the colony.

When the judge advocate, Ellis Bent, let Macquarie know that emancipists should not be forced into office or society contrary to the feeling of the respectable, and that to appoint a man of such dubious moral character and social station as Simeon Lord degraded the office of magistrate, Macquarie interpreted his stand as base ingratitude for all the favours and courtesies he had lavished on Bent. Bent, however, drew a different conclusion. Macquarie, he said, wanted the judge advocate to act like a subaltern, or a cypher; he, on the other hand, believed the judiciary should be independent of the executive government. The officers of the regiment mocked the emancipist policy at their dinners, and one officer pinned a cartoon on the wall of the guard room showing Macquarie in a position of ignominy. The officers also declined invitations to dine at Government House. They made it plain that they gloried in refusing to associate with men who were so much their inferiors in rank and situation, and welcomed the prospect of leaving a country in no point of view congenial to military feelings. Macquarie was incensed by their insubordination rather than the arrogance and haughtiness of their social principles.

When Marsden refused to co-operate in the emancipist policy, Macquarie described him as a malevolent man clothed in the garb of humanity and hyp-

GOVERNOR DAVEY'S
PROCLAMATION
TO THE ABORIGINES
1816

ocritical religious cant. Again Macquarie saw Marsden's opposition as an affront to his own authority. Early in 1818 he commanded Marsden to appear at Government House, and after reminding the chaplain of his indispensable duty to support the governor's high station and authority, and to preserve the tranquillity of the country, he commanded him never to set foot again in Government House except upon public duty.

Thomas 'Mad Tom' Davey, Lieutenant-Governor of Van Diemen's Land from 1813 to 1817, devised this proclamation to the Aborigines.

Two years earlier those in the colony who believed they had suffered from Macquarie's high-handed behaviour had drawn up a petition and forwarded it by the Reverend Vale to the British House of Commons. In it they had accused Macquarie of influencing the decisions of juries, of having free men flogged without the order of a magistrate, of selling pardons to convicts, of prohibiting banns of marriage, and influencing the courts of justice. Macquarie had castigated it as the work of a mischievous and mean faction; and up to a point it was. A wiser man might have let it go at that, but not Macquarie. He was so deeply wounded that the vindication of his name and honour became from that time the ruling passion of his life.

This obsession with his honour and his power began to overwhelm him just at a time when his creative talents, his exuberance, and his enthusiasm might have been more usefully employed on the problems of the colony. Between 1817 and 1819 the number of convicts transported to New South Wales increased sharply as more shipping became available after the Napoleonic wars and the British Isles were plunged into the disturbed conditions of the postwar years. In May 1818 five convict ships arrived at Sydney. Macquarie, believing the settlers did not wish to employ them, assumed that the government would have to feed and employ them. In Sydney they were set to work on a new convict barracks, on a house for the judge of the Supreme Court, and at Windsor and Liverpool on building new churches. In this way the expenses of government increased enormously. Posterity in Australia inherited the glory and the honour of the Francis Greenway churches at Windsor and Liverpool, while Macquarie's vision had shrunk to thoughts on how the new barracks at Sydney would improve the morals of the convicts by preventing nocturnal robberies, theft, and other depredations.

At the same time economic developments in both New South Wales and Van Diemen's Land were taking both settlements further and further away from their original purpose of extensive gaols for the punishment and reformation of British criminals. In 1817 the merchants and more opulent settlers combined to found the Bank of New South Wales. The trade of both settlements increased; wool was being exported successfully from Sydney to England; whale oil and sealskins were also successful exports; the trade in salt pork, sandalwood, and trepang was becoming more and more lucrative. In New South Wales settlers were farming in the Hunter River district, in the Bathurst district, in the area south-west from Camden towards Moss Vale, and along the coast from Illawarra to Jervis Bay. In Van Diemen's Land settlement was spreading from Hobart Town along the valley of the Derwent, and there were plans to use the Huon pine growing in abundance at Macquarie Harbour on the south-west coast of the island. By 1819 the population of New South Wales was 26,026, with 9,986 or 38.3 per cent convicts; the population of Van Diemen's Land in the same year was 4,270, 2,190 or 47.1 per cent being convicts. Contemporaries estimated that over three-quarters of the population in both settlements were either convicts or the children of convicts.

In January and February of 1819 the merchants of Sydney held two meetings under the chairmanship of Sir John Jamison to discuss their future and the future of the colony. They decided to draw up a petition that in effect requested the abolition of those features in the government of the colony that sprang,

Among Greenway's most important buildings is Hyde Park Barracks in Sydney. For this notable achievement, completed in 1819, Macquarie made his pardon complete.

at least in part, from its origins as a convict settlement. They denounced the judge advocate's court as contrary to all their habits, feelings and opinions as Englishmen. They asked for trial by jury; if Hindus, Hottentots, and Negro slaves had such a right, then they as Englishmen and the sons of Englishmen were surely worthy of it, too. For the most part they concentrated on the steps that should be taken to improve their opportunities to accumulate wealth; they wanted markets for their grain, the repeal of the statute forbidding ships of less than three hundred and fifty tons burthen to trade with the colony, and the abolition of British duties on such colonial goods as wool and whale oil. They also wanted the recognition in England that the numerous and rapidly increasing colonial generation was just as moral and sober in its habits as the people of the mother country. At the same time Macquarie himself suggested that the British government might like to take up the suggestion originally made by Flinders to call the whole continent Australia.

Observers from England noticed how the native-born were beginning to differ from the migrant both in appearance and speech. The currency lads, or native-born, were tall in person, slender of limb, and fair in complexion. They were capable of great feats of physical strength but were somewhat ungainly in their movements. By temperament they were quick to anger, though not vindictive towards those who provoked them. In speech most of them copied the flash or giddy language of their convict parents; in addition, they were developing a distinctive pronunciation of their own. Some of them believed that, since Australia was a convict colony whose wealth and civilization had been created by convict labour, it therefore belonged to the convicts and their descendants, and that settlers and immigrant free workers were all 'bloody foreigners'. This xenophobia of the native-born was the first of a long line of claims to exclusive possession, and the forerunner of later slogans such as 'Australia for the Australians', or 'Australia for the white man'. It was fed by an ardent patriotism and nurtured later by a vision of what the native-born could achieve in a country that had not inherited the Old World evils of social class, war, and poverty. It was this tradition of xenophobia amongst the descendants of the convicts that later gave some distinctive twists to secular humanism in Australia.

In the age of Macquarie, however, the tone of civilization was still set by the evangelicals. From press and pulpit came warnings that the drunkard, the philanderer, the gambler, and the idler, would not gain those prizes of affluence and respectability in this world, while, as for the next, remorse would be their scourge and eternity their dread. While the native-born tended to be silent on their heritage from the British Isles, the apologists for the Protestant ascendancy tended to take inordinate pride and pleasure in being British. 'Great and miraculous Providence!' wrote the *Sydney Gazette* in praise of their being British, 'the author of all Good! how we are indebted to your saving Power!' While the native-born were beginning to take pride in their natural environment and to look on it with the eye of a lover rather than the eye of an alien, the apologists for the Protestant ascendancy tended to write of Australia in the early Dutch-English tradition as an exceedingly barren land. An early poet, Barron Field, the second judge of the Supreme Court, wrote of the country as a place which:

> '. . . emerg'd at the first sinning,
> When the ground was therefore curst;
> —And hence this barren wood!'

Towards the end of the age of Macquarie the voice of the other view of the world that has influenced the development of civilization in Australia began to be heard publicly in New South Wales and Van Diemen's Land. In May 1820 two priests, J. J. Therry and P. Conolly, arrived from Ireland to minister to the Catholics in both colonies. They were not the first priests on the continent, as they had been preceded by three transported during the troubles of 1798 in Ireland. In 1817 Father O'Flynn had arrived without formal credentials from the Secretary of State and had been promptly forced to leave by Macquarie, who was piqued as much by O'Flynn's low insolence towards the Protestant clergy and his claims for the magical power of the sacramental bread as by his lack of credentials. The arrival of Therry and Conolly ensured that the Irish Catholics in New South Wales and Van Diemen's Land would continue to be instructed in those ideals of charity, compassion, love of God, and the preservation of their holy faith by men who at times confounded these ideals with the worldly aspirations of the Irish people, just as the religious sentiments of the Protestants, their profession of faith in one God, the Maker of heaven and earth, were confounded with the worldly aspirations of the British. The Protestant mocked at the Catholics' low standard of living, their stooping to their priests, their superstitions, the tinsel and ornament surrounding their acts of religious devotion. The Catholic grieved at the Protestant for sundering the unity of Christendom, for performing ceremonies that were but a pale shadow of their own rich liturgy, and for seeming to condemn a portion of God's children to a perpetual position of inferiority in society. So by the end of the age of Macquarie two different views of man and his destiny confronted each other in Australia.

In the meantime wild reports were beginning to circulate in England about what was happening in the colony. Those with grievances against Macquarie had been doing their best to convince those of like mind in London that the governor was a hopelessly corrupt tyrant. The more responsible were alarmed by the increase in crime in the British Isles as well as by doubt of the efficacy of transportation in deterring from crime. In an attempt to find out the true situation the House of Commons in 1819 appointed a committee of inquiry into the state of the gaols. The Secretary of State for the Colonies, Lord Bathurst, was pondering over similar problems. He came to the conclusion that permission to settle in New South Wales had become the aim of all who desired to leave their native country.

How then could transportation continue to be an object of apprehension to criminals in the United Kingdom? Had it not lost its efficacy as a punishment? In 1819 Bathurst appointed John Thomas Bigge as commissioner of inquiry to report on whether transportation was any longer efficient as a punishment. He was also instructed to report on all the officials of the colony no matter how exalted their rank, or how sacred their character; to report on the case for restoring severity of punishment; on the possibility of improving religion and education; on the agricultural and commercial interests of the colony; and on the propriety of admitting into society persons who originally came to the settlement as convicts. In effect Bigge was invited to recommend what sort of society and civilization should be developed in Australia; whether it should be primarily a gaol for the punishment and reformation of British criminals or a colony using convict labour for the exploitation of its wealth. Bigge was then thirty-nine, a lawyer by education whose only previous experience had been his years as Chief Justice at Trinidad, which probably influenced him in favour of the use of slaves and convicts to create the wealth of the planters. Macquarie by then was fifty-nine, and had well over thirty years of service to the British crown in four parts of the world. This difference in years and experience began his deep division with Bigge and his dark, undying pain from the moment Bigge arrived in Sydney in October 1819.

The British flag was raised on Norfolk Island in February 1788, and it became a convict settlement until 1814, when it was abandoned. In 1825 it was resettled as a prison for hardened offenders.

Between October 1819 and February 1821 Bigge collected both oral and written evidence from the inhabitants of New South Wales and Van Diemen's Land, travelling extensively in both settlements. Almost from the beginning of his stay he heard much of the extravagance of Macquarie, much on the impropriety of the emancipist policy, and much on those quirks of character that had bedevilled relations between Macquarie and the senior officers in New South Wales. Bigge had the gifts of the novelist and, in his private correspondence with Bathurst, sketched the characters of colonial society with a breadth of understanding and a sympathy for all points of view. Above all he

heard of the clamour of the settlers for more convicts. Chaplain Marsden told him that sheep would be the source of unknown national wealth, if the government supplied convicts of the most experience and best characters to sheep farmers. By contrast, under the Macquarie system, as another settler reminded Bigge, the labour of an immense proportion of the convicts was being retained for the use of government at enormous public expense.

John Macarthur showed Bigge how the British interest in the reformation of the convicts could harmonize with the interest of the settlers in their labour. The very labour necessary for the rearing of sheep and cattle was also calculated to lead to the correction of vicious habits. Shepherds spent their days in solitude, where they had time for that reflection and self-examination that might lead to amendment of life, and where they no longer saw the dazzling sights or heard the tempting sounds of the towns. He suggested to Bigge that the British government should recommend land grants of not less than ten thousand acres to enable men with capital to become a powerful aristocracy: this in contrast to the democratic feeling that, he asserted, had already taken deep root in the colony as a result of the absurd and mischievous policies pursued by Governor Macquarie. The convicts would enable the settlers to grow wool; the manufacturers of Great Britain would buy the wool; the convicts would be reformed; New South Wales society would develop into a plantation-type society.

From the more opulent emancipists Bigge heard about their legal grievances, their contribution to the wealth of New South Wales, and their claim that this was a convict colony whose future development and ownership should be left in their hands. He heard, too, all the gossip of the colony, the personal feuds, the frictions, the grievances of Mad Tom Davey against the upright and censorious Macquarie—all the petty disputes of both societies. He listened to all with patience and dignity. But from the first his mind was set on the major issues of the colony of New South Wales.

On his return to England he emphasized again and again these issues in the three reports he published in 1822 and 1823. He recommended that the employment of convicts in the management of sheep might be made highly conducive to the improvement and reform of all but the most hardened criminals, who should be transported to penal settlements at Moreton Bay, Port Curtis, and Port Bowen. For the rest he recommended the abolition of the main features of the convict system as administered by Macquarie. He recommended severity of punishment rather than leniency, the restriction of the privileges of ticket of leave holders, and the abolition of land grants for emancipists. He also recommended the end of the Macquarie policy of appointing emancipists to positions of trust and responsibility. Macquarie, as Bigge saw it, had been influenced by the dictates of humanity. Bigge, on the other hand, was concerned with the stability of society, and he believed that to promote a man such as Simeon Lord, whose domestic life had been notorious and who was engaged in the low and common pursuit of selling things, could only degrade the office of magistrate in the eyes of people all too free of any sentiment for the might, majesty, and power of the law.

On the future institutions of New South Wales and Van Diemen's Land, Bigge was just as conservative. The emancipists were clamouring for trial by jury and a legislative council on the grounds that these belonged to all Englishmen as a birthright and that free institutions would contribute to their material wealth. Besides, they argued, their wealth and behaviour were already such as to render them worthy of the character of useful and respectable citizens. Bigge, however, was impressed only by their argument for the restitution of their legal rights as free men on their emancipation from servitude. As for trial by jury it was, he believed, highly inexpedient and dangerous to expose the life or property of a free man to a jury of ex-convicts; they would have to be educated before they received their birthright as Englishmen. He saw a case for an improvement but not for a fundamental change in the judicial institutions of the colony. He did, however, recommend the granting of separate judicial institutions to Van Diemen's Land.

The British government accepted these recommendations. Macquarie's successor, Brisbane, was instructed to abolish most of the features of the old convict system, and every effort was to be made to separate the convicts from the mass of the population. An act of parliament, an Act to Provide for the Better Administration of Justice in New South Wales and Van Diemen's Land, passed in 1823, created a legislative council of not more than seven nor less than five to be appointed by His Majesty. The right to initiate legislation was reserved to the governor, who could also proclaim an act without the consent of the council provided he stated in writing his reason for doing so. The governor was required to submit each bill to the chief justice, who was to certify whether the bill was repugnant to the laws of the United Kingdom. To preserve the sovereignty of the parliament of the United Kingdom, the crown might disallow any act within three years of its enactment. The trial of criminal cases was to be held under prosecution by the attorney-general, and all questions of fact were to be submitted to a jury of seven commissioned naval or military officers. A pardon by the governor was to restore a man to the full legal rights he had forfeited on becoming an attainted felon. The crown was empowered to create a separate colony in Van Diemen's Land. By this series of administrative decisions and an act of parliament, the government proclaimed that whereas hitherto New South Wales had been treated as a penitentiary for convicts, from 1823 they proposed to treat it as a British colony.

Opinion in the colony greeted the promised change with enthusiasm. John Macarthur rejoiced that the changes had been already productive of much pleasure to his son in England and of much land to himself. The Reverend Marsden rejoiced because God, as he put it, had 'filled his basket'. The young William Wentworth, then doing terms at Cambridge, wrote a poem prophesying the day when the convict blot had been forgotten and Australia had become 'a new Britannia in another world'. Only one man was deeply hurt, and that was Macquarie, for by one of those ironies in human affairs the man who presided over the transition from gaol to colony was by then more concerned with the vindication of his name and his honour than with the future of New South Wales. Like most human beings he could not have what he most desperately wanted; he died in grief and anguish, not knowing that posterity would confer on him a more lasting gift than the confounding of his enemies: the title of Father of Australia.

Far right: John Macarthur, who was one of the pioneers in perceiving how the natural wealth of New South Wales could be exploited to harmonize with Great Britain's interests.

Mrs Macquarie's Chair. At the end of the three mile harbour-side walk, a seat was cut into a rock. The inscription, dated 1816, commemorates Elizabeth's part in beautifying Sydney.

CHAPTER FOUR

THE TRANSITION
1821—1831

BIGGE HAD RECOMMENDED the abolition of the old convict system, and its replacement by sheep men who put the proceeds from convict labour into their own pockets in return for reforming their assigned servants. Just as the development of a society sometimes suggests after the event a pattern not in the minds of its creators, the transition from the old convict system to the new did not always follow the recommendations of Bigge. Between 1821 and 1831 the economic power in the colony belonged to the large settlers and the merchants, and by the end of that period political and social power were beginning to belong to the same group. But all this happened in such a chaotic way, and was so disturbed by the clamour and uproar of faction fights and personal feuds, that the transition might easily be attributed to chance rather than human design.

The transition began with radical changes in the convict system. Brisbane, who succeeded Macquarie as governor in December 1821, was instructed to remove from the towns all convicts capable of being reformed and assign them to the settlers in the country districts, where they would be free from all evil associations and temptations. The government would also benefit by being freed from the expense of victualling, clothing, and housing those convicts. Incorrigible convicts were to be sent to Port Macquarie to the north of Newcastle or to Moreton Bay, the site of the present city of Brisbane. When Moreton Bay proved unsuitable as a convict settlement, Governor Brisbane was ordered to re-occupy Norfolk Island.

At the same time the incentives to reformation in the old convict system were removed. Land grants to emancipists and expirees were abolished. Brisbane was warned that if he did not distinguish between emancipist and immigrant in society he might disgust the free section of the population. He was advised, too, that he should make it as difficult for an emancipist to be appointed to a public office as it was for a camel to pass through the eye of a needle. In this way the economic, social, and political avenues to preferment for an emancipist were blocked off. The British government was determined that the society of New South Wales should not be rocked by faction fights caused by the accident of its convict origins, and so it was resolved to cut the ground from under the feet of any future Simeon Lords, or William Redferns, or Samuel Terrys. At the same time the convicts in the penal settlements were not to be pampered by a higher standard of living than that provided by a life of crime in the United Kingdom. But the hope for a society not agitated by hatreds, fears and suspicions between the emancipists and the immigrants did not allow for the longevity of some emancipists, the clannishness of their children, or the supercilious arrogance of the immigrants towards the emancipists and their

Lady Darling, the wife of Sir Ralph Darling, Governor of New South Wales from 1825 to 1831, and two of their children.

Convicts in Sydney, wearing 'magpie' clothing, which was yellow and black, and irons round their ankles. The colour of the clothing was a mark of deep disgrace.

descendants, which caused the convict question to intrude into every public question in the colony.

In Van Diemen's Land, on the other hand, the emancipists did not possess sufficient wealth to rouse the fears of the immigrants. In Van Diemen's Land, too, the supply of convict labour was more able to meet the demand of both government and settler. On the mainland of New South Wales the settlers were clamouring for more and more convict labour. To meet this demand, as well as to reduce still further the cost to the government of feeding the convicts, Darling, who had taken over from Brisbane in 1825, closed down most of the government farms in New South Wales and distributed the convicts amongst the settlers. But still the settlers were not satisfied, mainly because by the end of the decade the number of immigrant settlers had substantially increased.

As early as 1820 the English press had singled out New South Wales as a suitable place to which men of capital might emigrate. With the change of convict policy the British government began to encourage the migration of men of capital and genteel birth to New South Wales and Van Diemen's Land. In this way New South Wales and Van Diemen's Land, and later the Western District of Victoria, became lands of opportunity where ploughboys, Scottish crofters, and Irish peasants became landed gentry, and the genteel poor of the United Kingdom were rescued from the fate of becoming ploughboys in their native land. In 1828 one James Henty, a merchant and manager of a bank at Worthing in Kent, who belonged to a family that could trace its history back to the Doomsday Book, wrote to his brother William on the advantages of emigration to New South Wales:

I have come to the conclusion that New South Wales will do more for our family than England ever will . . . . It would be silly to suppose that he [i.e., his brother Charles] can live many years longer on less than two hundred pounds a year, brought up as we all have been unless indeed we chose to descend many steps in the scale of Society and which our feelings could ill stand, having at the same time an opportunity of doing as well and perhaps considerably better in New South Wales, under British Dominion and a fine climate. . . . At the expiration of ten years in New South Wales I shall be much disappointed if we individually are not worth double that sum [i.e., four hundred forty to five hundred pounds a year] . . . . Our amusements would be in sporting and improving our estates and our business growing fine wool and breeding blood horses for both of which we have good markets.

There were others like the Henty brothers who received from the Colonial Office a letter to the governor of New South Wales or the lieutenant-governor of Van Diemen's Land instructing him to grant the holder land commensurate with the capital at his disposal and every assistance in his power to enable the holder to settle successfully on the land. In this way gentlemen farmers, retired army and naval officers, as well as some needy adventurers, were added to the top layers of colonial society. This meant there was less good land for the men born in the colony, and this heightened the xenophobia of the native-born towards the immigrants. So the faction fight between emancipists and immigrants, which had begun because of the social exclusiveness of the latter, developed into a contest for the landed wealth of New South Wales, with the emancipists fighting for the right of their children to come into their inheritance.

The fears and suspicions of the emancipists were heightened by the grant of a charter to the Australian Agricultural Company in 1825. In return for a grant of one million acres in the hinterland of Port Stephens, a port on the coast of New South Wales to the north of Newcastle, the promoters of the company promised to rear flocks of sheep of the purest and finest breed, to introduce large capital and agricultural skill into the colony, to increase the amount of fine wool for export, and to employ so many convicts that the expenses of government would decrease. The promoters also promised to employ the convicts in a manner conducive to their punishment and reformation. The emancipists protested vociferously against the proposal: the managers of the company, they said, would lay their paws upon the best land they could find. These fears were fed by reports that members of the Macarthur family, notorious for their insolence and exclusiveness to all emancipists, were the main promoters of the scheme in London. At the same time the laws for the ownership and use of land and the exploitation of the labour of the convicts became more favourable to immigrants with capital than to the successful emancipists. So the emancipists came to believe that the British government was handing over to the immigrants the land that belonged to the native-born and their descendants. Experience in New South Wales tended to push the emancipists towards being radicals and Anglophobes and the immigrants towards being conservatives and Anglophiles. As a measure of the difference between the society of New South Wales and Van Diemen's Land, the grant of a charter to the Van Diemen's Land Company in 1825 neither excited the immigrants nor soured the emancipists in that colony.

In the meantime the increase in the number of settlers caused an expansion of settlement in New South Wales. Gentlemen immigrants and emancipists took up land in the valley of the Hunter River on the Patrick and Wallis Plains, with the large grants going to the immigrants and the smaller to the emancipists. The Dangar family, whose founder had served under Governor Darling, took up land in the district, as did the Dumaresqs, to found family dynasties at the expense of the Aborigines, the convicts, and possibly the land. The number of settlers in the Bathurst district and in the fertile valley of the Macquarie

In London in the 1790s the kangaroo became an important topic of conversation, and one proved to be 'an extraordinary phenomenon' at the Royal Gardens at Richmond.

River also increased. The same pattern of expansion was occurring in the Goulburn-Canberra district, where Robert Campbell, in compensation for earlier losses, was granted twenty thousand acres of land by the governor. The ladder of both social preferment and social prestige was not unlike that of the other European societies, where the founders of a family made their wealth from trade and then took up land to acquire that social prestige wealth alone could not confer. At the same time the settlers in Van Diemen's Land were less obtrusively occupying the upper reaches of the Derwent from Hobart Town and the valley of the Esk from Port Dalrymple.

To discover more land for prospective settlers as well as to clear up mysteries about the directions and mouths of the inland rivers, the government in New South Wales promoted journeys of exploration. In 1824 Hume and Hovell were instructed by Brisbane to walk to Spencer's Gulf in South Australia. They walked as far as Corio Bay in Port Phillip. On their way they discovered a river that they named the Hume, but another explorer, Charles Sturt, later inadvertently cheated the original discoverer of his glory by calling it the Murray. After crossing the river they came on a country that was the finest in soil and incomparably the most English-like in point of climate they had seen, with an admirable port and a river not inferior in magnitude to any known in the colony. When they reported their discoveries in Sydney, the press enthused over this amazing range of pasture, the possible extension to commerce and agriculture, and the advantages of establishing a settlement at Western Port, which Hume and Hovell believed they had reached—whereas in fact they had camped on the western shores of Port Phillip.

In some ways the most significant result of their journey was the unseemly bickering between Hume and Hovell for the glory and honour of being the promoter, leader, and main discoverer. Hamilton Hume was native-born, the son of a somewhat unsteady overseer of convicts in New South Wales, and given to boasting of his achievements as a native youth or 'currency lad', while William Hovell was an immigrant and a gentleman by birth. Hume said that the idea of the expedition had originated with him, that if it had not been for his perseverance and abilities the object of the journey would never have been accomplished, that Hovell had poor abilities as a bushman and knew little of the interior of the country. With the passage of time Hume's charges of incompetence against Hovell descended into malicious and spiteful jibes at his cowardice.

In the beginning of the long and anguished struggle of the native-born for recognition, then, they behaved not as those innocents who wandered over the face of the earth before the Fall of Adam, but with the truculence of men with a chip on their shoulder. Hovell bore all these attacks with patience and dignity, though without any overt awareness that he was but the victim of that implacable hatred that characterized the relations between emancipists and immigrants during this period. Hovell saw himself as the man who had first shown how to walk from Sydney to Western Port over a country that, to the south of the Murray, was 'extremely beautiful, clothed with a luxuriant herbage, and both hill and lowland thickly wooded'. Alan Cunningham, a botanist by profession, performed the same sort of service for the country to the far north of Sydney in two journeys. On the first of these, in 1827, he discovered extensive tracts of clear pastoral country in a district subsequently named the Darling Downs in honour of the governor. In the following year he discovered a pass from the Darling Downs down to Moreton Bay.

In the same year Charles Sturt, who was born the son of an English judge in Bengal, India, in 1795, set out to follow the course of the Macquarie River to its mouth. He found a large river, which he named the Darling. He believed this river gave a fresh importance to the distant interior, for it was evident that it was the chief drain for carrying off the waters falling westerly from the coast. It soon became his great objective to ascertain the river's further direction. He believed, too, that something more powerful than human foresight or human prudence appeared to avert the calamities and dangers with which he and his companions were so frequently threatened. Sturt had a deep and abiding faith in the Providence of that good and all-wise Being to whose care he committed himself.

To clear up the mystery of the mouths of the Murrumbidgee and the Darling, Sturt set out again from Sydney on 10 November, 1829, for the Murrumbidgee, humbly committing the safety of his person and his companions to the protection of Almighty God. With drays and horses the expedition proceeded down the banks of the Murrumbidgee over melancholy tracts of land till January 1830, when progress was impeded by a swamp. Then Sturt and a small party set out in a whale boat, travelling through dreary plains till they came onto a broad and noble river, which Sturt named the Murray, after the gentleman who then presided over the Colonial Office, not realizing this was the same river on which Hume had conferred his own name. Once again chance, rather than spite or malice, robbed the native-born of immortality and conferred it instead on an English official.

On their way down the Murray, Sturt's party was threatened by the natives, but, thanks to the miraculous intervention of Providence, as Sturt put it, they were saved. Sturt's faith was too strong to attribute their salvation to chance, and he was too modest to attribute it to his own charismatic powers as a leader, or to the terror of the Aborigine on first meeting gunpowder. Like their predecessors in the interior, Sturt's men found the effects of syphilis amongst the native tribes truly disgusting: many had lost their noses, and all the glandular parts were considerably affected. On 23 January they discovered the junction of the Murray and the Darling, and then began to pass through an unprofitable and inhospitable country. The men were beginning to complain of sore eyes: they were down to a ration of flour and what they could get with gun and hook, since the meat they had was needed for the dogs they had brought along.

On 9 February, 1830, they arrived at a beautiful lake, which Sturt called Alexandrina Reservoir, where the Murray flowed into the sea. From the top of a hill they saw the waves breaking upon the distant headland. That mystery of the rivers that had perplexed all the explorers of the inland from Oxley to Sturt had been resolved. They then faced the hardships of rowing upstream through an inhospitable land with the men already weakened by their exertions and their poor diet. All this they overcame by that strength to endure and that compassion for all men that religious faith conferred on Sturt.

As a result of the journeys of Hume and Hovell, Cunningham and Sturt, the way was open for the expansion of settlement south to Victoria, north to Queensland, and south-west to South Australia.

Ever since the middle of the eighteenth century the discussion in England on the possible uses of New Holland and New South Wales had centred around the role they could play in the capture of the spice trade with the East Indies and the trade with China and the Pacific, and as a possible base for naval operations in the Pacific. To forestall the French, the British government had established an abortive settlement at Port Phillip in 1803 and permanent settlements at Hobart Town and Port Dalrymple in 1804. Fears of French colonization on the south coasts of New Holland and New South Wales again caused the British to establish garrisons manned by convict labour at King George's Sound, on the south coast of Western Australia, and Western Port, on the south coast of Victoria, in 1826. In another vain and quixotic attempt to entice trade from Dutch to English merchants they established a settlement at Melville Island off the north coast of Australia, where officers, soldiers, and convicts rotted away their lives in the service of English greed and duplicity, for the English had solemnly handed back Java to the Dutch in 1815. Yet the dream

Inadequate soil and vegetation brought the Swan River settlement in Western Australia close to ruin.

of New Holland as a stepping-stone to the islands of gold and the spices of the Moluccas survived in the minds of the men of the 'Eastern interest' in London.

It played a part in the decision to establish a colony on the Swan River in 1829. In July 1828 Captain James Stirling had reported enthusiastically to the Colonial Office on the climate, soil, and water supply of the Swan River area. The desire to forestall the French was still influencing official opinion in London, while the 'Eastern interest' snatched at yet another opportunity to exploit the wealth of the Indies. An emancipist merchant in Sydney, Solomon Levey, was prepared to invest capital in a colony on the south-west coast of New Holland, and he entered into partnership with Thomas Peel in London. Yet, paradoxically, when the British government accepted the terms under which it was prepared to promote the foundation of a colony on the Swan River, it excluded convicts from the colony and stated that land should be granted to settlers in proportion to the capital they invested. They appointed Stirling the first lieutenant-governor and instructed him to take possession of New Holland under the name of Western Australia. The settlers, workers, officials, and a small party of soldiers landed and officially proclaimed the colony on 18 June, 1829, when Stirling swore, as had Phillip in 1788, that he would not attempt to restore a member of the House of Stuart to the throne of Great Britain and took other oaths to maintain the Protestant ascendancy.

But neither the lofty aims of the Protestant ascendancy nor the more worldly aspirations of the founders were brought to fruition in the early history of Western Australia. In the beginning the inadequate soil and vegetation, rather than the system of land tenure or the folly and greed of the settlers, brought the colony close to ruin. The men who had dreamt of tapping the wealth of Asia were soon confronted with a struggle for survival. The colonial reformers in London, ignorant of the true causes of the anguish and material hardships of the early settlers, added insult to injury by attributing the failure to the stupidity of the men who had drafted the land laws. When the Colonial Office accepted this criticism and imposed a minimum price for crown land in all the Australian colonies, the proceeds to form a fund to pay the passages of immigrants to that colony, the sale of land almost ceased in Western Australia, and with it the emigration fund disappeared. Some settlers in Western Australia migrated to the eastern colonies, while those who remained suffered from a chronic shortage of labour. In 1846 the despairing settlers begged the British Government to make and declare this colony 'a penal settlement upon an extensive scale'. So another society that had been conceived on the grand scale of putting a part of Australia into a world setting, connecting it with the civilizations of Europe and Asia, was metamorphosed by a barren land and human contrivance into a society concerned with the more elementary problems of food and shelter and the dependence of workers on their employers. Once again the European discovered to his regret that to transplant a civilization it was necessary to use a slave or semi-slave labour force to lay its foundations.

By contrast the politics of the mother colony of New South Wales were disturbed and stormy as a consequence of the use of convict labour. The suspicions and ill-feeling between emancipists and immigrants had introduced a factiousness into its politics as misrepresentation and vilification set the tone of public life. Chaplain Samuel Marsden, who belonged to the immigrant faction, accused Dr Douglass, an emancipist sympathizer, of drunkenness and lifting the skirts of convict girls for most improper purposes. Governor Brisbane accused Marsden of the daily neglect of the spiritual concerns of his parish for the sake of attending to his own multitudinous temporal affairs. Sir John Jamison, a large settler on the Nepean, accused the Macarthurs of disturbing the peace of the colonies for thirty years and of diabolical and self-designing

William Charles Wentworth, the Blue Mountains explorer, was the son of a surgeon, D'Arcy Wentworth, and a convict woman, Catherine Crowley.

intrigues. To add to the confusion of observers searching for a pattern in the politics of the period, Jamison also accused Governor Brisbane, whose sympathies lay with the emancipists, of encouraging the prostitution of female convicts at Emu Plains. In January 1824 Brisbane accused the Judge of the Supreme Court, Barron Field, who had not visited Government House for two years, of not succeeding in keeping his court free from the spirit of party.

By 1825, the year in which Darling took over from Brisbane as governor, the exclusive section of the immigrant faction had been discredited. A court of inquiry had acquitted Dr Douglass of the charges of drunkenness and fornication. On instructions from Lord Bathurst, Darling sent for Marsden and rebuked him for the party spirit and intemperance that befitted his age as little as the sacred profession to which he belonged. It was the end of Marsden's career in politics in New South Wales, the end of a sincere and at times tragic attempt to satisfy both God and Mammon. He had failed to win favour from men in high places, or to win the respect of his fellow-men. From that day his lips were often seen to move in prayer as he turned to ask that divine favour that he had also desperately coveted from his earliest years.

Macarthur's public career also seemed finished. He began to absent himself from the meetings of the legislative council; he ceased to visit Government House. He spoke in private of his plans to aggrandize the Australian Agricultural Company; at other times he spoke of his plans to visit China; again at times he spoke of his plans to visit South America to study the breeding of asses. He was beginning to behave like a wayward child, and spent so much time sitting at home brooding and muttering to himself that doubts were entertained for his sanity. At a time when riches, honour, and affection might have been his desert for his great contribution to the prosperity of the colony in his early days, he had to endure his opponents' rancour and resentment for his policy of social exclusiveness. Thomas Hobbes Scott, who had accepted the office of Archdeacon of New South Wales in 1823, was also paying the penalty of too-close association with the Macarthur faction, and had become a victim of the scurrilities of the other side. James Bowman, the other public figure in the exclusives' faction, was a nonentity who owed his public position to his marriage into the Macarthur family. The exclusives had become the victims of their own snobbishness, men haunted by the evil in their past, men who were seeking solace in their religion or in the bosom of their families rather than men with a vision for the future of New South Wales.

By contrast, the emancipists were buoyed up by the belief in the righteousness of their cause and by the enthusiasm of a group of young men of talent who had joined them. The chief of these was William Charles Wentworth, whose great natural talents were driven on by ambition and by wounded pride. He was born in 1790, the son of a surgeon, D'Arcy Wentworth, and a convict woman, Catherine Crowley, who had been transported to Norfolk Island. He grew up in the belief that he belonged by birth to a family of ancient lineage in England and Ireland. He went to England for his early education, returned to the colony, where he was a member of the party that first showed how to cross the Blue Mountains in 1813, and then returned to England to recuperate and to continue his education. By then, apart from his career and his deep affection for his father, the other passion of his life was the prospect of marrying a daughter of the Macarthurs and so aggrandizing his property while ministering to the dictates of his heart. Then the blow fell. In a pamphlet written in London by H. G. Bennet he read that his father had himself been transported. He decided there and then to avenge the honour of his father against this vile slander and to make his own career one of such glory that the honour of his family would be vindicated. The glory of New South Wales became

confounded with the promotion of his own career. At the same time he heard
that the Macarthurs were implacably opposed to his marriage. So when his
private hurts revealed to him what he would fight for, the wound to his heart
influenced what he would fight against.

Shortly after his return to the colony he presided at the dinner to commemorate the anniversary of the founding of the colony. His angry and aggressive voice converted the traditional conviviality into a call for action for
the emancipist side in politics. To drunken shouts of approval, the poet of the
emancipists, M. M. Robinson, recited the line 'That a birthright at *home* was
an inheritance *here*!' With fervour they drank the toast 'The land, boys, we live
in', for the great emancipist dream was that the land belonged to them and
their posterity, not to the immigrants. At a public meeting called to draft an
address to present to Brisbane, Wentworth, in that ruthless language that
damaged both his own prestige and the reputation of the cause with which he
was identified, described the exclusives as the 'yellow snakes of the Colony'
who should be deprived of their venom and their fangs by the emancipists.

He demanded the immediate establishment of the two fundamental principles of the British constitution, trial by jury and a house of assembly. The population was adequate: they excelled all other British societies in the great particular of good morals; Sydney was orderly; a free people was entitled to their ancient and free institutions. Only the 'yellow snakes', the colonists of rank and wealth, were inimical to the establishment in New South Wales of the British constitution.

In 1825 it looked within their grasp. The new Governor Darling was feeling his way. Young men of ability were serving the emancipist cause. There was Wardell, a lawyer and joint editor with Wentworth of the *Australian*. There was E. S. Hall, an ex-evangelist and, by 1826, editor of the *Monitor*. There was Robert Howe, the editor of the *Sydney Gazette*. The *Australian* and the *Monitor* by 1826 were propaganda sheets for the emancipist cause. The clergy had been commanded by the archdeacon not to take part in political life. So, in influencing opinion, the press and public meetings were on the emancipists' side, while the Protestant pulpit was neutral (the priests of the Catholic Church were under the threat of expulsion if they used their pulpits for political propaganda).

Part of the town of Sydney and the entrance to Port Jackson in 1823.

By the end of 1827 the emancipists had squandered the advantage they enjoyed. Political comment in the *Monitor* and the *Australian* became so slanderous and inflammatory that Darling became alarmed lest the Irish and the convicts be incited to the destruction of all law and order. Events came to a boil when Darling sentenced two soldiers, Sudds and Thompson, who had committed an offence to secure their discharge from military service, to seven years' hard labour. They were drummed out of the regiment in a ceremony wherein they wore neck collars and chains. Sudds died soon after. The *Australian* unjustly and irresponsibly attributed his death to wearing 'the instruments of torture'. Darling began to be exasperated by the use of the case for political purposes. In private Wentworth talked of his plan to impeach Darling for cruelty and tyranny. From all this Darling concluded that Wentworth was a vulgar, ill-bred fellow utterly unconscious of the civilities due from one gentleman to another; that he was a demagogue who was trying to lead the emancipists for his own personal aggrandizement. When Darling made two attempts to control the press, to protect his senior officers from wicked slanders and the lower orders from the evils of sedition, Chief Justice Forbes refused to certify that the bills were not repugnant to the laws of England. The emancipists howled for joy as Darling in his zeal seemed to be illustrating their argument that his government was an arbitrary despotism while their group was merely asking for the birthright of Englishmen.

All through 1827 Darling was harried by the emancipists. At the Turf Club dinner in November Wentworth again overstepped the bounds of propriety and decorum in his speech, and Wardell was so carried away by strong drink and the spirit of the evening as to call out to the band to strike up the tune 'Over the Hills and Far Away' after they drank a formal toast to the health of the governor. When Darling heard of this fresh insult, he promptly dismissed the officers of his government who had identified themselves publicly with the political demands of Wentworth's extreme group. The more cautious of the emancipists, who put career before principles, and those who were not touched by the passions driving Wentworth, took fright. At the dinner to commemorate the anniversary of the founding of the colony in January 1828 the name of Wentworth was greeted with uneasy silence by men traditionally sympathetic to the cause of the emancipists.

At the same time Darling had got round to putting down on paper his ideas for the future constitution of the colony. The people, he believed, were not ready for a house of assembly; the thoughtful part of the community saw this, and the people in general were indifferent, though a few had been worked upon by Wentworth's inflammatory speeches and the radical articles in the *Monitor* and *Australian*. If they were guided by their friends, Darling believed, the colonists would not have to boast of any great extension of their privileges, and it was altogether better that it should be so. For his part he advised the British government against surrendering to the demand by the Wentworth faction within the emancipists for trial by jury and a house of assembly. This was, in effect, the same advice Macarthur had given to the Colonial Office when he informed them that the opinions of emancipated convicts were not the opinions of the moral and respectable part of the community, who were in fact anxious to disclaim the violent and absurd demands of publicans, bakers, Jews, and other common people.

The views of Darling and Macarthur were incorporated in the Act to Provide for the Administration of Justice in New South Wales and Van Diemen's Land, which was passed by parliament in 1828. The members of the legislative council were to be appointed by the secretary of state on the recommendation of the governor. There were to be ten to fifteen members consisting of the officials of the government and men chosen from the leading landholders and merchants in the colony. The right of initiative in legislation still rested with the governor, but no law could be passed under any circumstances without the assent of a majority of the members. Any act of the council could be disallowed by parliament within three years of its receiving the governor's consent. Summaries of new bills had to be published in the press eight days before their introduction to the council. Members of the council were not compelled to take an oath of secrecy. In civil cases the Supreme Court could order trial by jury if both parties required it. In criminal cases the government was empowered to introduce trial by jury when it saw fit. So the degeneration of the emancipists in the eyes of Darling into a drunken, irresponsible rabble prepared the way for the political institutions of New South Wales to be manipulated by those who enjoyed economic power. The curtain was rising on the pastoral age in New South Wales.

In Van Diemen's Land over the same period political life was not enlivened by any faction fights between immigrants and emancipists. In that colony the supply of convict labour often equalled the demand by government and settlers. Nor was there any group of wealthy emancipists competing with immigrants for land. Nor did any section of the officers or immigrants form themselves into a coterie of exclusives. As in New South Wales, the public life of the colony was influenced by the character and values of the lieutenant-governor. In 1824 Colonel George Arthur took over the seals of office from William Sorell. He was then just forty years of age and enjoyed a reputation as a soldier, an organizer, and an administrator. He belonged to the evangelical group in religion and shared their assumption that the Roman Catholic Church destroyed liberty and reduced its members to poverty. Like most puritans of the time, he behaved with a chilling formality to other men, though the few who stayed with him at the table to lower a second bottle of port found to their surprise that the man had a heart. For in public he behaved with all the implacable austerity of the strong towards the weak and with contempt and disgust for the liar, the drunkard, and the adulterer. With that high seriousness and high-mindedness of the evangelicals, he used the strong arm of the state and the teachings of the parsons to reduce the drunkenness, the gambling, the whoring, and all the other abominations in Van Diemen's Land.

In 1825, to the delight of the free population of Hobart Town and Port Dalrymple, the British government accepted their requests for the independence of Van Diemen's Land from New South Wales. After a royal salute was fired, Governor Darling officially proclaimed independence and announced that Van Diemen's Land was to have a constitution similar to that of New South Wales, a lieutenant-governor, and a legislative council of three to five members. That night the houses of the most loyal and public-spirited inhabitants were illuminated, and many a rosy bumper was emptied round festive boards in toasts to the future prosperity of Ultima Thule.

The next day, when the trivial round and the common tasks were resumed, difficulties and hardships returned to plague the colonists. They had always resented the practice of the government of New South Wales of sending incorrigible criminals to Van Diemen's Land. They feared their lovely island was being turned into a cage for the vultures of Australia. In an attempt to counter this tendency, and as an indication of how much his mind had been spotted by prejudice against Irish Catholics, Lieutenant-Governor Arthur requested the British government not to send Irish convicts to Van Diemen's Land: to the impoverishment of Tasmanian society and the future impoverishment of its intellectual and spiritual life. For whereas the culture of New South Wales was enriched by and, up to a point, fashioned by the confrontation of the

Protestant upright man and the Irish Catholic image of Christ, Irish Catholics in Van Diemen's Land were never strong enough in numbers or sufficiently various in social type to emancipate themselves from the ghetto mentality of an oppressed and degraded minority.

The settlers were constantly besieged by bushrangers, who were recruited in the main from absconding Irish convicts. They had taken to the bush to pursue a life of plunder, as their sense of themselves as victims of an ancient wrong lent both savagery and revenge to their plunder of the Protestant settlers. The settlers, too, were constantly besieged by the Aborigines, who travelled in packs of one hundred-odd, so that their numbers compensated for their primitive arms. They surrounded houses, and then, to the accompaniment of blood-curdling yells and the savage barking of their kangaroo dogs, they clubbed settlers and stock-keepers to death. The settlers demanded reprisals. In their rage they forgot just how disastrous their civilization had been to the Aborigines. Of the three to seven thousand Aborigines estimated to be living on the island when the white man established his first settlement in 1804, there were probably three hundred left in 1830. In the towns of Hobart and Port Dalrymple a few high-minded people realized that the hunting of the kangaroo and possum by the European had brought starvation to the Aborigine. A few, too, were puzzled by the disastrous effects of contact with civilization on the Aborigine, and were pained to see that the gift of 'higher civilization' degraded the Aborigine into a wretched cadger of alcohol and tobacco. Arthur still believed they should be treated with kindness and compassion. When a group of them came to Hobart Town, he ordered the commissary to feed and clothe them and the police to protect them against insult. But others less high-minded served the Aborigines with drink, provoked them into a fight, and then roared with laughter as they mangled and butchered each other.

Scenes such as these convinced the evangelicals that their first task was to convert and civilize their own people. Their voice of piety was heard more frequently and more effectively during Arthur's governorship, when chaplains of the Church of England, Wesleyans, Presbyterians, and Catholic priests united at least in accepting the role of the clergyman as a moral policeman for the state. To the evangelicals of all Protestant persuasions, but not to the Catholic, Great Britain was a distinguished nation renowned on earth and highly favoured of heaven. When the evangelical surveyed the material achievements of the first twenty-seven years in the Australian colonies, he was inclined to marvel at such a creation. 'Britain, and Britain alone,' a pious evangelical told his flock, 'could bring about so wondrous an achievement—such a monument of the stupendous energies of a mighty nation.'

During the same time education and religion in New South Wales were being fashioned to serve the interests of a society in which economic and political power was concentrated in the officials, the large proprietors of land, and the wealthy merchants. In 1823 Bathurst asked Thomas Hobbes Scott to advise

A skirmish between bushrangers and constables at Illawarra, New South Wales. Settlers were constantly besieged by bushrangers who had taken to the bush.

him on the future education in the schools. Scott, who subsequently became the first archdeacon of New South Wales, recommended a system under which there would be attached to every parish church a school where children would be taught reading, writing, arithmetic, and the catechism of the Church of England. In addition Scott recommended a secondary school for all who could afford it, with bursaries for the talented but indigent, for Scott, though Tory at heart, had ideas in his head of a career open to talent. He also recommended the future creation of a university; in the meantime he favoured a system of scholarships to enable the gifted to take their degrees at Oxford or Cambridge, thus strengthening the ties between mother country and colony. Scott was inspired by the highest ideals of Christian humanism, though in his attempts to gain converts in New South Wales his seed fell on the stony ground of colonial philistinism, or was choked by the weeds of his own self-esteem and concern for the dignity of his office. With the creation of the Church and Schools Corporation in 1825 the government of New South Wales conferred a monopoly, at least for primary education, on the clergy of the Church of England.

The Presbyterians, the Methodists, and the Catholics were thus driven into an alliance of expediency to destroy the Anglican monopoly. In this setting a Presbyterian clergyman began his stormy career in New South Wales. He was the Reverend J. Dunmore Lang, who was born in Scotland in 1799, educated in the best Presbyterian tradition to fear the Catholic Church and all its works, and became a convert to the ideas of the 'Voluntarys' in education. From his teachers he received a lively impression of the joys of the elect and the eternal torments of the damned. He arrived in Sydney in 1823. By temperament he was driven to reckless and at times perverse support for the weak and the inferior, not so much out of sympathy with the humble and meek but from pleasure in hurting the proud. So by principle as well as by inclination he was driven to oppose and humble the Anglicans in New South Wales. With him he brought to New South Wales an association between Calvinism and the rights of man, a dream of reconciling Christian teaching with the ideal of the brotherhood of man, and a doubt of man's ability to create the terrestrial while God created the celestial paradise.

To defeat the Anglicans Lang was prepared to work with the Catholics—to the astonishment and disgust of the Anglican establishment in Sydney and Parramatta. The men of the establishment in Sydney thought the Irish Catholics so benighted and so bereft of every advantage that should adorn the mind of man that, in their eyes, there was nothing but the shade of a Catholic's skin to distinguish him from an Aborigine. A proof of this seemed to be the fact that these Catholics, who lived in such appalling squalor, were erecting at enormous expense a church in Sydney decorated with tinsel and extravagant ornaments.

By contrast the chaplains of the establishment saw themselves as the guardians of higher civilization and true religion. The God of the Protestants was not a God of social confusion and anarchy, but that creator of rank and order in the natural world and man's world as described by Ulysses in Shakespeare's *Troilus and Cressida*. The Bible, the Book of Common Prayer, and Shakespeare were their teachers. They were guarding society against the inroads of anarchy, infidel atheism, false doctrine, heresy, and schism. To preserve order in society they prayed in their churches for the welfare of their sovereign—'Long may a Protestant crown flourish on the head of England's King, and let the hierarchy of our country, let every member of the Church of England, let every subject of the realm, let every friend to virtue and social order in every land say, AMEN.' So one clergyman counselled his flock at St James' Church on 6

September, 1827. The Protestant clergy preached the duty and utility of keeping holy the Sabbath day; they urged the faithful to kneel devoutly during prayer. They urged them to avoid the sins of thieving, swearing, drunkenness, lying, fornication, and adultery. They believed that the teaching from the pulpit and a perusal of the Bible and other writings of a religious tendency produced honest and upright servants. The young, especially, were taught to read the Bible, to regard it as the guide of their path and the rule of their lives, so that, under the Divine blessing, they might advance to their eternal salvation. 'Sobriety and contentment,' argued one parson, 'decency and domestic peace will be united around them, and the dawn of that glorious day will have opened on our view, when the young shall grow up in every virtue and the old man finish his course with joy, and slumber in the grave in peace.'

The Anglican establishment still entertained hopes of raising the Aborigines from barbarism to civilization by education. They still hoped that if the minds of the Aborigines were expanded by useful knowledge and their sentiments refined by moral culture, and if, as they put it, 'they were taught to think as we think, to feel as we feel, to live as we live, then the Aborigines would be blended with the general population'. For, they argued, humanity and Christian mercy constrained them to raise the Aborigines from their abject wretchedness. They should also make some recompense for depriving them of their lands. The best recompense, as they saw it, was to teach the Aborigines to appreciate the advantages of Christian civilization. The difficulty was that, first, the Aborigines spurned the gift, and second, a drunken brawl between Aborigines provided the best spectator sport of the day.

In the up-country districts the Aborigines (known as 'the blacks') remained the most formidable enemy the settlers had to encounter. It was downright folly, the settlers argued, to talk of humanity and forbearance because the blacks never could be persuaded into good-fellowship, never could be conciliated, and never could be divested of their treacherous habits. Drop them, the settlers counselled, when they showed fight; strike terror into them, because they were irrational and brute-like. The blacks, they believed, must be treated as an open enemy because the progress of their hostile acts was marked with blood and murder and desolation for the white settlers. This policy, which was always ascendant, drove the Aborigines away from the settled districts and thinned their numbers, though not so catastrophically on the mainland, for the very vastness of the interior provided an opportunity to escape total annihilation.

The behaviour and values of the white men were beginning to be influenced by the climate and environment and the peculiar composition of their society, as well as by their European past, whether Protestant, Catholic, or Enlightened. Before 1830 observers in Sydney were beginning to speculate on the effect of the uniformity of the climate and scenery. They predicted that it would produce such a tameness and feebleness of character that the inhabitants would write little or no poetry and would have no impulse to rise in the scale of morals. In New South Wales, they argued, there was no long summer day or long winter night, no fall of the leaf, no sudden exuberance of flowers in the spring, no song of birds, no deep, continuing twilight, no season of absolute gloom. Instead there was a plain, level uniformity. The imagery of English poetry was not understood by the children of New South Wales. The environment in which poetry had been written in England did not exist in New South Wales. Where, it was asked, were the 'blue-veined violets, hare-bells, butter-cups, daisies, soft silken primroses, the heather of hawthorn's bloom? Where were the lions, the tigers, elephant, hippopotamus, camel and other noble quadrupeds? The sequestered glens or purling streams, or mountains peaked with snow, the towering crags, or the gushing waterfalls—all that scenery which was sublime?' By contrast, they argued, New South Wales was flat, uniform, and sombre.

The same flatness and dullness prevailed in its society. Men sought distraction and comfort not in art, literature, or religion, but in drinking, making money, and eating. The rest of the heavy, dull hours were consumed in scandal, which had become, in the words of one captious observer, 'the unrectified, pernicious alcohol, which undermines the enjoyment of more lives, than that ever did which enters the mouth'. Scandal had made every man distrust his neighbour. Difficulties with servants robbed many of the higher use of their leisure. In Sydney the domestic servants were said to be 'of the worst description under the sun'. The settlers in the country who used convicts to work their estates and serve in the house were afraid to spend time in the towns in social intercourse because the Aborigines or the convict servants might steal or destroy their possessions. Women with social aspirations protested that riding through rows of gum-trees or viewing cornstalks was not to their taste. 'As to conversation,' one woman wrote to the *Sydney Gazette* in 1823, 'nothing can be so *sheepish*. Young *Arable's* wits are gone a *wool gathering*—ever since he commenced grazing. Talks of music, and asks for a song, young Wholesale chaunts over an invoice, "Money is your friend, is it not?" '

While the life of the elite at Government House in Sydney and Hobart Town was all pomp, stiffness, and formality, the life of the lower classes was all riot, revelry and drunkenness. Some observers attributed such behaviour to the discrepancy between the sexes, especially amongst the convicts. In New South Wales in 1828, in a total population of 36,598, 16,442 convicts were men and 1,544 were women. In Van Diemen's Land, in a total population of 20,265, 6,724 convicts were men and 725 were women. All colonial societies in their early history have developed something singular in the relations between the sexes. In the United States the mystery of 'bundling' was resorted to by couples who proposed marriage but for economic or social reasons were in no position to consummate it. In South Africa the Dutch settlers, faced with the problem of an excess of males and what they called 'the first law of nature', intermarried with the native population. No such solution was open to the convicts. And the emancipists and their children were excluded from all social intercourse with the upper classes by that snobbishness and that policy of exclusion that provided the social cause for tension between immigrant and emancipist. In the early days there had been talk of importing women from the islands of the Pacific or even from China to produce a race of 'socially benevolent human beings' at Botany Bay.

The convicts and emancipists quickly found their own solution to the problem: they encouraged the convict women to be prostitutes, which had often caused their transportation in the first place. The clergy thundered against such wickedness, accused them of practising with each other the vices of the Cities of the Plain, or, in an attempt to interest them in marriage, reminded them that at the beginning of the world God had said, 'It is not good for man to be alone.' God's will, the clergy continued, was that man should be fruitful and multiply, and replenish the earth, and subdue it. But in this as in so much else the convicts ignored advice and followed inclination rather than duty, so that in time the convicts, like the Aborigines, became almost a vanishing race. The colony had the benefit of their labour without handing on to future generations the problem of an underprivileged class. In 1831, however, even the days of the convict domination of society in New South Wales, and to a lesser extent in Van Diemen's Land, were numbered by a decision in London to assist free workers to emigrate to those colonies.

CHAPTER FIVE

IMMIGRANTS AND SQUATTERS
1831—1842

BY THE 1820s it was a commonplace that there were districts in England and Scotland and especially in Ireland where there existed a distinct labour surplus. It was also a commonplace in public discussions that in the British colonies in North America, at the Cape of Good Hope, and in New South Wales and Van Diemen's Land there were tracts of fertile land capable of receiving and supporting any proportion of the redundant population of the British Isles. There was a chronic shortage of labour in colonies such as New South Wales. The problem was how to transplant the workers from the places of redundancy to the places of demand.

As early as 1820 the English newspapers had singled out New South Wales as a suitable place to which men of capital might emigrate.

In 1829 two serial articles began to appear in the London *Morning Chronicle*. The first, by Robert Gouger, was called *The Act of a proposal for colonising Australasia;* the other, by Edward Gibbon Wakefield, was *A Letter from Sydney*. Both recommended the sale of colonial lands at a price sufficient to deter labourers from becoming landowners too soon and to prevent dispersion of settlement, and then using the money thus gained to pay the passages of selected emigrants. At the same time news that Charles Sturt had discovered 'a magnificent river falling into the sea at Cape St Vincent' reached London. The followers of Gouger and Wakefield, who came to be known as the systematic colonizers, immediately suggested the use of the site to establish a colony where, by conforming to their laws of political economy, the colonists would achieve the maximum happiness. Others maintained the site provided an opportunity for investment by the men of the city, but the men of money were not prepared to invest in a scheme for a colony until the scheme had the approval of the Colonial Office. Others put forward high-flown reasons for a new settlement. George Fife Angas said:

My great object was in the first instance to provide a place of refuge for pious Dissenters of Great Britain who could in their new home discharge their consciences before God in civil and religious duties without any disabilities. Then to provide a place where the children of pious farmers might have farms in which to settle and provide bread for their families; and lastly that I may be the humble instrument of laying the foundation of a good system of education and religious instruction for the poorer settlers.

By 1831 Wakefield had drawn together his arguments for a new colony. Exportable commodities such as coal, woods, barks, gums, salt, saltfish, seals, and the products of the sperm and black whale fishery, abounded. The other Australian colonies had suffered from an insufficient supply of labour. In the new colony a concentration of people would ensure a combination of labour. The laws would prevent that dispersion of settlement that had ruined New South Wales, which was also adversely affected by an idle and vicious population who were almost totally unacquainted with the business of agriculture, because

Edward Gibbon Wakefield propounded his theory of systematic colonization while he was in Newgate gaol for having abducted a young heiress. His principles were used in part in the founding of South Austalia in 1836.

parishes that had defrayed the expenses of the emigration of paupers had poured into New South Wales the worst inhabitants of the workhouses. New South Wales also suffered from an undue proportion of males. Wakefield proposed to select none but young persons of the two sexes in nearly equal proportions. New South Wales had suffered from the use of convicts, whose presence was one of the causes of the inadequate supply of labour. In the new colony there would be no convicts. The pious agreed, not because of the effect of convicts on supply of labour, but because of their tendency to promote sin.

A prospectus for the South Australian Land Company was published in 1832. Investors were assured that the British government wanted to promote the foundation of the colony. A minimum price was to be charged to ensure adequate cultivation of all land purchased and the most desirable concentration of settlers. The net produce of the sales of land would be employed in conveying to the colony young married or marriageable persons of both sexes in about equal numbers. The trade of the colony was to be perfectly free. As soon as the male adult population amounted to ten thousand the colony would be entitled to a legislative assembly to be elected annually under the best arrangements for securing independence of choice.

All through 1832 and 1833 the representative of the company, the friends of systematic colonization, the speculators, and those excited by the prospects of a colony of the pious, badgered the Colonial Office for official recognition. Finally, in 1834, parliament passed an act to erect South Australia into a province, which stated in the preamble that there were waste and unoccupied lands fit for the purposes of colonization, that divers of His Majesty's subjects who possessed considerable property were ready to embark, and that these persons desired a uniform mode in the disposing of waste lands. The act then proceeded to establish a deed of authority for the government of the province, vesting the control of colonization in three commissioners and the preservation of law and order in a governor. There was to be a fixed uniform price for land and systematic selection of migrants. No convicts would be transported to the colony. In this way speculators, systematic colonizers, and pious dissenters wrote their ideas on colonization into an act of parliament.

As first governor the Colonial Office chose Captain John Hindmarsh of the Royal Navy, who was said to be zealous, good-tempered, anxious to do right, brave and inured to hardship, though one man with an eye to the future wondered whether the methods of the quarterdeck equipped a man to govern a colony of men dedicated not to hurt or destroy each other on the fertile plains of South Australia. As for the other officers, government and commissioners looked for believers in religious equality and philanthropy, and even men who conformed with the puritan ideal of the upright man. They chose some who were dedicated to the moral and intellectual improvement of humanity, some who were out to further their ambitions, and some who pursued pleasure by repeated violations of the seventh commandment and frequent looks at the wine cup when it was red. The settlers included worldly-wise men, army officers who had sold their commissions, land buyers from New South Wales and Van Diemen's Land, and urban tradesmen. Those selecting the workers were instructed to entice the sober and the industrious by promising them that their courage and exertions would bring them an estate of their own within ten years of landing; on no account would men of bad character and dissolute habits be welcome.

As evidence of their high principles and their awareness of motives other than the pursuit of material gain, they proclaimed their intention to introduce the Aborigines to civilization and so lead them into a voluntary and peaceful acceptance of the Christian religion. No one was to be hindered from worshipping God in a peaceable and orderly manner. Angas advanced eight thousand pounds to some pious Lutherans from Prussia to enable them to come where they might worship God according to the dictates of their conscience, at the same time binding them to him as tenant farmers for thirty years—and so philanthropy and profit were often happily united. In this way the German Lutherans began to contribute to the Protestant ascendancy in the Australian colonies, and the numbers of the upright were strengthened.

The *Buffalo* sailed in from Portsmouth in August 1836. Government officials, commissioners, settlers and workers gathered on the east coast of St Vincent's Gulf in December 1836 to hear Hindmarsh swear, as had all his predecessors in the other Australian colonies, that he would preserve the laws protecting the Protestant ascendancy in the United Kingdom, though possibly with more point because the colony had been founded in part to prove the great Protestant assumption that riches belonged to men of understanding, men who had found favour in God's eyes. Almost immediately upon arrival unseemly arguments broke out between the worldly-wise and the god-fearing. The righteous and the upright clashed with the drunkards, the fornicators and the liars. The governor and the resident commissioner quarrelled about the site for the future capital as well as its name. Speculation in land began. Relations between the governor and the resident commissioner were bedevilled by the divided authority. Hindmarsh was recalled and the high-minded Gawler sent to recapture the earlier vision. But idealism was not enough, and Gawler, too, was recalled to London. In 1841 George Grey took over as governor and resident commissioner, and by a policy of ruthless economy as well as shrewd use of the native gifts of a worldly-wise man, he lifted the colony out of its financial mess. An act of the British parliament in 1842 vested the statutory powers of the governor and of the resident commissioner in one man and relieved the colony from its constitutional mess.

By then South Australia was beginning to turn to traditional methods rather than depend for welfare on theorists on colonization or the prayers and lamentations of the pious. In 1840 the pastoralists subscribed to pay the costs of an expedition to discover a route for stock between South Australia and Western Australia. Edward Eyre, who was chosen to lead the expedition, persuaded the subscribers to allow him to search first for suitable pastoral land to the north. He set out in June 1840 with a party that included two Aborigines, but

In 1840 pastoralists subscribed to the cost of an expedition to discover a route for stock between South Australia and Western Australia. After suffering great hardships, Edward Eyre and an Aboriginal companion arrived at King George's Sound in July 1841.

on finding neither feed nor water for stock he returned and began to search for an overland route to the west. After suffering great hardships Eyre and one of the Aborigines, Wylie, arrived at King George's Sound in July 1841, where Wylie was greeted with 'wordless weeping pleasure' by his own people, and Eyre took a glass of hot brandy and water, performed his ablutions, and put on a clean suit of borrowed clothes, all of which, he said, enabled him to feel comparatively comfortable. He had shown that along the coast a desert, rather than land suitable for farming and grazing, divided South Australia from Western Australia. In 1844 Charles Sturt set out to examine the nature of the country in the centre of Australia, where he believed there were large tracts of desert country. After they had penetrated to an area where water and feed had both failed, and where sandy undulations succeeded each other like the waves of the sea, his companion exclaimed, 'Good Heaven, did man ever see such country.' Sturt soon turned away with a feeling of bitter disappointment and returned to Adelaide. The inhabitants of South Australia had to make do with the land they already knew.

But progress came on other fronts. In 1845 copper mines were opened at Burra. In the same year John Ridley invented a reaping machine that reduced the number of workers needed for harvest. The wage expense of the large estates was thus reduced, but the small farmers continued to harvest by hand. Moves were afoot to improve the quality of the plough. Flour mills were built

Burra Burra copper mine. The depresssion in South Australia finally ended with the discovery of rich copper deposits at Kapunda in 1842 and at Burra Burra, 'the eighth wonder of the world', in 1845.

in the country to solve the transport problem of farmers. South Australian farmers were giving a lead to agriculture in Australia. The backwardness in the older colonies had been caused by the use of semi-slave labour and the concentration of capital and enterprise on the progress of the pastoral industry. Equality in numbers between the sexes freed South Australia from the social evils of the convict colonies. The creation of a society of farmers, a high proportion of whom had a stake in the survival of the existing society, removed the fears that any extension of political privileges might be used by the propertyless against the propertied. The existence of a large group of dissenters, influenced by the teaching of the Voluntarys on the relation between the state and religion, prepared the way for the abolition of state aid to religion in 1851. So South Australia pioneered two great movements in the social history of Australia: how to appear radical and be conservative, or how to be a puritan without doctrines.

At the same time as the foundation of South Australia was being discussed in London, moves were afoot in New South Wales and Van Diemen's Land to settle the Port Phillip area. As early as 1831 Hamilton Hume, who had walked with Hovell from Sydney to Port Phillip in 1824, was predicting that if the country at Bass Strait were thrown open to emigration it would prove in a short time to be the granary of the colony and one of the greatest sheep countries in Australia. In 1836 the Surveyor-General of New South Wales, Thomas Mitchell, reported that he had travelled from the Murray River to Portland on the coast to the west of Port Phillip, over land that for natural fertility and beauty could scarcely be surpassed, across streams of unfailing abundance and plains covered with the richest pasturage. Stately trees and majestic mountains adorned the ever-varying scenery of this region, the most southern of all Australia and the most fertile. In his enthusiasm he called the new country Australia Felix. Immediately the land seekers amongst the settlers in southern New South Wales began to go 'overland' in drays with their flocks and herds, following the major's line. New settlers arriving in Sydney were attracted by the reports and followed the crowd.

At the same time settlers and businessmen in Launceston (formerly Port Dalrymple) and Hobart were speculating on the possibilities of a settlement at Port Phillip. John Batman formed the Port Phillip Association and solemnly purchased one hundred thousand acres round Port Phillip from the Aborigines in consideration of twenty pairs of blankets, thirty knives, twelve tomahawks, ten looking-glasses, twelve pairs of scissors, fifty handkerchiefs, twelve red

Kapunda copper mine, 'a wonder of the world', was discovered in 1842. The copper mines attracted skilled miners from Cornwall and Germany.

The oldest surviving building in Victoria. Captain William Lonsdale, the administrator of the Port Phillip District from 1836 to 1839, lived in this simple, five-roomed prefabricated house.

shirts, four flannel jackets, four suits of clothes, and fifty pounds of flour. John Pascoe Fawkner, the son of a convict, who as a child had seen the lieutenant-governor of Van Diemen's Land take snuff in handfuls while convicts were flogged before his eyes, looked to Port Phillip as the land of opportunity. In 1835 both Batman and Fawkner took up land on the Yarra at the northern head of Port Phillip Bay and began an unseemly brawl over who was the real pioneer of the new district.

By 1836 sufficient overlanders had moved into Australia Felix, or the Western District, and to Port Phillip for the government of New South Wales to proclaim the country of Port Phillip as a district open to settlement and to appoint Captain William Lonsdale its administrator. In 1839 the surveyor Robert Hoddle drew up a plan for a city of rectangles within a square mile; the main thoroughfare ran due north, thus exposing all future inhabitants to the hot north winds in summer and the cold south winds in winter. The town, on which the future city was to be built, was named Melbourne after the Prime Minister in the United Kingdom. By 1840 there were 10,291 people in the district, and its history began to be caught up in those problems of immigration,

Caroline Chisholm, moved by compassion for the fate of immigrant girls, and by sympathy for the labour needs of the settlers, shepherded the girls from Sydney to outlying districts.

land laws, transportation, education, and self-government. With sufficient sense of community, the settlers began to raise their voices in favour of the separation of Port Phillip from New South Wales.

In the meantime the way of life in New South Wales was being greatly influenced by the increase in the immigration of free workers as well as by the expansion of the pastoral industry. In 1831, under the influence of the ideas of the systematic colonizers on the advantages of concentration of settlement, Lord Goderich introduced a minimum upset price of five shillings per acre for the sale of crown land, the proceeds to pay the passages of migrants to New South Wales and Van Diemen's Land. Between 1835 and 1840 the amount paid and the categories of people entitled to assistance were increased. Some attempt was made to meet the principle of selection of immigrants by drafting regulations defining types considered suitable. As colonial criticism swelled against what they described as the sweepings of the poorhouses, a bounty system was introduced in 1835 by which the passage was paid only when the immigrants produced on arrival testimonials of good character, signed by clergymen and other respectable inhabitants of note, and evidence that they were within the age groups for which a bounty was paid.

Between 1831 and 1850 over two hundred thousand emigrated to the Australian colonies under the government and the bounty scheme. So emigration schemes appeared to contribute towards reducing redundancy in the United Kingdom. In the colonies the immigration systems caused both anger and dismay. Employers in the towns and settlers in the up-country were appalled by the quality of the immigrants' labour. The settlers complained that the immigrant was reluctant to leave the towns; whereas the convict could be forced to put up with the hardships and loneliness of the bush, the immigrant either jibbed at leaving the town, or if he did go inland he bolted back to the city so fast that neither persuasion nor bullying could make him honour his contract to work. In the 1840s Caroline Chisholm, the wife of an Indian Army officer, moved by Christ-like compassion for the fate of the immigrant girls, as well as by sympathy for the labour needs of the settlers, shepherded immigrant girls from the town of Sydney across country to the more outlying districts.

Males usually outnumbered females by three to one during the early years. The imbalance contributed to proposals to assist immigrants, especially women.

The settlers also complained that the ruinously high wages either encouraged the free workers to squander their earnings at a bush inn, or to use the money to buy land and so vacate the labour market. The demand for workers in the country districts was insatiable. 'The fact is,' wrote one settler early in the 1840s, 'we must have Labour in some Shape or other—free Labour if we can get it,— if not, then Prison Labour, and failing either, Coolie Labour.'

In the towns the arrival of immigrants from Ireland as well as England and Scotland exacerbated those sectarian sentiments that had taken root during the convict period. The *Sydney Herald* wrote on 17 March, 1840, that the sale-of-land funds had been handed over to agents who swept the gaols and parishes of the cumberers of the property of popish landlords for the contemptible purpose of establishing a popish ascendancy in New South Wales. On the other hand the priests of the Catholic Church grieved lest the scheme be used by the Protestant ascendancy to deprive Irish paupers of their faith: those monsters of iniquity who had already converted the most beautiful island of God's earth into a land of skulls were probably plotting to pervert the minds of Catholic immigrants with the poison of their apostasy.

The immigration schemes certainly provided the occasion for the sharpening of tensions between Protestant and Catholic in New South Wales and to a lesser extent in Van Diemen's Land. The Irish immigrants brought the same way of life and values as the Irish convicts. No earthly inducement would allow them to go against the wishes or opinions of their priest, since they considered that their salvation hereafter depended upon following his instructions. They brought with them that charity of the poor towards each other even where there was no claim to any relationship, and that compassion for the multitude they had learnt from their holy faith. They also brought with them the memories of their melancholy history, believing there was no justice for a Catholic in a court presided over by Protestants; and so, to outwit the traditional enemy of their people, lying, informing, treachery, arson, theft, outrage, and even murder was permissible. The priests grieved and warned the faithful not to endanger their eternal salvation by the satisfaction of the primitive passion of revenge. Although the Australian colonies and the United States of America were the best cures the English ever discovered for Irish lawlessness, colonial society became the setting for a desperate confrontation of the Catholic and Protestant views of the world.

Whereas the English and Scottish Protestant—and even the Irish Protestant—knew how to make wealth, understood the laws of political economy, and saw the connection between the upright man and the successful man, the Irish knew the secret of charity, compassion, and togetherness. In the United Kingdom the Irish lived in appalling filth and squalor, sustained in part by a sense of outrage and abomination against a whole people, in part by their holy faith. In New South Wales and Van Diemen's Land they confronted again the traditional enemies of their people, who with the effrontery of the successful told them that their success depended on their embracing British institutions and the Protestant religion. At the same time the Protestants took fright lest their standard of living be lowered by these waves of free immigrants from Catholic Ireland, or their minds perverted and degraded by their superstitious and idolatrous practices.

In the 1830s the other great subject of public discussion was the future of transportation. In 1835 five convicts on the estate of a Major Mudie at Castle Forbes, driven to desperation by perpetual and excessive floggings, fired at the manager, wounded him, and then took to the bush. After their arrest they were tried and found guilty. When the judge called on them to say why sentence of death should not be pronounced upon them, they requested permission to

exhibit their lacerated backs to the court to show what tortures they had endured. The people in the court shuddered in horror; so, briefly, did the
humanitarians in the colony. But those who were outraged by the 'legalized
abomination' of flogging were few, as were the numbers whose moral sensi-
bilities were offended by the servitude and degradation of the convict system.
A Catholic priest, the Reverend W. Ullathorne, wrote:

We have been doing an ungracious and an ungodly thing. We have taken a vast portion
of God's earth, and have made it a cess-pool; we have taken the oceans, which, with
their wonders, gird the globe, and have made them the channels of a sink; we have
poured down scum upon scum, and dregs upon dregs, of the offscourings of mankind,
and as these harden and become consistent together, we are building with them a nation
of crime, to be, unless something be speedily done, a curse and a plague, and a by-
word to all the people of the earth . . . . The removal of such a plague from the earth
concerns the whole human race.

But those were not the terms in which the leading settlers discussed the future
of the convict system. They discussed its success or failure as a source of labour.
Up to the middle of the 1830s they were prepared to put up with all the
inconveniences of convict labour—the petty thefts, the debauchery, and the
possible moral contamination of their families—because convicts were cheap
and could be forced to perform work that no free labourer would do. By 1840
some of the wealthy free settlers in New South Wales doubted whether the
transportation system was an efficient source of labour. In 1835 the British
government had instructed the government of New South Wales to pay for
police and gaols out of the land funds; that is, some of the money the settlers
believed to be earmarked to pay the passages of immigrants was to be used to
meet the costs of the convict system.

In 1840 James Macarthur, the son of John Macarthur, told the legislative
council of New South Wales that a great portion of the distress felt by the
colonists for want of labour arose from the diversion of this fund from the
purpose to which it was pledged. Free labour, he went on, was preferable to
convict labour, for free labour was always preferable to slave labour, because
the latter always was and always must be unprofitable. The diversion of the
land fund had prevented them from getting free labourers. As he saw it,
transportation had been of great advantage to the colony, as the convicts' labour
had laid the foundations of civilization and created the wealth of the settlers,

*A government gaol
gang in Sydney. In the
late 1830s a great
subject of public
discussion was the
future of
transportation.*

but by 1840 it had performed its historic mission: the colony had now arrived at such a degree of wealth, thanks to convict labour, as to be able to populate the country with a free and virtuous people. Not all the wealthy settlers agreed with Macarthur. Those who still believed that their economic future depended on the use of convicts tended to argue that the system of transportation and assignment was the most humane and reformatory punishment that had hitherto been devised. The most impassioned defender of transportation was William Charles Wentworth, who had become one of the largest landholders in New South Wales.

By contrast, the discussion in England on the future of transportation concentrated on its success or failure in punishing and reforming convicts. In 1837-38 a committee of the House of Commons on transportation under the chairmanship of Sir William Molesworth inquired into the system and reported that transportation had been ineffective in deterring from crime but remarkably effective in still further corrupting those who underwent the punishment. They found these qualities to be inherent in the system, which therefore was not susceptible of any improvement. They added that there belonged to the system the 'yet more curious and monstrous evil of calling into existence, and continually extending, societies, or the germs of nations most thoroughly depraved, as respects both the character and degree of their vicious propensities'. They therefore recommended that transportation to New South Wales and to the settled districts of Van Diemen's Land should be discontinued as soon as practicable.

This was not quite the way in which the British government discussed the question. In 1840 the Secretary of State for the Colonies, Lord John Russell, told the House of Commons that assignment was nothing less than slavery, since it consigned a man who had committed a crime to slavery in a penal colony. Where there was slavery, there also were the evils of slavery. On the one side there was the man existing in a mere state of dependence, actuated by fear, the desire for revenge, and every motive that debased human nature; on the other hand there was the master exposed to motives equally debasing, to temptations to tyranny, caprice, arrogance, and the indulgence of all the degrading passions. The assignment system ought not, therefore, he thought, to exist any longer. For these reasons, in 1837 the governor of New South Wales had been instructed to prepare the way for the abolition of assignment, which tended more to degrade the character both of master and slave than all the rest of the evils attendant on the system of transportation. Convinced by the report of the transportation committee that the system did not deter from crime, in 1839 the British government ordered the abolition of assign-

Hobart, 1840. The whaling industry of Hobart was at its height and whaling ships crowded the harbour.
Transportation to New South Wales had ceased that year but in Van Diemen's Land it would continue for thirteen years.

ment in New South Wales and Van Diemen's Land. In 1840 they abolished transportation to New South Wales.

When the news reached Sydney in October 1840, the enlightened settlers and free workers celebrated the occasion as a triumph for their own ideas of morality, though other settlers shouted that these groups did not fear an influx of crime but an interference with the monopoly of labour. The Anglican Bishop of Australia, William Broughton, congratulated those who were born in the colony upon the removal of an opprobrious imputation under which their country had too long laboured. In Hobart the decision to continue transportation to Van Diemen's Land aroused neither fear nor moral indignation, because the convicts were still making a useful contribution to the wealth of the community. When the abolition of transportation to New South Wales produced a glut of convicts in Van Diemen's Land, the settlers there joined with chaplains and philanthropists in cries of horror at the Sodom and Gomorrah in their midst.

All through the 1830s, however, anger and indignation, both in New South Wales and Van Diemen's Land, were directed in the main against the land laws imposed on them by the British government. As early as 1826 the government had tried to meet the criticism of favouritism and minor corruption levelled against the land-grant system by introducing a system of land sales. By 1831 they had become convinced that the combined system of land grant and land sales had not succeeded in making the landholder use his land, or in preventing dispersion of settlement. They were aware, too, of the emancipist's charge that the existing system greatly favoured the immigrant with capital rather than the native-born. To reduce dispersion of settlement they had defined in 1826 boundaries outside which it would be illegal to settle. These boundaries were redefined in 1829, but a line on a map proved no more successful as a deterrent against dispersion than the land laws in encouraging cultivation of the land held under freehold or lease. To promote cultivation and concentration of settlement, and to prevent labourers from becoming landowners too soon, in 1831 Lord Goderich introduced the sale of crown land at the minimum upset price of five shillings per acre. In 1838, believing that five shillings per acre was an inadequate check to dispersion of settlement, Lord Glenelg raised the minimum price to twelve shillings, and in 1842 Lord Stanley introduced a minimum price of one pound per acre.

The settlers howled at the absurdities and inequities of the system. Workers, they said, were not prevented from becoming landowners, and the land laws were not preventing dispersion of settlement. The settlers were paying money for the passage of immigrants who then worked in the towns. The settlers of Port Phillip complained that the revenue raised from the sale of land in their district was being used to bring immigrants to the settled districts of New South Wales, where the powerful settlers, the members of the ancient nobility of New South Wales, grabbed all the labour. The settlers in the Port Phillip district grumbled and began to agitate for separation from New South Wales. The settlers in New South Wales, fearing the loss of revenue from the sale of land in Port Phillip, closed ranks to concentrate on the demand for self-government from London. In their eyes the British government had so mishandled transportation, immigration, and the land laws that the first step to the preservation of their economic and social power was the transfer of political power from London to their own hands.

The settlers in the outlying districts maintained that the price of land was too high for them to accumulate much acreage, while the regulations for leasing and licensing gave them no security of tenure. Until such time as they acquired this security they did not propose to plant civilization on their runs, to build houses, schools, or churches. The land laws, they argued, were responsible for barbarism in the Australian bush. The laws were also responsible for another curious paradox of the period. The men on a one-year lease or licence were part of the landed wealth of New South Wales, Van Diemen's Land, Swan River, and, after 1836, South Australia, and as such they should have been pillars of law and order and subordination in society. But their very insecurity of tenure forced them into a wild and reckless abuse of government. So, in a society that knew no political traditions and was not surrounded by any monuments of the past, the men who might have spoken for authority and stability mouthed words of revolution. The settlers at the Swan River believed their colony was being ruined by political economists and a group of Whig incompetents. Nor were the working classes any happier about the introduction of a minimum price for land. The price was too high for them to invest their savings in a block large enough to give them a living. So the moralists shook their heads in grief and woe as the bush workers squandered their wages at the rum shanty instead of investing in blocks of land.

Land, after all, was the great source of wealth as well as the means to respectability and prestige, and of all the sources of wealth from the land the most romantic, the most popular, and possibly the most lucrative, was the grazing of sheep on crown land in return for the payment of an annual lease fee or licence. The men who did this were called squatters. According to the popular notion the squatter was a happy man, far removed from all the cares of the world, who lived a calm pastoral life and grew rich without much fuss or trouble, while contemplating and applauding the breeding powers of his sheep. There had been a time when men had grown wealthy quickly by the use of cheap convict labour which kept costs down, and by the sale of their wool in London. But by the middle 1830s the country had become more and more thickly settled, and the squatter was obliged to drive his sheep three to four hundred miles into the interior. They took up their runs in the new districts recently discovered by explorers, such as the New England district, the Darling Downs, the Bathurst plains, the Goulburn plains, and the Western District of Port Phillip.

The squatters were either men who were able to receive financial accom-

New South Wales had become more and more thickly settled by the mid-1830s and the squatter was obliged to drive his sheep into the interior.

modation from a bank or from a merchant, or men with sufficient capital to invest in their enterprise. Some formed partnerships, and some worked as agents and managers for city men or men with land in the settled districts. Their social origins were almost as diverse as their sources of capital. Some were British gentlemen who had been educated in the best schools and colleges and belonged by birth to a class in whose halls hung 'the armour of the invisible knights of old'. Others were successful merchants or farmers who had arrived in New South Wales or Van Diemen's Land in a state of penury and had risen to affluence by their own exertions. Others were the sons of convicts. Others again were commissioned officers who were attracted to the Australian colonies by the special concessions in the land laws for officers in the army and the navy.

Exploring parties looking for land filled drays with provisions and set off across country which for the most part had neither road nor track.

After filling the drays with provisions to meet the human needs of food, clothing, shelter, and liquid and spiritual refreshment, the squatter, with his stock, his workers, and possibly his wife, set out for the bush. They travelled for the most part over country where there was neither road nor track. At times the way lay across deep gullies; the drays descended easily into these depressions and were pulled up the other side by the bullocks to a volley of oaths from the driver. At times they were halted by rivers in flood, or by swamps through which they could pass only by frequent unloading. At times the drays sank up to the axles in mud, and at other times bullocks and men laboured against flies and dust. On a good day they travelled twelve miles, on a bad day as few as three or four, so that the journey to a run took between forty and sixty days.

After selecting the run, master and men put up a simple bark hut, dug deep into the side of a hill to make a coolhouse for their food, and erected the hurdles inside which the stock were folded down at night for protection against the wild animals. Then the master, or manager, set out on the long journey to stake his claim to the run at the lands department and pay the lease or licence fee. The shepherds remained to watch the sheep, beguiling the time by reading if they were 'scholars', playing on the Jew's harp, or carousing at the nearest bush-hut or shanty, where they were warmly welcomed.

Dipping sheep. After selecting a sheep run, master and men put up simple huts, dug deep into the side of a hill to make a coolhouse for food, and erected the hurdles inside which the stock were folded down for the night.

The evenings at the bush-hut were spent in cheerful conversation and merriment. As one observer put it, two-thirds of the shepherds and pastoral workers of the country were in perpetual migration, and so the bush-hut developed to meet their needs at a time when almost everyone in the colonies of New South Wales and Van Diemen's Land knew each other. The great scarcity of cash in the up-country districts contributed to a tradition of bartering and sharing. At night, after supper was over, the short pipes were taken out and quart pots of tea were placed in front of the fire. One man sang a song, another told a tale of the early days in the colony, another described the exploits of the bushrangers, others bragged about or cursed their bullocks, and the recent immigrants told the latest news from 'home' and put up as best they could with the colonial jokes about 'bloody immigrants'. At midnight they stretched out on the floor, their heads protruding from the blankets at one end and their feet at the other. At a rum shanty the aim of the drinkers was to seek oblivion as quickly as possible in rum, and the aim of the publican was to rob them of their earnings as quickly as possible. As one reformed drunkard put it, after earning their money like bullocks they spent it like asses. To such men the sight of a white woman was a novelty, and they spent their lives as strangers to the refining influence of religion and education.

The life of the masters was characterized by the same loneliness and the same absence of the refinements of civilization. In the beginning the life of the squatter was a hard one. 'A Settler's life here,' wrote one squatter, 'is very much that of a gipsy living a great part of his time under a hedge hut doubled up in an opposum cloak before a fire at Night and on Horseback all day.' The squatter was plagued by his own ignorance and inexperience, by diseases in his sheep that might rob him overnight of all his working capital, and by the vagaries of the seasons, which threatened to cheat him of that profit to gain which he had steeled himself to face such hardships. Some tired of roaming about a 'beastly ugly sterile country' without finding a safe investment for their capital.

For their life was one long emergency. In February 1839 a squatter near Braidwood in southern New South Wales went for a bath on a hot, sticky day when the temperature was in the nineties and the humidity very high. On returning he was alarmed to see smoke billowing down the gully. All hands turned out and found the whole bush on fire, and the flames bearing down on the huts fanned by a hot searing wind. They worked until they were nearly blind, when the wind turned to the south, the temperature dropped in five minutes to sixty degrees, and the huts and stock were saved. In that year the whole of New South Wales assumed a poor, barren appearance after two years of drought. All through the Murrumbidgee area travellers came upon dead horses and working bullocks. Sheep and cattle crawled to almost-dry water-holes, became bogged down in the mud and died, leaving their rotting carcasses as a testimony to the series of dry seasons.

Gentlemen squatters were appalled by the dirty work some of their fellow squatters practised to make money. Gully-raking, or sheep and cattle stealing, was common in most districts. The gentlemen blamed the ex-convict squatters for such practices and wrote long letters to their friends and relations in the British Isles complaining that this was not a country for gentlemen or men of honour and integrity, as gentlemen could not compete with the rascality of every transaction and the deceit and lies that were made use of every hour. The genteel, the weak, and those not able to adapt themselves to the rough-and-tumble of the new life held up their hands in horror or cried to their Lord to save them from such dens of iniquity.

The greatest difficulty for the squatters was the shortage of labour, or what one man called 'the want of hands'. With the abolition of assignment in New South Wales in 1838 every newspaper in Sydney, Melbourne, and the country districts was filled with advertisements for men, some asking for ten, twelve, and even twenty shepherds at a station. The incompetence and waywardness of the shepherds drove the squatters at times to desperation. Convict workers could be flogged for disobedience or negligence. Free workers behaved with all the independence conferred by the acute labour shortage. If the boss displeased them, they bolted. In December 1839 Learmonth, a squatter near Ballarat in the Western District of Victoria, lost nine hundred lambs from his fold during a severe storm. He sent two shepherds, Mooney and Gabb, to search for them, but they procured rum from a dray that arrived at the run and became as drunk as fiddlers. The two of them and all the men who had come for the shearing spent the next day in bed recovering from the debauch. Two weeks later Learmonth discharged all the shearers for repeated drunkenness, whereupon they celebrated their departure with such gusto that his cook-housekeeper, Ben Good, did nothing for two days, being, as his master put it, 'unwell from the effects of drink brought up by the dray'. On one beautiful bright day in April 1840 Learmonth went up to see the fence-splitters on his run, and when he returned he found all the men raving drunk from the wine that had been brought up from Melbourne the previous day. For days the men remained drunken and unruly and threatened to bolt till Learmonth appeased them, at least for the moment, by handing out more bottles of wine.

The other great plague of the squatter was the Aborigine. By the end of the 1830s the British government, influenced by special pleading from the humanitarians in London, had decided to take action to protect the Aborigines of New South Wales and the few survivors in Van Diemen's Land. 'The inhabitants of New Holland in their original condition,' wrote a committee of the House of Commons in 1837, 'have been described by travellers as the most degraded of the human race; but it is to be feared that intercourse with Europeans has cast over their original debasement a yet deeper shade of wretchedness.' For the better protection and civilization of the natives the British government ordered Governor Gipps in 1838 to divide Port Phillip into four districts and to appoint a protector of Aborigines to each district. These protectors were to be both missionaries and teachers, and were charged with the protection of the Aborigines against the greed and cruelty of the white man. The squatters were not impressed. To them this appointment, like all other appointments by London, seemed useless and expensive, for no man could or should preserve peace between white and black. When the black men stole their stock or threw a fire-stick in their dry grass, they retaliated by putting poison in the flour given to the blacks.

In 1838 a party of white men near Myall Creek, driven to desperation by

A group of Tasmanian Aborigines at Oyster Cove in the 1860s. In 1847 the remnants of this dying race – 14 adult males, 22 adult females, 5 boys and 5 girls – were moved from Flinders Island in Bass Strait to the site of a former convict station at Oyster Cove near Hobart. Ten years later only five men and ten women were alive.

the behaviour of the blacks, captured some, tied them together with a rope, shot them, and then burnt their bodies. Eleven of the white men were tried and acquitted, but the governor ordered a retrial. Seven were found guilty and sentenced to death by hanging. The colony was in uproar. The press in Sydney accused humanitarians and philanthropists of squeamishness. But Gipps stood firm, and the men were hanged in Sydney. In the frontiers of settlement the cause of the Aborigines remained as hopeless as ever: all attempts to civilize them were derided as 'founded in delusion and supported in folly'. Earlier, in Van Diemen's Land, in a last desperate attempt to save the few hundred survivors from total destruction, Lieutenant-Governor Arthur had organized a man-hunt in 1830 across the whole island. Only one woman and one boy were caught, and the days of the remainder were numbered, for in 1869 the last male Aborigine died, and in 1888 an East Tasmanian Aboriginal woman died at Kangaroo Island. So the race became extinct. Both on the mainland and in Van Diemen's Land the expansion of settlement with the increase in the number of squatters had spelt doom to the Aborigine.

For the squatters who survived the ordeals of the early days there were great compensations. The festivals of the Christian year were observed with much ceremony. On Christmas Day 1839, for example, a large party sat down to dinner in a squatter's hut near the shores of Western Port. The table was covered with the usual English cheer of roast beef, roast potatoes, and roast vegetables, washed down by champagne. 'We were a merry party that evening,' wrote the squatter to his friends in England, 'though sitting in a hut which a beggar in England would hardly live in, the walls full of holes, the floor the natural earth, and situated in the middle of the eternal forest where till eighteen

Truganini, who died at Hobart in 1876, aged 76 years. In her last years she lived in a house at Hobart known as Lalla Rookh, and was cared for by the Dandrige family, of whom she was very fond.

months before, a white man had never trod.' It was this sense of achievement, this sense of creating a new way of life, of planting civilization in areas where hitherto barbarism and savagery had prevailed, which sustained them in their dark days. Some relieved their boredom by reading. Some sweated out their days in the bush in the knowledge that each year there was relief and pleasure to be tasted in the towns of Sydney, Melbourne, or Hobart. All were sustained by the hope of material gain, for some earned between one thousand and two thousand five hundred pounds in a year, while their stock multiplied and the value of their run soared as competition for land intensified.

All were looking to the towns or to London for their supplies, their pleasures, the education of their children, and the redress of their grievances against the land laws and the Aborigines. They paid little attention to strictly local or regional affairs. The dispersion of settlement and the absence of any other cause forcing them to co-operate with each other, together with the pressures to remain at home to protect families and stock against convict servants, drunken shepherds, or marauding Aborigines, made most settlers centre their lives on their own runs. Where closer settlement and the strength of Indian bands forced the settler in the northern British colonies into that co-operation in defence of their possessions that became their first rude school of local and self-government, the tendencies in the Australian colonies were towards centralization. The conditions in the bush that nurtured feelings of equality and mateship amongst the bush workers did not promote their combination for political purposes. So a society in which one section was passionately attached to equality was also creating administrative centralization that brought with it the possibility of conformity and equality under the tyranny of the majority.

To educate the sons of these settlers to act as a governing class in society, William Grant Broughton, who succeeded Scott as archdeacon of New South Wales in 1829, recommended in 1830 the creation of colleges in which scholars would be given 'a liberal education'. He had been shocked to find in his first year in the colony that the inheritors of large properties, young men who were to take the lead in society and occupy a station of importance in the country, were too often destitute of the acquirements that should qualify them for such a station. To his horror, these young men were sacrificing all their respectability and influence by associating with their own convict servants. Such a forgetfulness, he believed, would disappear if their minds were duly cultivated. He proposed to teach them to exercise their powers of reason and to encourage habits of patient investigation by steeping them in a classical education and by providing a general instruction in the chief articles of the Christian faith. In these King's Schools, as they were to be called, the sons of the squatters were to be groomed as a governing class. The first school was opened at Parramatta in 1832, but the pupils proved stony ground for the seeds of Christian humanism. The rapacity with which the squatters pursued their material interests in the 1840s, especially in agitating for convicts or coolies to meet their labour demands, alienated the rest of the community. So while their sons were surprised to learn at The King's School that in addition to the horse there was also the idea of the horse the fathers were depriving themselves of political and social power and prestige by their own folly and greed.

At the same time the public life of New South Wales and to a lesser extent of Van Diemen's Land was disturbed by an acrimonious debate over the future of education. In both colonies Catholics, Presbyterians, Methodists and dissenters resented the Anglican monopoly of education. Governor Bourke, who took over from Darling in 1831, was a Whig in politics and a liberal in religion. He wanted to promote the religious instruction and general education of the people. In a colony that included members of all the religious persuasions, it was, he believed, impossible to establish a dominant and endowed church without much hostility. The inclination of the colonists, which kept pace with the spirit of the age, was decidedly averse to such an institution. So he proposed to give financial assistance to every one of the three grand divisions of Christians indifferently—that is, to Anglicans, Catholics, and Presbyterians. Immediately Anglicans and Presbyterians howled that the proposal would subvert Protestantism. Broughton demanded that all children should be taught to read the Bible upon the principle that Holy Scripture contained all that was necessary to salvation. The Anglican Church, he went on, had given the English-speaking world the Bible in its native language. That was its glory and its claim to their gratitude and favour. By such bombast the Protestants forced Bourke to abandon his plans.

But when Bourke's successor, Gipps, a liberal in religious questions, announced in 1840 that the highest interests of mankind required that the youth of the country be nurtured in feelings of love and charity towards each other irrespective of religious creeds, the Anglicans and the Catholics took fright. For Gipps insisted that if each separate denomination had its own school in each district, then even in the towns a large proportion of the population would remain uneducated. He proposed a comprehensive scheme to include all Protestants. But Broughton was still unhappy. From the persuasion that all forms of religion are alike, he argued, it was but a step to the more total persuasion that all religions are unimportant. When Ullathorne and Polding, two Eng'ish Benedictine priests who had arrived in Sydney in the early 1830s, remonstrated with Gipps, he told them it was his duty to adhere to the strongest party, and he added, 'I don't think you are the strongest.' So Ullathorne and Polding organized a procession through the streets of Sydney. Preceded by a huge cross, with magnificent banners flying, three hundred girls dressed in white as a symbol of the mystical purity of Christ's church, followed by the laity, acolytes, priests in their sacred robes, and the saintly Polding in full canonical dress bringing up the rear, marched to demonstrate that if they had to choose between Christ and secular truth and enlightenment, they would choose Christ. It was on this altar of varying religious truth as seen by Anglican, Catholic, and Presbyterian that secular education was sacrificed in both New South Wales and Van Diemen's Land. In South Australia, by contrast, the greater number of dissenters, and the numerical weakness of the Anglicans and the Catholics, allowed religious education to be sacrificed on the altar of secular education.

In the meantime the politics of New South Wales and to a lesser extent of Van Diemen's Land were concerned less and less with issues between emancipists and immigrants. So long as the immigrants, and more particularly the exclusive faction of the immigrants, continued to be favoured in land grants and continued to propose such measures as the exclusion of emancipists from jury lists, the franchise, and membership of any future house of assembly, the emancipists and the native-born had an interest in common in resisting their proposals. On the other hand, so long as the emancipists demanded trial by jury and a house of assembly and opposed exclusion of emancipists from jury lists and electoral rolls, the obvious course for the immigrants in general, and certainly the exclusives in particular, was to oppose them, arguing that the colony was not ripe for such developments. By the middle of the 1830s the governor's patronage was sufficiently extensive for the emancipists to demand the right of the native-born to be appointed to public positions, which added a 'job' argument to the emancipists' case against the immigrants.

In 1835 the emancipists formed the Australian Patriotic Association to agitate for their claims both in Sydney and through their representative in London. But by then the winds of change had begun to blow through the politics of New South Wales. The introduction of a minimum upset price for land in 1831 removed ill-feeling between the native-born and the immigrants over land grants. By 1838 wealthy emancipists and wealthy immigrants were beginning to find common ground in opposing British proposals on the sale of crown land, on immigration, and the future of transportation. In July of that year some emancipists and some exclusives had joined together in the legislative council of New South Wales on the convict question. Three more years of British control of land policy, immigration policy, and convict policy, together with the threat to allow Port Phillip to secede, converted the immigrants to the need for self-government. At the same time wealthy emancipists such as Wentworth were alarmed by the radical proposals of the rank and file of the emancipists. So at a meeting in Sydney on 4 February, 1841, to protest against the dismemberment of New South Wales, James Macarthur urged emancipists and exclusives to join forces to show they were ripe for representative institutions. For his part he was prepared to forget the past, to drop the long-agitated emancipist question, and concentrate on the demand for self-government.

The decisions of the British government in 1842 gave added point to that demand. By an act of 1842 they changed the legislative council of New South Wales from a nominated council to a council of which twelve members were to be nominated by the crown and twenty-four elected by inhabitants who possessed a high property qualification. But the right to legislate on the disposal of crown lands was reserved to parliament, which also retained the power to disallow any act of the legislative council within three years of its passing. Another act of parliament in the same year enlarged the legislative council of South Australia to seven, to enable the Queen in council to nominate some unofficial members. The legislative council of Van Diemen's Land remained a nominee council, as Her Majesty's government did not feel justified in proposing to parliament the extension to Van Diemen's Land of a similar form of legislation because of the incompatibility they considered to exist between the grant of such a form of constitution and the continuance of transportation to the colony. Within a decade, however, the convict question in Van Diemen's Land started an angry campaign for self-government, while in New South Wales angry cries of 'no taxation without representation' suggested that the colonies of Australia might be on the eve of a Boston Tea Party.

CHAPTER SIX

POLITICS AND CULTURE 1843—1851

BETWEEN THE YEARS 1825 and 1827, according to the Reverend J. Dunmore Lang, it had pleased Divine Providence to visit the colony, in the midst of speculations in land and stock, with an afflictive drought that lasted nearly three years. The effect of this, he continued, combined with the natural result of the sheep and cattle mania, had been to open the eyes of the colonists to their own folly and madness, to blast the golden hopes of multitudes, and to bring many respectable families to poverty and ruin. The years 1840 and 1843 seemed to repeat these events. Speculation in land and stock was again rife: sheep, cattle and land were bought for sums far beyond their real value. Then the crash came. Payments to the banks and other finance companies fell due. Land and stock were offered for sale on a falling market to meet obligations. Prices toppled. Sheep were sold at sixpence per head; cattle, which had been bought at up to six guineas a head, were sold for as low as seven shillings and sixpence; and carriages, which had cost up to one hundred and forty pounds in the days of plenty, were sold for three pounds in the lean months of March and April 1843. Bankruptcy became widespread, and unemployment and distress became so common that in Sydney the legislative council appointed a committee to inquire into the conditions of distressed labourers and mechanics. In Adelaide, as an economy measure, Governor Grey closed down most government works and had one in seven in Adelaide on unemployment relief under conditions, he was proud to say, from which he had deliberately removed all 'ease and enjoyment'.

Again the clergy pounded their pulpits and implored their congregations to contemplate such suffering as a sign of the displeasure of Almighty God for their sins as well as their madness and their folly. But this time, as evidence of that increasing secular spirit of the age, others put forward empirical causes for the monetary crisis, such as the high minimum price of land, while others argued that it began from supposing that the wealth of a community could be increased by any other means than human industry and economy. The United States consul in Sydney reported to the State Department in 1842 that the depression was caused in part by local issues, in part by the depression in the United States, which had so materially affected the demand for European manufactures as almost entirely to prostrate the wool-growing interests of New South Wales.

In the depth of this depression, in June 1843, the writs were issued for the first election of twenty-four members to the legislative council of New South Wales. The *Sydney Morning Herald* told its readers that the issues of the election were whether the executive government was to have an undue preponderance of power, whether labour should be bond or free, whether to protect native

A pencil drawing by William Hardy Wilson of Panshanger, near Longford in Tasmania. Described as the finest colonial house in the State, it was completed before 1835 and built in front of the original simple brick structure erected by Joseph Archer.

An aquatic fete on Sydney's Domain, 1840, by an artist with a quaint sense of humour.

industries, how to finance immigration, and the eligibility of emancipists for municipal and legislative honours. The candidates could, the paper believed, be divided into three groups—a government party, a landowner party led by James Macarthur and W. C. Wentworth, and city radicals led by Robert Cooper. A week later the same paper was regretting that the elections generally had taken a personal turn, as with scarcely one exception the contests would not be upon principles. On 1 August, 1843, the new legislative council of twelve government nominees was sworn in, including five official members, large landowners such as Berry and Blaxland, and twenty-four elected members, dominated by such large landowners as James Macarthur, Hannibal Macarthur, James Macarthur, Junior, W. C. Wentworth, and W. Lawson, and including Robert Cooper, the workingman's friend, and the stormy J. D. Lang, who had stood for election for Port Phillip, it was said, because he was too well-known in Sydney.

Within six months the proceedings of the legislative council were plunged into uproar by the publication of new squatting regulations by Governor Gipps. Gipps said that three million acres of crown land were out on lease or licence to the squatters from which the crown collected only seven thousand pounds a year in revenue. He conceded that the squatters could legitimately claim security of tenure on their runs in return for the contribution they were making to the wealth of the community. To raise the revenue of government, to enact a just price for the use of the land from the squatters, and to give them security of tenure, Gipps proposed in April 1844 that the squatters should pay a separate annual licence fee of ten pounds per run, which was not to exceed twenty square miles. No single run should cover an area capable of depasturing more than five hundred head of cattle and seven thousand sheep. Pandemonium broke loose in the squatting community of New South Wales. Meetings were hastily summoned at Scone, Goulburn, Penrith, Mudgee, Camden, Singleton, Melbourne and Sydney. At the Sydney meeting on 9 April Wentworth spoke of his deepest alarm about these regulations, which were unconstitutional in their application, oppressive in their influence, and calculated to add materially to the existing distress of the colony. To thunderous and possibly even drunken applause he called on all present to use every constitutional means to force the government to change the regulations.

The uproar led to renewed agitation for the grant of self-government. Wentworth immediately moved in the legislative council for the appointment of a select committee, with himself in the chair and other landowners and professional and business men of like mind to support him, to inquire into general grievances. In their report they wrote of the evil tendencies that followed from the entire separation of the legislative and executive powers. They wrote, too, of the utter state of pupilage in which the governors of the colonies were held by the necessity of constant reference to Downing Street. The lack in London of the necessary information to decide correctly on questions of a purely local nature, which naturally resulted in wrong decisions and imperfect legislation, was a still greater evil. To remedy the evil of the separation of the legislative and executive power the committee recommended responsible government; to remedy the greater evil of reference to Downing Street the committee recommended self-government, or the absence of all interference on the part of the same authorities, except on questions purely imperial. They wanted the colonial parliament to have the power to legislate on land, immigration, education, posts and telegraphs, and customs, while defence and foreign policy and all related questions were reserved to the Imperial Parliament.

As it had in the agitation for trial by jury and a house of assembly in the 1820s, the intemperate language of Wentworth damaged the cause in official circles in Sydney and London. If true wisdom, wrote the *Sydney Morning Herald*, consists in the pursuit of the best end by the best means, Wentworth was not a wise man. Often, they went on, his strongest arguments were neutralized by the coarseness and violence with which they were mixed up, and his intentions, though in the main uprightly patriotic, were misunderstood and condemned by the rancorous personalities in which his tongue ran riot. Wentworth, they concluded, had a self-destroying fatality that convinced others that his resolutions on responsible government and self-government were not inspired by a generous love of country, or zeal for the public good, but rather by a wish to annoy and degrade the distinguished officer whom he sneeringly called 'the Imperial Officer'.

In London the demands were confronted by people who were masters in the art of evasion. Lord Stanley wrote on the demand for responsible government:

Her Majesty must decline to enter into any stipulation at once so abstract and so vague. . . . In neither case [i.e. neither in Canada nor in New South Wales] has the Queen entered into any statement of any Theory or abstract principle of Colonial Government, nor is Her Majesty advised that to discuss such Theories, or to propound such abstract principles, forms any branch of the duties which the laws and constitution of the British Empire call on Her to discharge.

It was the English way of saying 'not now', and using the opportunity to lecture the colonials on the first principles of government.

The squatters were more successful with their demand for security of tenure. Under the power conferred on it by the Sale of Waste Land Act of 1846 the Privy Council issued an Order in Council, which was published in the Sydney papers in October 1847. The colony was to be divided into three districts, the settled, the intermediate, and the unsettled, in each of which the squatters could take out leases for up to fourteen years in return for a small annual rental. Freehold in the land could be bought at a minimum price of one pound per acre. Again the squatters howled that all the fruits of their labour were put in jeopardy by armchair theorists in London. By an odd irony the price of one pound, which was intended as a declaration that land should not be sold till it realized more than it was worth, became in effect a declaration that it should not be sold at all.

This meant the accumulation of landed property in the hands of the few to the exclusion of the many. For the squatters acquired *de facto* their security

When settlers became more prosperous, they made improvements to their homesteads, as illustrated by this watercolour of the old and new homesteads.

of tenure and with it a monopoly of the grazing and agricultural land of Australia: in New South Wales alone the Order in Council handed over 180,000,000 acres of land to about 1,800 persons. So the regulations that had been designed to prevent dispersion of settlement ended by allotting one hundred thousand acres to some squatters outside the boundaries of location in New South Wales, and this, as a committee of the legislative council pointed out in 1847, could not have been outdone by even the wildest abuse of free grants.

With security, the squatters began to make improvements on their runs, fencing their paddocks and putting up homesteads in brick and stone worthy of their rank and prestige in society. In the settled districts, such as New England, Canberra, the Western District of Victoria, the valley of the Derwent, and the south-eastern districts of South Australia, they began to co-operate with the governments in Sydney, Hobart, or Adelaide to erect schools and churches as outward and visible signs of order and civilization. Some squatters at Yass in southern New South Wales summed up their anguish and their nostalgia for older civilization by carving on the bell tower of the Church of England the words, 'I sing the Lord's song in a strange land'. The squatters also devoted their energies to the solution of the problem of the chronic shortage of labour in the up-country districts; but the very desperation of their situation caused them to snatch at remedies that robbed them of the reputation and respect they might have enjoyed as stewards of the countryside. Ironically that security of tenure had presented them with the opportunity to adopt such measures.

In the meantime the politics of all the colonies continued to be disturbed by the argument over education. By 1844 it was clear that the denominational system had failed to provide education for the children, and that its failures were more marked in the country districts than in the towns. It was also criticized for its wastefulness, its expense, its aggravation of sectarian sentiment, for enforcing the subservience of the schoolmaster to the parson, and for the poor quality of the teachers since the low stipends attracted only the odd, the bizarre,

A pencil and French crayon drawing by William Hardy Wilson of a brick cottage in Davey Street, Hobart.

and the picaresque. The government, the Presbyterians and the dissenters suggested a system of national schools, in which the children would be taught religious opinions but not religious doctrines. But neither the Anglicans nor the Catholics would have a bar of it. To both all attempts to teach something so vague as a religion on which all agreed would lead to indifference and unbelief. Broughton went so far as to tell the chairman of a select committee of the legislative council on education in 1844 that if the children were not to be taught the doctrines of their own persuasion he would rather they were not taught at all. Bishop Polding took the same stand, though he cleverly evaded giving the appearance of preferring ignorance to error.

This time in New South Wales, Van Diemen's Land, and South Australia the government had the courage to ignore the prophecies of the priests and parsons on national schools as seedbeds of immorality and unbelief. In the first two colonies between 1848 and 1849 a dual system of education was introduced. A denominational board had the responsibility of dividing among the denominations the money provided by the state. A national board had the finances and power to build schools, equip them, and pay teachers, who were to be persons of Christian sentiment, of calm temper and discretion, and imbued with a spirit of peace, and who were to teach obedience to the law and loyalty to the sovereign. Textbooks were selected in which would be found a large infusion of what all Christians agreed upon as the most important elements of religious truth. Doctrinal religious instruction was to be given at set periods by the clergy of the various Christian persuasions.

The Catholics branded the national schools as Protestant seminaries. Some Protestants were beguiled into accepting them as preferable to surrendering to 'popish' domination. In an attempt to reconcile the irreconcilable both the denominational and the national schools were starved of funds, and so the quality of both types of education paid the price of sectarian folly. The state was consenting to the growth of an education system wherein three types of schools, Protestant, Catholic, and those run by followers of the Enlightenment, presented fundamentally different views of the nature of man and the meaning of his life.

By contrast in 1851 South Australia created a central board of education from which representatives of the religious denominations as such were specifically excluded. Under its supervision schools were established in which children were given a good secular education based on the Christian religion, apart from all theological and controversial differences on discipline and doctrine, and no denominational catechism was used. The Anglicans and the Catholics protested against the attempt to teach religion without doctrine; the Presbyterians and the dissenters celebrated another victory for the voluntary principle and contemptuously brushed aside the warning of Anglican and Catholic that religion without doctrine prepared the way for an age of unbelief.

While priests and parsons wrangled over the role of religion in education, the squatters were driven to desperate remedies to solve their labour shortage. In 1843, believing they were threatened with inevitable ruin by the scarcity of labour, they proposed to introduce Indian coolies. These men, they argued, were well adapted for the role of shepherds, and had exhibited a remarkable example of honesty and sobriety. Besides, the squatters argued, their residence in this country could not fail to communicate to them the habits of civilized life and, by the removal of prejudices, render them more accessible to the influence and adoption of Christian principles. Impatiently dismissing the cackle about civilization and Christ, Ben Boyd, a whaler from Boyd Town near Eden on the south coast of New South Wales with extensive squatting runs in the Eden-Monaro district, recruited shepherds from the islands of the Pacific. The liberals and humanitarians in the towns reviled him as a greedy monster who was trying to create a new slave trade in the Pacific. The workers in the towns protested against the wickedness of lowering the rate of wages by methods that they said could not fail to hinder the growth of virtue and morality, for coolies, they argued, meant slavery and inferiority. Besides, they went on, the labourers here were Europeans, or the descendants of Europeans.

So in their first attempt to preserve their standard of living the workers consciously argued that Australia should be preserved for the white man. They began to see the squatters as traitors to this idea of a White Australia. The squatters, as a group, would preserve the benefits they had enjoyed under the convict system, to the manifest injury of the other classes of the community. At the same time in London the permanent head of the Colonial Office, James Stephen, wrote two minutes on the squatters' proposals. In July 1843 he wrote:

... introducing the black race there [from India to New South Wales] would, in my mind, be one of the most unreasonable preferences of the present to the future .... There is not in the globe a social interest more momentous—if we look forward for five or six generations—than that of reserving the Continent of New Holland as a place

Miss Debney's establishment for young ladies in Van Diemen's Land in 1831.

where the English race shall be spread from sea to sea unmixed with any lower caste
. . . . we now regret the folly of our ancestors in colonizing North America from Africa.

Again in September 1843 he minuted that 'the [coloured people] would debase
by their intermixture the nobler European race'.

Faced with the opposition to coloured labour of the professional classes, the
middle classes, the workers, and the members of the establishment in England,
some squatters turned their minds to the possibility of renewing transportation.
When transportation to New South Wales was abolished in 1840, Lord John
Russell had planned to reduce the number transported to Van Diemen's Land
by keeping some of the convicts in the United Kingdom. A change of government had upset these plans, and so Van Diemen's Land was swamped with
convicts. Between 1829 and 1840 an average of 1,658 convicts each year had
been transported to Van Diemen's Land; between 1841 and 1846 that number
shot up to 3,527. At the same time no provision was made to increase the
buildings to house the convicts, nor was the number of officials increased. The
settlers did not benefit from the glut of labour because assignment was abolished in Van Diemen's Land in July 1841 and replaced by the probation system,
under which the convicts worked in gangs on government farms or public
works. The government of Van Diemen's Land could not use them because
it had been instructed to pay for their services, and the revenue of the colonial
government could not meet the cost. So the convicts in the probation gangs,
or parties, were employed in producing food for themselves.

Very soon the settlers in the country districts and the inhabitants of the towns
began to complain that these probation parties that were intended to be the
scenes of reformatory influences were nothing else than the schools of advanced depravity. The parsons wrung their hands in horror at a system of penal
discipline that encouraged members of probation gangs to practise nightly the
'horrid, debasing, disgusting, detestable sin of the Cities of the Plain, who were
denounced by Divine fire to extinguish their abominations'. The economic and
administrative chaos of the years 1841-46 opened the eyes of the inhabitants
of Van Diemen's Land to the moral evils of transportation. As soon as
Gladstone, the new Secretary of State for the Colonies, heard there was sodomy
again in the Australian colonies, he suspended transportation to Van Diemen's
Land in 1846 for two years.

Some squatters in New South Wales used the opportunity to invite the British
government to renew transportation to New South Wales. Under the chairmanship of Wentworth, a committee of the legislative council, well stacked with
members of the landed interest, boldly suggested in 1846 that the life of a
shepherd or a hutkeeper would humanize and restore a fallen human being
and estrange him from his former tastes and pursuits, especially as the way
of life would provide ample opportunities to contemplate the power and be-

Settlers attacked by Aborigines.

THE CONVICT SHIP HAS ARRIVED!

THE GREAT MEETING will be held on the **CIRCULAR WHARF, TO-DAY, at Noon, to Protest against the Landing of the Convicts.**
The Chair will be taken by **Robert Lowe, Esq., the Member for the City.**
Let all places of business be closed!
Let every man be at his post!   9600

Nine years after transportation in New South Wales ended, a meeting was held at the Circular Wharf on 11 June, 1849, to protest against the arrival of the Hashemy with convicts on board.

neficence of the 'Great Author of the Universe'. 'This grand system of National education and immigration,' as they put it, 'would ultimately reduce to a mere nominal amount crime and pauperism in Great Britain and, at the same time, solve the labour problems of the squatter.' In the meantime the British government, under the pressure of an increase in crime, decided to renew transportation to New South Wales, provided the convicts were not assigned to settlers. When the announcement was made in New South Wales, the inhabitants spoke of treachery and breaches of solemn pledges by members of the government.

On 11 June, 1849, a great protest meeting was held at Circular Quay in Sydney to demonstrate against the arrival of the ship *Hashemy* from London with convicts on board. In spite of continued rain, four or five thousand persons gathered to hear the speakers. To enthusiastic applause, Robert Lowe, an albino who was driven to spite and malice to compensate for all the humiliations he had suffered at boarding school in England, came forward to second the protest. The threat of degradation, he said, had been fulfilled. The stately presence of their city, the beautiful waters of their harbour, were this day again polluted with the presence of that floating hell, a convict ship. To the accompaniment of immense cheers he told them that once again New South Wales must be the university at which those scholars in vice and iniquity finished their course. Again the moral filth of Great Britain had been tipped into New South Wales. This was a breeches-pocket question for the working classes: convicts might increase the profits of the squatters, but for them it was a struggle for liberty and against a system that in every country had destroyed freedom. As in America oppression had been the parent of independence, so it would be in this country. Here, too, injustice and tyranny would ripen into rebellion, and rebellion into independence. After other speeches the meeting dispersed without any noise or tumult, and the conduct of the people throughout, according to the reporter of the *Sydney Morning Herald*, was grave, decorous, and becoming. In the heat and passion of the moment the meeting entertained wild ideas of taking Government House by storm and forcing the timid Governor Fitz Roy to order the captain to take his cargo of moral filth out on to the high seas. But Government House agreed to receive a deputation, and in the upshot some convicts were sent to the up-country districts and the rest sailed in the *Hashemy* for Moreton Bay, where the squatters were clamouring for labour and there was no middle or working class to oppose them.

Not all the squatters in eastern Australia had abandoned the hope of convict labour in the face of angry opposition from the working and the middle classes in the towns. The squatters of the Moreton Bay district petitioned for independence from New South Wales provided they could have convicts. Some squatters in Port Phillip did likewise, so that from 1847 in Port Phillip there was a pro-convict group agitating for independence from New South Wales in co-operation with an independence group in Melbourne that was implacably opposed to the renewal of transportation. At the same time anti-transportation associations were formed in all the colonies except Western Australia to agitate against the renewal of transportation on moral grounds. When the convict ship *Randolph* anchored in Hobson's Bay in Port Phillip in August 1849, excitement ran high in Melbourne. At a public meeting the inhabitants pledged themselves to co-operate with other colonies determined to reject the use of convicts. On 1 October, 1850, the legislative council of New South Wales, after receiving many petitions against transportation, resolved that no more convicts ought to be sent to any part of the colony.

In the meantime Fitz Roy was writing secretly to London that the anti-transportation movement was the work of designing and disaffected persons who were instilling in the minds of the lower orders of the community sentiments of disloyalty to the government of the mother country. To give the lie to such reports an anti-transportation league was formed in Melbourne in February 1851 whose members pledged themselves to prevent the establishment of English prisons or penal settlements in Australia. Within three months there were branches in all the colonies except Western Australia, and the league had chosen the Southern Cross as the national emblem for the movement. In this way the convict question fostered sentiments of some community of interest between the inhabitants of the Australian colonies. But Lord Grey, relying on the Fitz Roy reports about designing and disaffected persons, was playing into the hands of the hotheads and the extremists by flatly rejecting the resolution of the legislative council of New South Wales and the requests of the anti-transportation league.

So it was the transportation question that had infused a note of urgency into the demands for self-government and responsible government. The inhabitants were so caught up with their heated and acrimonious denunciations of existing constitutions that they devoted no time to thinking about what sort of constitutions they wanted. Most of such thinking was being done in England by men such as Grey and Stephen who had been greatly influenced by the writings of de Tocqueville, especially his work *De la Démocratie en Amérique*. While the colonists thundered about British oppression, Grey was turning over in his mind the problem of how to introduce that nursery of self-government, experience in local government, in colonies where dispersion of settlement and the use of convicts had developed a high degree of administrative centralization. Grey was also pondering the problem of what provision there could be in the new constitutions against the tyranny of the majority in a society without an aristocracy. He was considering, too, the disadvantages of four colonial parliaments legislating on such subjects as railways, or customs duties, in which the colonies had a common interest, and on which variations in legislation might prove costly. In magnificent periods of language, redolent of the rhythm and cadences of the Book of Common Prayer, he drew the attention of the colonists to the case for a federal assembly that could pass legislation binding on all the colonies in certain specified fields.

But the colonists remained implacably single-minded. They sang again their song for self-government, while members of the legislative council of New South Wales added that they were not interested in a federal assembly that could not be dominated by New South Wales; and South Australia, as a hint of future provincial loyalties, rejected the proposal as in a British sense unconstitutional. In their eyes a federation such as existed in the United States was an un-British activity, since it was opposed to the social institutions of the colony, and endangered their colonial experience. Intercolonial customs and different railway gauges were part of the price paid for indulging in such folly. For Grey, after reflecting on the colonial reactions, provided in the final draft of the Australian Colonies Government Act, which passed through parliament in 1850, for the separation of Port Phillip from New South Wales, for legislative councils for New South Wales, Van Diemen's Land, South Australia, and Victoria in which one-third of the members were nominated and two-thirds elected on a high property qualification. He also included a clause that conferred on these legislative councils the power to draft new constitutions to be submitted for approval to the Imperial Parliament.

When the news of the contents of the Australian Colonies Government Act reached Sydney towards the end of 1850, it was greeted with howls of disappointment. In a 'Declaration, Protest and Remonstrance', adopted early in 1851, the legislative council of New South Wales recorded deep disappointment and dissatisfaction at the constitution conferred by the act on the colony. They protested that the power to tax should be exercised only by the colonial legislature, that the revenue arising from sale of crown land ought to be subject to their control and application, that customs and all other government departments should be subject to the direct supervision and control of the colonial legislature, that offices of trust and emolument should be conferred on the settled inhabitants (the office of governor alone excepted), and that plenary powers of legislation should be conferred upon and exercised by the colonial legislature. They solemnly warned Her Majesty and their fellow-countrymen in the United Kingdom that it would be impossible much longer to maintain the authority of a local executive that was obliged to refer all measures of importance, no matter how great the urgency, to an inexperienced, remote and irresponsible department in London. In Hobart the act was greeted without enthusiasm. The press urged the new council to get more control over local affairs and rescue the colony from the infamy of convictism. The old nominee council, wrote the *Hobart Courier*, had outlived public respect. Adelaide received the news quietly, with that grave decorum with which the upright are wont to discuss the decisions of their social superiors. In return for the material gains from convicts, the inhabitants of Perth were prepared to forego that birthright of Englishmen to self-government.

When the news reached Melbourne in November 1850, the city gave itself up to a week of celebrations. Special issues of the local papers were published; the Union Jack was hoisted over Flagstaff Hill to a salute of guns; by night the city was illuminated; the churches held special services of thanksgiving; the celebrations lasted a week and ended with a fancy dress ball. During the week the bridge over the Yarra, Prince's Bridge, was officially opened to traffic. Melbourne was beginning to contemplate that juxtaposition of material and political progress that beguiled the Protestants into declaring themselves the recipients of divine favours, and others to reflect on the superiority of their civilization. Then one day in February 1851 the Colonial Secretary of New South Wales, Deas Thomson, who loathed the colonial tendencies towards equality of conditions, opened a letter from a Mr Edward Hargraves announcing that gold had been discovered near Bathurst. History does not record whether Thomson, when he read the letter at the end of a long hot summer in Sydney, perceived that the colonial society he had hoped to see develop in the Australian colonies, headed by a colonial aristocracy that earned its wealth from the growth of fine wool, would disappear like snow before the wind when it confronted the changes that followed the discovery of gold.

In August 1849, in one of those perennial complaints of immigrants against the absence of intellectual culture in colonial societies, a writer to the *Sydney Morning Herald* posed the question: 'Gentlemen, is our Australia to become a second Boeotia, a proverb among Nations? What single building or institution do we possess connected with art or science worthy of an enlightened people? Or are there none who care about them?' He was wrong on the last point, for there were the few, as in all societies, who cared; but they were hopelessly divided in their view of the nature of man and the meaning of his life. Of the 265,503 who lived in New South Wales on the eve of the discovery of gold, the 70,130 in Van Diemen's Land, the 63,700 in South Australia, and the 4,600-odd who lived in Western Australia, all had been influenced by at least one of the three creative forces in their civilization—Protestant Christianity, Catholicism, and the Enlightenment.

At first sight it appeared that all these colonial societies were agitated and consumed by a never-ending sectarian argument between Protestant and Catholic. The press, the pulpit, the public platforms, the pamphlets, and even at times the proceedings of law courts, were given over to unseemly exchanges between Protestant and Catholic. At the end of July 1838 the town of Sydney was placarded with notices summoning Catholics to a meeting convened by Bishop Polding to protest because Judge Willis of the Supreme Court had charged them with the worship of idols. In 1848 Protestant congregations throughout New South Wales declared the day on which two Anglican clergymen, Sconce and Mackensen, were received into the Roman Catholic Church as a day of mourning and a chastisement by God because in their wickedness they had turned away from Him like lost sheep. A priest of the Catholic Church, John McEncroe, called John Calvin a sodomite and all the leaders of the Protestant revolt in the sixteenth century the slaves of sensual lust. As in earlier periods, the Protestant was obsessed with the horrid nightmare that his high material standard and his personal liberty might be swept aside by an increase in Catholic power. He was affronted, too, by men from poverty-stricken Ireland who had the colossal impertinence to inform him that there was no salvation outside the church of Rome. To the Protestant this opinion could only have been held by men who were morally mad. The Catholic was obsessed by the feeling that exposure to a Protestant-dominated society, whose schools, public buildings, and public ceremonies breathed the very spirit of the Protestant religion, might cause shipwreck to the faith. They harboured, too, the grievance that their inferior position in society was the price to be paid for being Catholic, as the top places in the professions, the business world, and the services were, they believed, reserved for Protestants. So with all the passion of men afraid both for their temporal and their eternal welfare both Protestant and Catholic blackened the hearts of each other in wanton displays of human madness and folly.

Appearances deceived, however, for they distracted attention from the quickening of both Protestant and Catholic culture during the period. The Protestants were enlivened partly by the coming of the 'Anglo-Catholic' Tractarian movement to the Australian colonies—the two main proselytizers were Broughton in New South Wales and Nixon in Van Diemen's Land. Outside the Anglican church the Protestants were enlivened and strengthened by the coming of the Voluntarys and by the evangelical revival in England and Scotland. They were strengthened, too, at least temporarily, by the arrival of men such as Carmichael and Mansfield who believed there was such a thing as the religion of everyman, a religion without a catechism and without doctrines, firmly based on revelation of God's word in the Old and the New Testament. At the same time their religion drew inspiration from the teaching of the Enlightenment on human brotherhood and the possibility of achieving happiness on earth. By the 1840s the Protestants were not only split into a bewildering variety of sects, but were beginning to be divided in their vision of the world. Amongst the Anglicans, the Presbyterians, and even some Methodists there were those who viewed the life of man as an act of tragic grandeur. They had learnt their vision of life in a stern school. From Shakespeare they learnt that the flaws in the clay of men who had the stuff of greatness in them brought them deep damnation on earth. From the stories of Absalom, and Suzannah and the Elders, from the books of Proverbs, Job, and Ecclesiastes, and from some of the Psalms, they learnt that evil men were more powerful than good, that the righteous were not rewarded in this world, and that men endowed with charity and compassion were impotent against the wicked.

By contrast the piety preached for the many by the Protestants was still concerned with morality. A correspondent at Burra, South Australia, was pleased to report in 1849 that that bane of the human race, inebriety, was fast fleeing from Burra through the instrumentality of the total abstinence society. At a recent tea party, he was pleased to report, there was barely elbow room, and the tables were loaded with tea and biscuits and cake. Many who could not obtain standing room within thronged the building outside. 'The congregated sons and daughters of sobriety and rational enjoyment,' he continued, 'were addressed by some eight or ten speakers, the speeches being interspersed with temperance hymns, to which every effort was given by a band of able musicians.' By their fulsome support for temperance movements, as well as for the reduction of prostitution and gambling, the Protestant clergy were identified in the public eye as moral policemen for a particular way of life rather than teachers by precept and example of the way to salvation. By continuing to counsel subordination and to urge the poor to accept their lowly station in life, they prostituted their religion to the service of the social needs of the classes in power in the Australian colonies and in London. For good or evil the Protestant clergy had allowed their religion to become a religion of social utility and its reputation to depend on the survival in that society of the need for moral policemen.

On the other hand the Catholic priests from Ireland behaved in such a way as to cause those outside their church to identify it with the worldly aspirations of the Irish people. From the priests the faithful were taught the wrongs against Ireland and the sins of the Protestants with the same zeal as they were taught to say the rosary. In this way the Catholic Church, like the Protestant churches, tended to become a religion of social utility. Like the Protestant clergy, the priests assumed the role of moral policemen, denouncing drunkenness, whoring, and gambling. But again appearances deceived, for the Catholic Church in New South Wales, Van Diemen's Land, and Western Australia began to be affected by the Catholic intellectual revival in England during this period. This was brought to the Australian colonies by such Benedictine priests as Ullathorne and Polding in New South Wales, Willson in Van Diemen's Land, and the Spanish Benedictines at New Norcia near Perth. They spoke of the Catholic Church as the creator of European civilization, and of its lofty and noble traditions rather than of that priest-ridden, sectarian-tainted, bigoted, and superstitious corruption of Christianity that had emerged from centuries of poverty and oppression in Ireland, still preserving by some miracle the image of Christ and the Holy Mother of God. While the Irish priests were sympathetic to the worldly aspirations of the Irish lower classes, the Benedictines taught the case for rank and for inequality in society.

At the same time the bush workers were groping towards quite a different set of values. Ignorant of the consolations of religion, untouched by the traditions and conventions of European society, they looked for a comforter to offset the loneliness of their lives and to protect them against its dangers. They found it in mateship. One observer noted:

From the veranda of an Australian sheep station.

> There is a great deal of this mutual regard and trust engendered by two men working thus together in the otherwise solitary bush; habits of mutual helpfulness arise, and these elicit gratitude, and that leads on to regard. Men under these circumstances often stand by one another through thick and thin; in fact it is a universal feeling that a man ought to be able to trust his own mate in anything.

The same conditions promoted a belief in equality and the habit of judging a man by his performance rather than his inheritance. Prepared to stand by each other in anything, the bushmen were at the same time morbidly suspicious of the newcomer or the intruder who might upset their monopoly of labour, or disturb their way of life. The sentiments of mateship tended to be reserved for the native-born, and the ideals that were the offspring of their loneliness and isolation became in turn forces to strengthen their provincialism and their xenophobia.

The merie Gold buyer discussed
Eagle Hotel

CHAPTER SEVEN

GOLD
1851—1861

IN JANUARY 1851 E. H. Hargraves returned to Sydney from the Californian gold-fields with an anxious heart. Without any real knowledge of geology he had compared the geological formations in California with what he had seen in New South Wales eighteen years before, and concluded that gold must exist in Australia. On arrival in Sydney he told friends and acquaintances of his expectations, and one and all derided him as mad. Undaunted by their ridicule, he travelled from Sydney to Bathurst, from where, in the company of a bush-man named Lister, he set out down the Macquarie River, followed one of its tributaries, then went along a creek that flowed into that tributary, and finally found himself in the country he was so anxious to see. In his excitement he told Lister that gold lay under their very feet. But the bushman was just as incredulous as the mockers in Sydney. So Hargraves dug a panful of earth, washed it in a waterhole, and exclaimed 'Here it is. This is a memorable day in the history of New South Wales. I shall be a baronet, and you will be knighted, and my old horse will be stuffed, put into a glass case, and sent to the British Museum!' On his return to the inn at Guyong that night Hargraves wrote a memorandum on the discovery which he sent to the Colonial Secretary, Deas Thomson, who announced the discovery in the *Sydney Morning Herald* on 15 May, 1851.

Immediately a wave of excitement passed over the city. Government and employers trembled as more and more workers deserted to run to the end of the rainbow. The prices of commodities required at the diggings began to soar: flour rose to thirty or thirty-five pounds a ton, bread sold at sixpence to eight-pence a pound loaf. Shop-fronts began to display goods for diggers—blue and red serge shirts, California hats, leather belts, mining boots and camping blan-kets. On the pavements picks, pans, pots and Virginian cradles were offered for sale. Each day more and more extravagant reports of the nuggets picked out of the ground, or even lying on the surface waiting to be snatched by the first comer, circulated through the city.

By August the centre of interest shifted to Melbourne, for in that month Thomas Hiscock discovered the rich alluvial field at Ballarat. Again excitement ran high. The towns of Melbourne and Geelong were almost emptied of men. Cottages were deserted; businesses were deserted; ships in Port Phillip Bay were deserted. Even some masters of ships, accepting the loss of the crew as inevitable, teamed up with their men and set off for the diggings. Few families were able to retain their domestic servants in the first flush of excitement during that wet and depressing August in Melbourne. But by December large numbers had discovered the life of the digger was not for them and had drifted back to their positions. The clerks and the timid men in secure places were as

Buying and selling gold at Eaglehawk in Victoria.

Above: The cover of a sheet-music song entitled 'I'm Off to the Diggings'.

Above right: Edward Hammond Hargraves, who returned from the Californian goldfields in 1851, was sure that gold must exist in Australia. Ridiculed by his friends, he set out to find gold, and did. His discovery was announced in May 1851.

reluctant as ever to risk their all on such a gamble. More and more the diggings attracted the adventurers and the men of brawn. By January of 1852 enough men had returned to accomplish the season's shearing, and by March there were enough men to bring in the harvest.

By October 1851 wise men on the fields were reporting that gold finding was a matter of pure chance. Others were shaking their heads at the drivelling idiots who expected to accumulate bags of gold with a minimum of labour. The latter soon drifted back to the cities, where they whined about their hardships. On the other hand those who were well-equipped, who worked hard for three or four months, and who put up with the hardships were often very successful. The men of brawn and muscle succeeded, while the educated and the refined succumbed before the ordeal. Conditions on the fields in the early days were primitive. The diggers lived in tents, with the cooking and other chores being done either by one of their team or by a wife. Tents and bark huts were of primitive construction. A few yards of calico stretched between a few poles provided all the protection most diggers needed against wind or rain. Nor did the diggers shave, as 'beardies' became the fashion for men who were pursuing their fortunes with single-mindedness. Slightly more substantial tents were put up by storekeepers, sly-grog-sellers, and, from time to time, prostitutes. For six days of the week the diggers laboured from sun-up to sundown, but on the Sabbath the secular-minded spruced themselves and the religious joined a group listening to a parson perched on a stump who led them in the singing of hymns or recited with them their belief in the resurrection of the dead and the life of the world to come.

Most of the diggers worked in teams of four to six. One man picked and shovelled the earth out of the hole; two wheelbarrowed the earth from the hole to the water, where the other members of the team dollied or cradled it till any gold was separated from the earth. A team would probably get an ounce of gold in a day, for which they received probably three pounds from the merchants on the fields, or three pounds and six to ten shillings if they sold it direct to the government assayer in Melbourne or Sydney. Work began each day after an early breakfast of steak and chops washed down with huge cans of tea. Then with pick, spade, cart, wheelbarrow and cradle the work began in earnest. At times a man with a stentorian voice might call the diggers to a meeting where the chairman elected by the diggers would mount the stump and urge them in their own interests to observe the regulations.

In the meantime life in the towns went stark, staring gold-mad. According to the Melbourne *Argus* young misses whose fathers had been to Bathurst began to appear in brand-new bonnets, perhaps carrying a parasol, and strut about like India-rubber dolls. Several once-respectable and sedate matrons came out on the streets in gaudy silk dresses and wafted strong perfume over passers-by. Successful diggers, together with women whose morals provided material for the sermons by the parsons, sat in low-class inns with a roll of notes in one hand and half a pint of gin in the other, treating all and sundry who came their way. A doctor in Geelong compared the madness to the symptoms of a fever where the patient displayed restlessness, anxiety, and a disinclination to follow his ordinary avocation. Such excitement could, he predicted, terminate in delirium. Yet for the most part order and decorum prevailed on the fields, while the towns quickly accustomed themselves to the sight of diggers squandering the fruits of hard labour on ephemeral pleasures.

By October the government of the new colony of Victoria had improvised a government for the goldfields. All fields were placed under the control of a chief commissioner, and under him there was an assistant commissioner for each field. The commissioners were responsible for the general enforcement of the regulations under which the goldfields were worked. No person was permitted to dig, search for, or remove gold on or from any land without paying one pound ten shillings per month for a licence which had to be shown to the commissioner on demand, or to any person acting under the authority of the government. For failure to produce a licence a digger was fined. Later in Victoria the licence fee was changed to one pound a month, two pounds for three months, four pounds for six months, or eight pounds for twelve months, while licences to carry on business as storekeepers were sold at fifteen pounds for three months, twenty-five pounds for six months, or fifty pounds for twelve months. The diggers and storekeepers grumbled and groused at the height of the fee. 'What's the use of the separation?' called one digger when a stump orator read out the regulations. Another digger referred contemptuously to this 'specimen of independent government', while yet another shouted in anger that the licence was more than the squatter paid for twenty square miles, adding that the squatter, unlike the digger, was not a poor man. The government, however, needed the fees to pay for the cost of administering the fields, and so long as the legislative council, which was stacked with anti-digger men, withheld other financial support, there was no alternative but to collect the fees.

In the beginning the administration of the goldfields worked tolerably well. Observers praised the orderliness of the fields, and British columnists beat their breasts and thanked the God of the Anglo-Saxons that they were not as the Yankees in California, where lynch law had ruled unashamedly. According to one observer, the people were very well-behaved when the 'material' (i.e. their social origins) was considered, though they did not like gentlemen amongst them. Deaths were frequent, both from natural disasters such as a falling tree or the wall of a hole falling in on a digger, or from apoplexy brought on by hard labour and the excitement that surrounded everyday life. Doctors and even parsons worked for gold, too. The bearded parson indulged in open-air preaching on the Sunday. Each night bands struck up lively tunes, and the yells, whoops and shrieks of the successful, or the drunken cries of the failures, made the night hideous. Thefts were few, and murders were even rarer, for

*Conditions on the
goldfields were
primitive and human
tragedy frequent.
Doctors on the fields
were often quacks and
used their surgical
instruments for
cutting up tobacco or
spreading butter.
Their fees ranged
from one pound to
visit a sick miner, to
fifteen guineas for the
local squatter.*

by the end of the first summer the faint-hearted had departed, the parasites, the bludgers and sharpers had not arrived in numbers, and most diggers who remained were earning good wages, though not those fortunes that had first attracted them to the fields.

Where the officers of the law failed, diggers sometimes inflicted summary justice on those who stole from their neighbours. Early in 1852 some diggers on a Victorian field caught such a thief. While women shrieked, men shouted, and dogs barked, a rowdy discussion began on the appropriate punishment. Some wanted to tie him to a tree and lash him with a rope; others wanted to drown him, though they were somewhat at a loss to say where they would find enough water for the purpose; still others wanted to hurl him from a rock. A strange man asked, 'Has the culprit done anything worthy of murder?' Almost before the cries of 'No' had died away, the crowd rushed the culprit, hurried him off to a nearby gum-tree, stripped him, and whaled his bare back with a half-inch rope in such a manner that he could hardly walk. He hobbled off the goldfield into the bush, knowing that to return as a digger might cost him his life. Theft of water or gold was the only crime the diggers did not forgive, though they also judged a man harshly for any failure to endure the hardships of their daily lives.

By the end of 1851 the news of the discoveries had spread round the world. In England, Scotland, and Ireland gold-seekers scrambled for passages on ships bound for the Australian colonies. Australians who had joined the gold rush to California tried for passages home. Americans who believed the roaring days of '49 had vanished for ever took ship for Sydney or Melbourne. At the same time the British government began to ponder the effects on colonial policy of the discovery of gold, though it was not until December 1852, over a year after the early reports reached London, that they announced their decision in a dispatch to the governor of New South Wales. Numerous public meetings and all the legislative councils in the colonies had declared themselves strongly against transportation. 'It would appear a solecism,' the Secretary of State said, 'to convey offenders, at the public expense, with the intention of at no distant time setting them free, to the immediate vicinity of those very goldfields which thousands of honest labourers are in vain trying to reach.' In meeting the wishes of the colonists to end transportation the Secretary of State expressed the hope that they might recognize in it the desire of the government to consult their wishes and to strengthen their loyalty to the crown and to the British Empire. So the discovery of gold finally ended transportation to eastern Australia. The last convicts arrived in Van Diemen's Land in 1853. Approximately 168,000 convicts had been transported to Australia, including approximately 10,000 to Western Australia, between 1850 and 1868.

By the use of convict labour the Australian colonies reaped the advantages of semi-slave labour in transporting a civilization without handing on to posterity either the social problems or the sense of guilt that the use of slave or semi-slave labour often engenders. Opinion remains divided on the other effects of the use of convicts. Some, rather fancifully, have traced the Australian passion for equality to the sense of community in worthlessness amongst the convicts, as though the convicts perceived darkly the spiritual truth that he that is down need fear no fall. Others, pointing to the great disproportion of males to females in the early days of New South Wales and Van Diemen's Land, have traced to the convicts the beginning of a male-dominated society in Australia, from which developed the social habits of men and women collecting in different groups on social occasions and all the humiliations both great and small to which men subject women in Australia. Others have traced the attitude of defiance and hostility to the police back to the days when the police, who were often ex-convicts, taunted and mocked at the men in servitude. Others again have commented on the adverse effects on the large landowners of the use of convicts, to which they have traced the supercilious arrogance with which the upper classes have treated all members of the community. The use of convict labour, the same observers argued, began the alienation of the upper class of landowners from the rest of the community. But on that day in August 1853 when it was announced that transportation had ceased few paused to ponder the legacy of the convict labour system. Rejoicings and prayers of thanksgiving were offered in Sydney, while in Hobart a high festival was held on 10 August, which the inhabitants celebrated as a voluntary holiday. To mark the occasion the legislative council of Van Diemen's Land in the following year prayed to Her Majesty that the island might be called Tasmania in honour of the first European discoverer. On 21 July, 1855, an order in council in London proclaimed that from 1 January 1856 the said colony of Van Diemen's Land shall be called and known by the name of Tasmania.

At the same time the discovery of gold was causing British officials to have second thoughts on the future constitutions of the Australian colonies. By the end of 1852 the Secretary of State accepted the view that the most loyal, respectable, and influential members of the community wanted responsible self-government. He was influenced, too, by the discovery of gold, which would, he believed, stimulate the advance of population, wealth, and material prosperity with unparalleled rapidity. He therefore invited the legislative councils of New South Wales, Tasmania, South Australia, and Victoria to draft new constitutions and submit them for approval and ratification by Parliament. Those councils promptly appointed committees to draft such constitutions. It was during the debates in the legislative councils, in discussions in the press, and at public meetings that there emerged two quite different views on who should exercise political power in Australia.

All agreed that power to legislate on customs, disposal of crown lands, and, indeed, on all local questions should be vested in the colonial parliaments. But there the agreement ended. One group, representing the large landowners and conservative opinion in the cities, wanted the constitution to reflect the large interests in the community. They wanted a constitution in perpetuity for the colony, not one that could be set aside, altered, and shattered to pieces by every blast of popular opinion; they wanted, as Wentworth put it to the legislative council of New South Wales, 'a conservative one—a British, not a Yankee constitution'. To achieve this Wentworth proposed at first that the upper house should be composed of those holding hereditary titles, but he was laughed to scorn by the local wits, who talked with effect of a 'Bunyip Aristocracy' and suggested scurrilous titles for those whose wealth had been created by convict labour—James Macarthur would be called the Earl of Camden and have a rum keg on his heraldic emblem. So Wentworth compromised and suggested a nominated upper house of men of wealth, property, and education, 'men,' he said, 'not raised from any particular section of the community, but from every class that has the energy to aspire to rank and honour'. As a further safeguard for conservative interests he suggested a clause by which the constitution could only be amended by a two-thirds majority in both the assembly and the council.

The liberals in New South Wales were not happy with these proposals. They wanted a constitution in which population rather than the interests of property and education were represented in any parliament. At public meetings their speakers howled at and derided the Wentworth proposals. When W. R. Piddington, a liberal, came forward at a public meeting in Sydney in August 1853 and asked the people whether they submitted to be robbed of their rights, they shouted 'No'. When Piddington went on to mention the Wentworth proposal to create a colonial nobility with hereditary privileges, there were tremendous groans. 'Colonists,' Piddington concluded to loud cheers, 'speak now, or for ever hold your peace.' But power then rested in the pastoral interest, the city interest, and the official interest rather than with the people. So Wentworth won the day, and a bill went off for approval by parliament in which conservative interests were protected by a nominee legislative council, the two-thirds majority amending clause, plural voting, and property qualifications for electors to the legislative assembly.

In Victoria, by contrast, the conflict between pastoralists and bourgeoisie was not so sharp. There was less of that confrontation between conservative and liberal and more of a spirit of compromise between the two groups to resist the radical demands of the gold-diggers. The colonial secretary in the legislative council of Victoria declared in December 1853 that it would be a very poor policy to dam up the flood then setting in, saying that it would be a truer policy to direct that stream into the proper channels, and to develop

Crowds line a Sydney street as the Government escort and mail containing gold arrive at the Treasury.

properly that democratic element. It was the Tocqueville plea for a democracy guided by the educated and the intelligent rather than the opinions of any mob. He wanted the legislative assembly to represent both 'interests' and 'people', and the legislative council to represent the fixed and settled interests of the colony. So the legislative council sent off for approval by Parliament a constitution in which there was plural voting for both houses, a property qualification for voting for both houses, and a power to amend the constitution by an absolute majority of both houses. A similar constitution was sent by the legislative council of Tasmania.

In South Australia, on the other hand, where the subdivision of landed property prevailed to such a great extent that a high proportion of the population had a fixed interest in the soil, it was argued that a democratic constitution could be adopted without threatening the interests of property or education. So the South Australian constitution conferred the right to vote for the legislative assembly on all males of twenty-one years of age who had been on the electoral roll for six months before the election. At the same time the representation of 'interests', and especially property, was provided for by the property qualification for voters for the legislative council. In general, then, the constitutions were mixed constitutions, compromises between the representation of 'interests' and the representation of 'people', and between the conservative and liberal views on who should exercise power in a colonial society. In the constitutions, the Imperial Parliament remained sovereign. All bills passed by a colonial parliament dealing with subjects such as amendments of the constitution, the powers or salary of a governor, defence, foreign policy, or marriage and divorce had to be reserved by the governor for the assent of the British government. A copy of every act passed by a colonial parliament had to be transmitted to the Secretary of State for the Colonies and could be disallowed by him within two years of his receiving the text of the act. That was on paper. In practice the colonial parliaments were sovereign on local questions, and the British Parliament was sovereign on foreign or imperial questions. So the colonial parliaments of New South Wales, Tasmania, South Australia and Victoria received self-government on local questions and responsible government, i.e. the political and legal responsibility of the executive to the legislature, in the constitution acts passed for those colonies by Parliament between 1855 and 1856.

In the meantime observers in New South Wales and Victoria were commenting on the effect of the life on the goldfields on social values. One man in the Bathurst fields wrote at the end of 1851:

Nothing indeed can have a more levelling effect on society than the power of digging gold, for it can be done, for a time at least, without any capital but that of health and strength; and the man innured to toil, however ignorant, is on more equal terms with the educated and refined in a pursuit involving so much personal hardship.

By 1853 another English observer noted that on the Victorian goldfields all the aristocratic feelings and associations of the old country were at once annihilated. Plebeianism of the rankest and, in many instances, of the lowest kind prevailed. It was not what you had been but what you were that was the criterion. If you could not work, you were of no use, and would infallibly sink in the social rank in a society in which physical activity and industry were made the highest standards of a man's abilities for getting on in the world. Victoria, he concluded, had become 'an equalising colony of gold and beef and mutton'.

By the end of 1853 the decline in the income of the alluvial digger caused him to perceive a wider significance in the difference between the equality and mateship of the goldfields and the inequality and political and social privilege that prevailed in the society that surrounded him. By the end of 1853 the

My Newchum Mate.

stump orators on the goldfields were beginning to address their audiences on wider issues. They were beginning to talk of the three great grievances of the diggers: the licence grievance, the land grievance, and the political grievance. They complained that it was beyond their capacity to pay the licence fee, and that the police were unduly severe and tyrannical when searching for unlicensed persons. Diggers without licences were treated like felons, marched along the highway in charge of the mounted police, exposed to the gaze of the populace, and, if unable to pay the fee, put into a cell with thieves, horse-stealers, lags, and murderers amidst filth and vermin. Others were chained to posts where they were exposed to the sun and the ridicule of the rather insensitive troopers. All this was happening in colonies with a tradition of implacable hatred for the police by the working classes. Knots of diggers were heard murmuring that in California this state of things would soon be altered, or grumbling to others about the evils of a police-ridden country. They were grieved, too, by the lack of opportunity of acquiring land on reasonable terms. Some wanted to invest their earnings from gold in land and found it was impossible to do so. They were also grieved by their lack of political rights. As they saw it they had contributed to the wealth and greatness of the colony without enjoying any voice whatever in its administration.

On the night of 6 October, 1854, James Scobie was found murdered on the goldfield of Ballarat. The proprietor of the Eureka Hotel, James Bentley, his wife, and John Farrell were tried for the murder and found not guilty by the magistrates. The diggers, sensing in this acquittal the corruption and bribery in high places that plagued their class, gathered outside the hotel and burnt it to the ground. From that day the diggers began to hold a series of mass meetings in which the demand for justice against the murderers of Scobie was soon swallowed up in the demand for the redress of grievances. At Bakery Hill on 11 November a mass meeting of 10,000 diggers joined in a reform league and pledged themselves to work for (1) a full and fair representation; (2) manhood suffrage; (3) no property qualification for members of the legislative council; (4) payment of members; (5) short duration of parliament. In addition they demanded an immediate change in the management of the goldfields by the dismissal of the commissioners, and the abolition the diggers' and store-keepers' licence tax. The response of the government in Melbourne was to dispatch more troops to the goldfields and to organize more licence hunts.

On 29 November the diggers held a mass meeting that ended on a note of enthusiasm and passion when the diggers, inflamed by the stump orators, burnt their licences in a huge bonfire. With incredible folly the commissioner chose the next day for a general licence hunt, which precipitated a riot and the reading of the riot act. The more fanatical among the diggers then began to arm and to erect a stockade at Eureka in Ballarat, behind which they drilled. At night, when the flag of the Southern Cross was raised over the stockade, they solemnly took an oath of loyalty. On the morning of Sunday, 3 December, when all but one hundred and fifty diggers had become discouraged and left the stockade, the commander of the troops called on the remainder to surrender. When they refused, he ordered the troops to charge. After fifteen or twenty minutes the whole affair was over. Twenty-five of the diggers were killed and thirty wounded, while three privates and one officer of the troops were killed and eleven privates wounded. When the soldiers had once tasted blood, they became violent. The mounted troops began to mangle the diggers till they were stopped by their commanding officers. The police also bullied

Administering the oath at Eureka Stockade in 1854. On 29 November the diggers at Ballarat held a mass meeting and burnt their licences. Next day, the commissioners held a general licence hunt, which precipitated a riot. The diggers erected Eureka stockade and solemnly took an oath of loyalty.

V. R.

NOTICE!!

Recent events at the Mines at Ballaarat render it necessary for all true subjects of the Queen, and all strangers who have received hospitality and protection under Her flag, to assist in preserving

Social Order

AND

Maintaining the Supremacy of the Law.

The question now agitated by the disaffected is not whether an enactment can be amended or ought to be repealed, but whether the Law is, or is not, to be administered in the name of HER MAJESTY. Anarchy and confusion must ensue unless those who cling to the Institutions and the soil of their adopted Country step prominently forward.

His Excellency relies upon the loyalty and sound feeling of the Colonists.

All faithful subjects, and all strangers who have had equal rights extended to them, are therefore called upon to

ENROL THEMSELVES

and be prepared to assemble at such places as may be appointed by the Civic Authorities in Melbourne and Geelong, and by the Magistrates in the several Towns of the Colony.

CHAS. HOTHAM.

BY AUTHORITY: JOHN FERRES, GOVERNMENT PRINTER, MELBOURNE.

A notice calling on true subjects of Queen Victoria to assist in preserving social order.

the correspondents of the newspapers on the goldfields for publishing accounts of their abominations against the diggers. The leader of the diggers, Peter Lalor, having lost an arm in the fighting, hid for a season to escape the vengeance of the authorities and reappeared years later as a conservative in the Victorian legislative assembly.

It looked as though the appeal by the governor for all true subjects of the Queen, and all strangers who had received hospitality and protection under her flag, to assist in preserving social order and maintaining the supremacy of the law had triumphed over the forces of rebellion and the demands of the radicals. The government hastened to redress the grievances of the diggers: A miner's right of one pound per year replaced the hated licence; an export duty on gold of two and sixpence per ounce was imposed to raise money for the administration of the fields; the administration of the goldfields was changed with the substitution of wardens for commissioners; the goldfields were made part of electoral districts, and the possession of a miner's right became a qualification for voting for the legislative assembly in Victoria. Once again the Anglo-Saxon seemed to have silenced the radical by acceding to the demands of the moderates. But the idea of Eureka was to prove more tenacious than the original defenders of the stockade. In the 1890s the alluvial diggers at Kalgoorlie in Western Australia used Eureka as their inspiration in another fight for the rights of diggers. At the turn of the century the poets of the radicals began to write of Eureka as the origin of all the democratic and radical achievements since that time. Victor Daley wrote:

> Yet, ere the year was over,
> Freedom rolled in like a flood:
> They gave us all we asked for—
> When we asked for it in blood.

At the same time Henry Lawson wrote in his ballad 'Eureka':

> But not in vain those diggers died. Their comrades may rejoice
> For o'er the voice of tyranny is heard the people's voice;
> It says: 'Reform your rotten law, the diggers' wrongs make right,
> Or else with them, our brothers now, we'll gather to the fight.'

In this way Eureka became a part of the tradition of those of the Australian people who viewed their history as a steady progress from the dark and bloody days of the birth-stain to their great and glorious future when the people would be liberated from capitalist and imperialist enslavement.

But no such vision crossed the mind of the diggers chafing under the indignity and ignominy of the licence tax. Once that indignity was removed they were soon caught up in other obsessions. The first of these was the Chinese. They began to arrive in the goldfields of Victoria in large numbers during the years 1855-56, when the income of the alluvial diggers was sinking to that of unskilled manual workers, and when gold was being found at such depths that gold mining by companies, employing diggers as wage earners, was beginning to replace alluvial digging by teams of four to six independent diggers. The Chinese came from southern China, generally bound to some headman to work under his orders to pay debts in the homeland. They arrived in groups of six or seven hundred, each man with a pole and two baskets and a hat like the top of a haystack nearly a yard across. In the beginning their manners were those of the old world; the young respected the old, and would not sit down till the aged bade them. But as one cynic observed: 'I expect they would lose their good manners when they got colonised.'

By 1857 there were 23,623 Chinese on the Victorian goldfields and by 1861 there were 24,062, of whom only six were women. At that time there were 203,966 Europeans on the fields in Victoria, of whom 130,535 were men and 73,431 were women. By 1857 the Europeans both in the towns and on the goldfields had become afraid of the Chinese. John Pascoe Fawkner asked the legislative council of Victoria to appoint a committee to frame a bill to control the flood of Chinese settling in the colony, and 'effectually prevent the Gold Fields of Australia Felix from becoming the property of the Emperor of China and of the Mongolian and Tartar hordes of Asia'. The diggers accused the Chinese of immorality caused by the absence of women, of not contributing to the wealth of the country but on the contrary exporting all their wealth to China, and of crimes of great magnitude. But the principal grievance was the great diminution in the yield of gold and the lowering of the price of labour. The Europeans took fright. The Chinese retorted that they thought the English very kind and were delighted by the mercy manifested. They said:

We Chinamen who are here get no gold only by working, headings and tailings, and from old holes abandoned by Europeans, and from which we can but barely make a living. We having only the refuse cannot make as much as Europeans, but with their chances we should not be so poor. As soon as we get a little money we will try to get home to our aged parents, for our ancient books teach that we must look after our parents. . . . Now we hear you are going to put a tax of a pound a month and we much sorry we do not know what to do. . . . We pray your Honourable House will feel for the poor man, and not exact this money, and then all the Chinese will be happy and ever honor the Governor and Legislators and never forget those who are so kind to poor people, and when we get to our own country we will ever speak in honor of such rulers of poor people.

The shanty town of Mount Alexander goldfields in Victoria. These fields yielded nearly £3 million worth of surface gold in six months.

The Europeans were not moved by such tugs at the heart strings. The parliaments of New South Wales and Victoria passed legislation to restrict the entry of Chinese and to discriminate against those resident on the goldfields. Undaunted, the Chinese began to land in South Australia and walk overland in single file in groups of six to seven hundred from Adelaide to the Victorian goldfields. On the fields the Anglo-Saxon diggers took the law into their own hands. On the Buckland River in Victoria in 1857 there was an ugly riot against the Chinese. At Lambing Flat near Young in New South Wales on 30 June, 1861, the storm of anti-Chinese feeling broke with astonishing violence. To cries of 'Roll up', upwards of a thousand men armed with bludgeons and pick-handles assembled round a 'No Chinese' standard. Forming themselves into a rough line, to the accompaniment of martial music supplied by a local band, the men rode to the Chinese quarters at Lambing Flat, shouting, yelling, and singing to high heaven of their undying hatred for the Chinese. These monsters on horseback, as they were described by the correspondent of the *Sydney Morning Herald*, armed still with their bludgeons and their whips, took hold of the pigtails of the Chinese, pulled them towards the rump of their horses, where they cut off their pigtails and left them to the fury of others who surrounded them. One Chinese boy went down on his knees and, with tears running down his cheeks, begged for mercy. A ruffian gave him a blow sufficient to kill a giant, knocking him to the ground. A European woman married to a Chinese was assaulted, and her clothing and that of her children was torn to pieces

while her tormentors took counsel on how to rape her, only to be foiled by the restraining influence of other Europeans. All day the outrage went on till police and troops, summoned from neighbouring districts by the bush telegraph, arrived to restore order. In September juries at Goulburn acquitted all the Europeans charged with riot, which, wrote the *Sydney Morning Herald,* was 'a fitting wind up for so disgraceful a commencement with which it is so perfectly in keeping'. With the decline in alluvial digging in the next decade the agitation against the Chinese declined, only to be fanned again to white heat by the passions roused during the last quarter of the century. The diggers had found a scapegoat for their subterranean passions; in time the minds of large sections of the community would be moved by the same emotions.

Experience on the goldfields infected the diggers' ideal of mateship with the poison of race hatred, but the levelling and egalitarian tendencies present before the discovery of gold continued to be strengthened by events. By the end of 1854 the diggers had begun their campaign for political equality. At Beechworth in Victoria in October 1855 the diggers' candidate for election shod his horse with gold shoes and led off a drunken and rowdy procession down the main street to a mass meeting in favour of votes for all. During 1856 reform associations were formed in Melbourne and Sydney and on the goldfields, and the members pledged themselves to work for manhood suffrage, perennial parliaments, no property qualifications for members, no compensation to the squatters, abolition of state aid to religion, and compulsory free secular education. Noisy demonstrations occurred outside the first parliament in Melbourne under responsible government when it assembled in November 1856. Inside the new parliaments both in Sydney and Melbourne, members from the goldfields electorates demanded the radicalizing of the constitution, while some members from city electorates demanded its liberalization. In May 1858 Henry Parkes told the legislative assembly of New South Wales:

Here all men, comparatively speaking, were on a level. . . . In principle, this country was essentially democratic, and the difference of grade, so far as it went amongst us, would be laughed at by men in the Mother country. They were bound to establish their institutions in accordance with the spirit of the country.

He therefore supported the proposal to introduce manhood suffrage for the legislative assembly, a distribution of electorates to provide representation of people rather than interests, a vote by ballot, the abolition of the two-thirds majority for amendments to the constitution, and the abolition of the property qualification for members of the assembly. He believed in the representation of majorities and the career open to talent, rather than birth or privilege.

Both in New South Wales and Victoria this bourgeois liberalism was strongly opposed by the large landowners or squatters, who continued to defend the principle of the representation of interests. They wanted the two houses to represent the main interests in society—the landed interest, the city interest, the gold interest (pained though they were to admit its existence), and an educated or professional interest. S. A. Donaldson, for example, argued in the legislative assembly of New South Wales that to concede such demands would convert the legislative assembly into a convention as dangerous, as damnable, and as destructive of property and of liberty as that which met in Paris in 1789. He believed the proposals of the liberals would convert a hitherto prosperous colony into a home of destitution and drive both credit and capital from it. In the legislative assembly of New South Wales Daniel Deniehy made an impassioned plea for special representation of the University of Sydney on the ground that men of education might soften the otherwise harsh materialist spirit of a colonial society; but the advocates of government by the majority defeated his proposal, and the advocate of sweetness and light was buried later in a pauper's grave, while the colony of New South Wales swept on over wave after wave of material prosperity.

In both New South Wales and Victoria between 1856 and 1858 the liberals succeeded in introducing manhood suffrage, vote by ballot, a redistribution of electoral districts, and the abolition of the property qualification for members of the assembly. The interests of property were protected by plural voting, by the nominated legislative council in New South Wales, and by the high property qualification for voters for the legislative council in Victoria. One by-product of this principle of majority rule was the decision of the British government to accede to the requests of the inhabitants of the northern districts to implement a clause in the Australian Colonies Government Act and proclaim them a separate colony with the name of Queensland. By letters patent of June 1859 the boundaries of the new colony were defined by an Order in Council. In the same month the new colony was given a constitution the same as that of New South Wales—that is, the Constitution Act of 1856 as amended by such acts as the Electoral Districts Act passed by the New South Wales parliament between 1856 and 1859.

While these changes were occurring in political institutions and values, the material setting of the colonies was changing rapidly. Between December 1851 and December 1861 the total population increased from 437,665 to 1,168,149. In Victoria alone the population increased from 97,489 to 539,764 within those years; South Australia—66,538 to 130,812; Tasmania—69,187 to 89,908; Western Australia—7,186 to 15,936; New South Wales—197,265 to 357,362. Queensland had 34,367 in 1861. The sudden increase did not change the pre-gold proportion between those from the United Kingdom and those from Europe or the Americas. The one significant change was the creation of a Chinese minority, of whom there were just over 24,000 in Victoria by 1861 and over 13,000 on the Queensland goldfields by 1877. Nor did it change the proportion of Catholic to Protestant in the colonies, for Catholics had approximately 23 per cent of the total population in 1861.

The discovery of gold permanently influenced the history of the several colonies. It raised Victoria from a district of New South Wales to a position where in twenty years it challenged the mother colony in population, production of wealth, and prestige in the United Kingdom. On the other hand failure to discover gold in Tasmania except in negligible quantities put an end to the dream of its free settlers that Hobart might develop into the Athens of the South Seas. Instead, Hobart and its hinterland sank back into provincial lethargy, as history or destiny passed it by. South Australians, too, failed to find gold in their colony, and in the beginning paid the price by losing a large portion of their working-class population to the Victorian goldfields. But by the use of those same gifts with which they had begun to turn the hard stones of their native land into standing water, they turned this new flintstone into a springing well. The Bullion Assay Act, which was passed by their legislative council early in 1852, prevented speculation in gold in Adelaide unless the proceeds were used for investment in South Australia. This promoted the shipment of merchandise to Melbourne and the return of gold dust in payment, gave a strong inducement to the South Australian diggers to return to the colony with their gold, and secured to the farmer a good price for his produce. By this device South Australia not only weathered the storm, but so exploited the situation as to confer on her, as Governor Young pointed out in 1852, 'much of the advantage, unalloyed with any of the inconvenience, attendant on the locality of a gold field'.

The increase in population began a boom in the building trades in the cities. As housing accommodation in Melbourne had not kept pace with the demand in the decade preceding the discovery of gold, hard-pressed builders improvised and used weatherboard or canvas rather than stone. In the gold decade weatherboarding and canvas again became the order of the day in Melbourne. Temporary accommodation became permanent, and the improvisations to meet an emergency set the standards of domestic housing for the working classes and the petty bourgeoisie for the next two decades. The principle of fair average quality had come to the cities.

At the same time improvements in transport and communication created opportunities for a more intensive exploitation of the wealth of the country. In 1853 G. F. Train, an American businessman who had come to Melbourne to exploit the possibilities on the goldfields, imported from America a coach with springs, which rapidly improved transportation between Melbourne and Sydney and the fields. In 1854 the first steam train ran from Williamstown to Melbourne; in 1855 suburban trains began running in Sydney. By 1862 the Victorian government had built railways from Melbourne to the Ballarat goldfield and to the Bendigo goldfield. This latter was extended to Echuca on the Murray River in 1864 in an attempt to attract the wool and wheat of the Riverina and the wool brought down from the western lands of New South Wales along the Darling and the Murray to the port at Melbourne rather than to Sydney. In October 1856 the Lord Mayor of London presided at an elegant dinner to wish bon voyage to the *Istanbool*, a combined sail and steam ship that was expected to reduce the voyage from London to Melbourne to sixty-five days, and thus, as the Lord Mayor pointed out, by a combination of sailing and steaming they would have arrived at perfection and be able to get to and from Australia in the shortest time and at the cheapest price. On 19 October, 1858, telegraphic communication was completed between Sydney and Melbourne and Adelaide.

So the discovery of gold became the occasion for, if not the cause of, material progress and a strong movement toward democracy. It was this juxtaposition of material progress and democracy that swept a wave of philistine optimism over the inhabitants of the Australian colonies. The Melbourne *Age* wrote on 13 May, 1858:

... let us recall the established fact that self-government is by incomparable odds the most potent engine for developing and elevating the intellectual and moral condition of the people—surpassing all other machinery for the purpose by as long odds as the steam-engine surpasses all anterior methods of locomotion.

In simple truth, the *Age* went on, the people of Victoria were far better adapted for this prerogative of a civilized man than any one of the most refined nations of the Old World. The people of Victoria were, as a matter of fact, the picked men of Europe, and as a consequence, intelligence, enterprise, energy and spirit were immeasurably more universal here.

Not all of the colonists' energy or thinking was devoted to the pursuit of material gain. In December 1853 the Anglican cathedral in Melbourne, St Paul's, was opened for divine service, and large and attentive congregations attended at both matins and evensong. When the news reached Melbourne that on 8 December, 1854, Pius IX had proclaimed it as a dogma of Catholic faith that 'the most Blessed Virgin Mary from the very first instant of her conception, by a unique grace and privilege of Almighty God, through the merits of Jesus Christ the Saviour of mankind, was preserved free from all stain of original sin', the Catholic community sent a medal struck from Victorian gold to His Holiness to commemorate what was to them a momentous event in human history.

Then at very end of the decade an event occurred that might well have pricked the bubble of colonial conceit and the colonists' belief in moral and spiritual progress following in the wake of democracy and material progress. For more than a decade the governments of South Australia and Victoria had taken an interest in the possibility of finding suitable grazing land between the centre of Australia and the Gulf of Carpentaria. In 1860, somewhat to the surprise of informed opinion, the Victorian government chose Robert O'Hara Burke to lead such an expedition. Burke was a man in whom nature had so

The lavishly equipped expedition of Robert O'Hara Burke ended in tragedy. Burke and William Wills and party set off in 1860 to seek grazing lands between the centre of Australia and the Gulf of Carpentaria.

mixed up the elements that at the very moment when he reached a pinnacle of human achievement his weaknesses brought him to destruction. As a young man in Ireland he had entered the army with dreams of achieving honour and glory on the field of battle, but when the Crimean War broke out, Burke was serving as a police inspector on the Victorian goldfields, and by the time he reached Europe the fighting had ceased. His Victorian expedition, which was lavishly equipped, left Melbourne in 1860 at the height of the enthusiasm and confidence that made it seem that earth and sky would bend to the wishes of the colonists of Victoria. The explorers travelled to Menindee on the Darling, then to a depot on Cooper's Creek, from where Burke and three others, Wills, Gray, and King, set out for the Gulf of Carpentaria, leaving a small party at the depot under Brahe to wait for their return.

With a display of that energy and skill that were efficient servants of his passion for worldly recognition and honour, Burke drove his party to the Gulf of Carpentaria by February 1861. But then things began to go wrong. On the way back, when Gray began to display signs of exhaustion, Burke, who believed Gray was feigning illness to justify getting more than his share of their provisions, thrashed him soundly. Seventeen days later Gray died, and Burke, overwhelmed with remorse and guilt, pushed on in the hope of finding fresh supplies and human companionship at the depot. But Brahe had struck out just that morning, leaving behind a bottle below the word 'Dig' carved on a tree. So with their legs almost paralysed by their severe travelling and privation Burke, Wills and King paused at the depot at Cooper's Creek till they were refreshed.

Then with incredible folly Burke decided to set out for Mount Hopeless in South Australia rather than follow their old track to Menindee on the Darling. With almost equal folly he buried a note for Brahe in the bottle but did not change the sign 'Dig' on the tree. When Brahe's party returned after Burke, Wills and King had left the depot, they did not dig up the bottle and so assumed that Burke's party had not returned. In the meantime the three explorers had become so weak from their diet of nardoo root and crow that Wills returned again to the Cooper's Creek depot, found the bottle untouched, and concluded that Brahe had not been back. By the time Wills rejoined Burke and King, Burke had been so weakened by his privations that he died, asking Wills to place a pistol in his hand so that presumably he might die as an officer and a gentleman. A few days later Wills died. King was kept alive by the Aborigines and was eventually found by one of the search parties sent to investigate what had happened to the expedition.

When the news reached Melbourne, some referred to Burke and Wills as two of the most gallant spirits who had ever sacrificed life for the extension of science or the cause of mankind. Squatters began seriously to contemplate the occupation of Burke's land south of the Gulf of Carpentaria. Within a few years, some said, the journey from Melbourne to Carpentaria would be made with comparative facility by passing from station to station. In the last days of his life Wills had written in his diary: 'It is a great consolation, at least, in this position of ours, to know that we have done all we could, and that our deaths will rather be the result of the mismanagement of others than any rash acts of our own.' It was beyond the range of believers in progress and human perfectibility to ponder what came from within a man to lead him to his destruction, or to ponder over the combinations of chance and circumstance that cheated a man like Burke, whose heart was hot within him, of what he most desperately craved. Twenty years later, when the voice of the nationalists was heard in the land, they remembered the English and the Irish had been tried in the desert and found wanting.

CHAPTER EIGHT

THE AGE OF THE BOURGEOISIE 1861—1883

DURING THE YEARS 1858 TO 1861 a colonial minstrel, Charles Thatcher, wandered from town to town in the colony of Victoria singing to audiences who clapped, catcalled, whistled, and cheered him to the echo as he boasted of the power of the people to:

> Upset squatterdom's domination,
> Give every poor man a home,
> Encourage our great population,
> And like wanderers no more we'll roam;
> Give, in mercy, a free scope to labour,
> Uphold purest bold industry,
> Then no one will envy his neighbour,
> But contented and happy will be.

A satirical painting of the pretensions of the white settler, who is observing with condescension the Aborigines bringing wood and water.

The bourgeoisie began to upset squatterdom's domination when they changed the land laws of the colonies. In the cities, towns and countryside the cry went up to 'unlock the lands'. The bourgeoisie in the cities took their stand on the principle of equality of opportunity. The bourgeoisie also argued that the squatters' use of the land had been wasteful. Out of the 31,467,816 acres in the hands of squatters as licensed runs in the colony of Victoria in 1858, the annual yield for home consumption in the colony and for export had a net value of only 1,997,469 pounds, or one shilling, three and one-half pence per acre. Besides, those who occupied the thirty-odd million acres could not supply the people of Victoria with food. The pastoral tenant had gathered the land's riches and left behind a crop of thistles and burrs and the dilapidated remnants of a few miserable huts. By the lavish alienation of immense tracts of land in the period before 1851 the richest and most accessible lands of the colony had been permanently placed out of the people's reach. In the eyes of the bourgeoisie the squatters' monopoly was wasteful and offended against their principle of equality of opportunity in access to the land. It also repressed the progress of agriculture and retarded the extension of settlement. Australia, they argued, was in danger of remaining a sheep walk for ever.

In the cities the radicals campaigned for homesteads for the people and manhood suffrage, and spoke recklessly to excited groups of the right of the people to take spoils from the landowning and monied interests to enable them to rise above the condition of labourers. At a meeting at the Denison Hotel in Sydney in December 1860 a Mr Cheater told an enthusiastic audience that the land was

all free at first, but them as had a big grip liked to keep it. It would be better for 'em to loose their grip, and let some of the little 'uns amongst them. It would be better to give land for nothing for six years to come. . . . Let them give the land, and not lock it up, so as they might not send out of the country for grain, while they had plenty of beautiful country to grow it in here.

*Hawkers displaying
goods for sale to
country settlers.*

To the *Sydney Morning Herald*—indeed, to all conservatives—the Cheater speech
and the meeting itself partook of the character of a burlesque. Earlier, in
Sydney in 1857, a Mr Read had harangued a group on equal electoral districts,
manhood suffrage, and free land for the people, but was checked with such
interjections as 'He's drunk' and 'Stop till you're sober', till he sat down and
the meeting closed in a rather chaotic way.

It was one thing to talk of equality of opportunity, or of free land, but another
thing to show how either was to be achieved. As John Robertson, a large landowner and businessman in Sydney and an advocate for land reform, explained
when he opened the second reading debate in the legislative assembly of New
South Wales on the Crown Land Alienation Bill in 1860: '. . . it would be
recollected that they had not a clean sheet upon which to legislate—that there
were existing interests. There was one of great importance—the pastoral interest.' He wanted to facilitate the permanent occupation of the country by
freeholders with as little injury as possible to the pastoral interest.

During the same debate in the parliament of New South Wales some of the
squatters, donning mantles in the fashion of those earlier prophets in the
wilderness from whom the parsons read to them during Sunday service, prophesied that land reform would bring everything to ruin. Free selection, they
argued, would aim a blow at the pastoral interest and injure a class that had
given to the colony its largest exports. It would lead to dispersion of settlement,
which would encourage crime and drunkenness; it would lead to over-pro-
duction, which in turn would pauperize and depress the selector. Where, the
squatters asked, was the market for the produce of the selector? Where was
the transport to move it to market? Where was the finance to stock and equip
the selector and tide him over the vagaries of prices and climate? The *Sydney
Morning Herald* warned its readers of the democratic torrent that was levelling
all barriers to tyranny; if the people used the rights of property at their discretion, then let them roar among their ruins, dance about their fires, and
revel among their pigs.

But the warnings were swept aside in the passions of the moment. In 1861
the parliament of New South Wales passed two acts—an Alienation Act and
an Occupation Act—that were intended to be a compromise 'to preserve old
rights while granting new ones—to keep faith with the past while doing justice
to the future'. From the first day of January 1862 any person could purchase
between forty and three hundred and twenty acres of crown land other than
town lands, suburban lands, or proclaimed goldfields at twenty shillings per

*'An English Primrose'
revived thoughts of
'home' in 1858 in
Melbourne, where it
was displayed to
crowds of people.*

*Country visitors
enjoying the city
during Christmas
1874.*

acre, provided he deposited twenty-five per cent of the purchase money and paid the balance within three years to the colonial treasurer, to whom he was to tender a declaration on improvements and effective residence. A portion of the money raised from such sales was to be used to pay the passages of immigrants.

In Victoria the Duffy Act of 1862 proclaimed ten million acres as agricultural areas. Any person, except infants or married women whose marriage was still valid, could select a block between forty and six hundred and forty acres for one pound an acre, part to be paid as a deposit on the day of selection and the balance over eight years at two shillings and sixpence per acre per year. The selector was to cultivate one acre in ten, or to erect a habitable dwelling, or to enclose his selection with a substantial fence. One quarter of the land fund was to be used to pay the passages of immigrants.

The Selection Act of 1868 in Queensland proclaimed crown land open for selection in two classes: agricultural land to be purchased at fifteen shillings an acre in ten annual instalments; second-class pastoral land at five shillings per acre in ten annual instalments of sixpence per acre. The selector was to erect and maintain boundary marks, and either his agent or his bailiff was to reside on the selection. No infant or married woman was entitled to select land.

In South Australia the Strangways Act of 1869 proclaimed certain agricultural areas open to selection, in which any person could purchase up to six hundred and forty acres of agricultural land at one pound per acre, on payment of a deposit and the balance at the end of four years.

The results varied from colony to colony. In New South Wales the selection acts divided the rural population into two hostile camps and encouraged a class war between squatter and selector for the possession of land. Each group practised every species of fraud and abuse against the other. 'Dummying', 'picking the eyes' of a run, bribery of officials in the lands department, arson and physical violence, became the order of the day. To protect what they believed to be their legitimate interests against aggression by the selectors, some squatters mortgaged their estates to the banks or the pastoral companies, and were reduced to the status of managers of lands over which they had once enjoyed the power and prestige of ownership. The methods to which the squatters stooped to protect their interests continued that alienation from the rest of the community that had begun when their fathers had attempted to revive the transportation of convicts, or to import coolie labour in the 1840s, in a desperate attempt to obtain cheap and servile workers on their estates.

The selectors fared no better. Of the 170,242 who lodged original applications to take up selections in the colony of New South Wales between 1861 and 1880, only eighteen to twenty thousand held homesteads according to the

A bush race meeting on the Darling Downs in Queensland.

intent of the law in 1880. In the district of Deniliquin, of the fourteen hundred who purchased selections between 1861 and 1880 only two hundred and forty-four remained in possession in 1880. In the electorate of Murray, to the south of Deniliquin, of twenty-one hundred who took up selections five hundred and ninety remained in occupation. During the same years the revenue to the New South Wales government from the sale of crown land increased from £212,750 15s 10d in 1862 to £2,351,226 6s 11d in 1882. Over the same years wheat cultivation in New South Wales increased from 128,829 acres in 1860-61 to 253,138 in 1880-81. But it was the squatters buying agricultural land under the selection acts, rather than the selectors, who boosted government revenue and doubled the area under wheat.

Most of the selectors in New South Wales lived in appalling squalor. Some lived in bark humpies where the rooms were partitioned off by bark and bag, with beaten earth as their flooring, bushel bags stretched between poles for beds, packing cases for dressing-tables, rough slab tables on stakes driven into the ground, seats made the same way as their furniture, and cuttings from old numbers of the *Illustrated London News* and family albums as the sole decoration on the walls. The crockery was cracked and dirty. In the districts of New South Wales opened up by the selectors there were many such slums in the wilderness, where father, mother and children slaved amid squalor, filth, ignorance and superstition to make a living on the land.

Vagaries of the climate and prices, the lack of agricultural equipment and capital, ignorance, and inadequate or expensive transport to market, contributed to their penury. Some obtained stock, seed, and supplies from stock and station agents, or local owners of the general stores, who sometimes charged interest rates as high as eighty per cent. When they were unable to meet their commitments, the creditors foreclosed. Such selectors either became workers for wages in the district or moved to the cities in search of work. Some hung on in the hope that one day they might earn a competence to reward them for the years of anguish and slavery. It was not until the twentieth century, when agricultural machinery was introduced on a fairly wide scale and when government financial assistance began to relieve the selector from the clutches of the money-lenders, that slavery and squalor began to disappear. It was not until World War II, when there was a boom in world prices for agricultural produce, that some small farmers in New South Wales could afford such creature comforts of civilization as sinks in the kitchen and boarded flooring, and so begin to relieve their wives and children from sun-up to sundown drudgery. The recurring sore that distinguished the descriptions of the life of the selectors in Henry Lawson's *Water Them Geraniums*, Barbara Baynton's *Bush Studies*, and Steele Rudd's *On Our Selection* was then covered up with a sentimental poultice and the slap-stick humour of Dad, Mum, Dave, and Mabel. So time converted human agony into a huge joke.

In Victoria and South Australia the attempt to substitute a numerous yeomanry owning their own farms for a few pastoral lessees met with more success. Within four years of the passing of the Grant Act of 1865 in Victoria over 30,000 persons had taken up selections. Swagmen who had tramped idly from one end of Victoria to the other and wandering miners settled down on their selections. In South Australia, according to one apologist, the land acts, if not an unqualified success, had certainly proved no failure, since settlement had actually taken place. In both colonies the financial difficulties of the selectors, rather than the cunning dodges of the squatters, the activities of the black-mailers, or the corruption of the officials in the lands departments, were the main cause of penury or failure. To make the improvements on the land prescribed by law, selectors often had to borrow from banks, money-lending

Right: Rupertswood at Sunbury near Melbourne was built by William John ('Big') Clarke. The vast garden had layer upon layer of terraced lawns and exotic trees and shrubs grew by the lake.

Above far right: A reception room at Government House, Sydney, in the 1870s.

Far right: 'Doing the block' consisted of walking up and down the fashionable quarter of Collins Street, Melbourne.

agents and storekeepers. When they failed to meet their commitments, the land fell into the hands of their creditors, who thus became the owners of large estates. In this way the shrewd country storekeeper or stock and station agent climbed a rung or two on the social ladder by adding the prestige of broad acres to the wealth accumulated in trade, though not all did, for as one man testified to a Victorian parliamentary committee in 1878, 'Bad debts do not make rich men.'

A few advanced to wealth and even respectability by sheep and cattle 'duffing' (stealing). William John 'Big' Clarke, who was so huge that in his declining years it took four men to carry him from his carriage into a house, made a fortune selling stolen cattle. By the 1870s he owned one hundred and twenty thousand acres in Victoria, fifty thousand acres in Tasmania, and was estimated to be worth two and a half million pounds. He was a director of the Colonial Bank, Melbourne, and a member of the legislative council. His private life was just as passionate as his greed for money: the colonies were sprinkled with the bastards he had fathered as well as the men he had defrauded. He died in 1874, at a time when at least lip service was paid to the belief that flagrant violators of the Ten Commandments should expect neither reward nor mercy in this world. The *Melbourne Punch* wrote: 'Mrs Grundy is by no means pleased at the disposition of his property [a reference to bequests to his illegitimate children], but really the old lady is riled at the man dying so rich.'

With a low cunning, Hugh Glass exploited the loopholes in the land laws of Victoria before the passing of the first selection act in 1862. He became the lessee of over a million acres by such a lavish use of dummies that at one time he had three hundred on his payroll. He put up an expensive house in Melbourne, with an artificial lake on which swans floated with a dignity their sponsor lacked, and there were tanks of strange fish and aviaries in which rare and exotic birds delighted his guests. Around his dining table he gathered men of wit, refinement and culture. In the late 1860s rumours of corruption by Glass were circulating in press and parliament. The respectable took fright.

When a fall in prices for wool in 1871 left Glass unable to meet his commitments, he drank poison rather than endure the humiliation and shame of failure.

Not all the squatters or large landowners lived with the flamboyancy and disregard for the laws of both God and man of 'Big' Clarke and Hugh Glass. Between 1850 and 1870 the squatters in the eastern colonies used the accumulated wealth and the *de facto* security of tenure conferred by the Order in Council of 1847 to make improvements on their runs. They fenced them off to enable them to dispense with shepherds; they dug holes in the ground (known as tanks in New South Wales and dams in Victoria) in which to store water. They built homesteads on their estates, quarried from local stone, so that limestone became the fashion in Yass and Canberra, redstone in New England, and bluestone throughout the Western District of Victoria. In front of each house there was generally a wide veranda over which creepers grew to provide shade in the long hot summers. There was also a croquet lawn, and flower gardens sloped away to a nearby watercourse. The drawing-room was richly ornamented with furnishings, paintings, and *objets d'art* collected during tours of Europe, and the library was filled with the principal works of English history, literature, and religion, and copies of such periodicals as *Blackwood's*, the *Edinburgh Review*, and the *Melbourne Punch*. The bedrooms, kitchens, and servants' quarters ran along the two arms of a U-shaped back courtyard. At a suitable distance there were huts for the men, or a house for a married couple, and sheds to house the shearers and other seasonal workers employed from time to time on the run.

Between the squatter and his men a great gulf began to open. The more opulent put up town houses in Melbourne, Sydney, or Adelaide, and during the spring the men yarned and drank and cursed the democratic tendencies of the age at the Melbourne Club, or the Australian Club in Sydney, or the Adelaide Club, while their women displayed their finery promenading the block in Collins Street, Melbourne, round Mrs Macquarie's drive in Sydney, and down King William Street in Adelaide. While parents laboured on their estates or pursued pleasure during the spring season in the cities, their children were instructed in the refinements of civilization at such schools as Melbourne and Geelong Grammar Schools or Scotch College in Victoria, The King's School in New South Wales, and St Peter's in South Australia. For all the eye could tell their world went well.

Yet some of the seeds that later deprived them of pre-eminence and glory had been sown before they erected these outward and visible signs of their opulence and achievement. Manhood suffrage, vote by ballot, and the abolition of property qualifications for members of the colonial parliaments had deprived them in 1856-58 of their majorities in the legislative assemblies of New South Wales, Victoria, Queensland, and South Australia. The nominee system of appointment to the legislative councils of New South Wales and Queensland, and the high property qualification for voters for the legislative councils of Victoria, Tasmania, and South Australia, presented them with the occasion as well as the temptation to present their idea of politics as the representation of 'interests', by which the interests of the minority were protected against the tyranny of the majority. But the price of supporting government by an elite of 'interests' was further ridicule and abuse from the bourgeoisie and workers in the towns.

This was the golden age of the bourgeoisie, and in the cities that class was laying up for itself treasures on earth, putting up monuments in brick and stone in wanton displays of their wealth and their vision of the meaning of life. In Sydney and Melbourne the bourgeoisie accumulated wealth from manufacturing, the building trades, the import trades, and law and medicine. In both cities the most important industries were clothing, printing, iron foundries, metal-working, carriage-building, furniture, food, brewing, tanning, sawmilling, and brick manufacture. Clothing workshops or factories employed an average of fifty workers per factory by 1871 in both Sydney and Melbourne. Employees in manufacturing comprised just over ten per cent of the labour force in both New South Wales and Victoria by 1891.

From 1861 to 1883 the great boom was in the building trades. In 1852 Joseph Reed, an architect from England, arrived in Melbourne to make his fortune on the goldfields, but found one instead in his own profession. Reed's work summed up the values of the period, especially his use of the baroque dome as the symbol of superfluous wealth and conspicuous waste. Between 1855 and 1880 he designed the town hall, the exhibition building, Wilson Hall at the university, the Independent and Scots Churches, the Bank of Australasia, the Bank of New South Wales, and the Trades Hall, thus indelibly imprinting his ideas on the appearance of Melbourne in buildings in which the quest of the bourgeoisie for display was reconciled with their passion for the solid and the secure. Over the same period in Sydney the baroque began to mingle and clash with the chaste lines of Regency buildings put up in the age of Macquarie. Hobart and Launceston suffered similar fates, while Adelaide and Brisbane suffered the baroque to grow in ostentatious and solitary splendour.

The same tendencies were reflected in the houses put up to meet the sudden increase in population caused by the gold rushes. During the decade 1851-61 half a generation of Australians had lived under canvas or in huts. In the towns the mansions of the successful were piles of grey and turreted masonry in 'Gothic' or 'Classic' or both. They were insulated by park-like grounds from endless unmade streets, which were rapidly lined with smaller separate or

The Victoria Tannery near Melbourne was an important industry.

The manufacturing of bricks. Employees in manufacturing comprised just over ten per cent of the labour force in both New South Wales and Victoria by 1891.

Above: Diggers celebrate at a ball in the Aruluen district of New South Wales. The occasion was 'highly characteristic of the rollicking kind of life in the interior'.

Above right: A charming view of Claremont House and garden near Ipswich in Queensland, 1881.

terraced dwellings. To flaunt their devotion to the bitch goddess of success, or, more charitably, to prove their devotion to the same ideals as the bourgeoisie, the veranda of the five-room villa of the petit bourgeois or worker sprouted the same iron lace edging, the same plaster urns, and the same stained-glass window framing to the front door as the master's mansion. Most houses were single-storied. The style was eclectic and European, but American influence in the shape of labour-saving devices began to penetrate the servantless houses by the back door. The kitchen, which was generally detached in the pre-gold period, began to be tacked on to the rear of the house. Like the homes of the squatters, the farmers, and the rich bourgeois, the houses in suburbia had verandas to protect their inhabitants against the summer sun.

By contrast, some of the working class in the cities lived in abject poverty. In Sydney, according to an observer in 1860, a block of twenty or twenty-five wretched hovels afforded shelter for perhaps a hundred human beings. A family lived in two rooms, each ten or twelve feet square and barely high enough for a man to stand erect. The floor was often lower than the ground, and the ceiling often leaked, so that water poured in off the streets, bringing filth of all kinds. Few of the houses had such domestic conveniences as indoor sinks, pantries, stoves, and clothes closets. The high rents caused overcrowding, so that in houses occupied by Europeans as many as seven men and seven women squeezed somehow into two rooms, while in houses occupied by the Chinese as many as three hundred and fifteen crowded into one building. In their daily lives the people were surrounded by ignorance and squalor, while their children, it was said, floated 'about the streets and lanes like fish in a pond'. Vagrant children infested the streets of Sydney; prostitution thrived as parents sold their daughters to supplement their incomes. The clergy grieved at such misery and vice, but the bourgeoisie looked only to their plenty and their virtue. In Melbourne, too, sweated labour, jerry-built houses and overcrowding created a contrast of bourgeois opulence south of the Yarra and working-class squalor in the industrial suburbs of Fitzroy, Collingwood, and even Carlton. Adelaide was saved from spawning 'two nations' within the one city by less overcrowding and the tradition of working-class ownership of the house and the block of land on which it stood. Religious dissent probably strengthened these bourgeois influences.

The politics of the period were disturbed not so much by the fundamental differences of opinion on the ownership of wealth and the exercise of political power as by fights within the bourgeoisie for the plums and social prestige that went with a seat in the ministry of the day. In the decade of gold (1851-61), society had been divided between conservatives and liberals, between squatters and bourgeoisie, or between country and town, on such questions as land policy, the constitution, immigration, and the tariff. By 1861 the victory of the bourgeoisie was so decisive that politics changed from an argument over fundamentals to a squabble over ways and means. In the 1850s there had been the semblance of a two-party system in both New South Wales and Victoria. After the amendments to the constitution in 1857-58, the passing of the selection acts in 1861, 1862, and 1865, and the decision on tariff policy, factions replaced parties.

Political principles were forced to yield to interest. In 1872, for example, in New South Wales, Sir James Martin and John Robertson, who had fought each other savagely for the preceding fifteen years over the tariff issue, buried the tomahawk. Martin's group had always been known as the Kookaburras, and Robertson's as the Rosellas. Now, said Sir Henry Parkes, the laughing jackasses were seizing on Robertson to get his fine feathers to decorate the Kookaburras. With the substitution of interest and personal ambition for political principle, the debates in all the parliaments became noisy, vulgar, and personal. In the legislative assembly of Queensland in January 1872 Mr Oscar de Satgé complained that a Mr Pring had been fiddle-faddling around Brisbane ever since the session and asked what he had been doing all this time. To which Mr Pring replied 'Making love', and Mr Satgé retorted that he did not propose to notice any remarks that fell from the honourable member after dinner. Mr Pring then became warm, shouted invectives against all and sundry, and, as he strode from the house, seized a member by the whiskers and shouted 'Come outside and we'll settle it', only to be interrupted by the Speaker, who called, 'Sergeant, arrest that Honourable Member.'

The proceedings of all the parliaments often degenerated into uproar, as members accused each other of drunkenness, favouritism or corruption. At a time when the test of a member's worth was his success in wheedling a school, a road, a bridge or a railway out of the government, politics became a contest between the 'ins' and the 'outs', between the 'ministerialists' and the 'opposition', with the groups contending not over fundamental questions of faith or the form of society, but over a seat on the ministerial benches. In the days before payment of members, members accepted a place in the opposition as a wound to their pride, though not to their pocket. The few such as Parkes, for whom politics was a reliable source of income, earned their keep from a ministerial salary, or took commissions (bribes would be too harsh a word) from such groups as the squatters and the banks who had interests to protect in politics. The professional politician thus became a paid hireling of the bourgeoisie.

In New South Wales the three main political factions were led by Parkes, Martin, and Robertson. Of these, Henry Parkes achieved pre-eminence both with his contemporaries and posterity by his histrionic gifts, the semi-tragedy of his public life, and his association with issues such as education that touched the faith by which people lived. With that lack of charity that characterizes the comments of the upright man on the behaviour of one of the insects to whom God gave sensual lust, Alfred Deakin said of Parkes that 'no actor ever more carefully posed for effect', and went on to add rather harshly that Parkes 'had always in his Mind's eye his own portrait as that of a great man, and constantly adjusted himself to it'. But there was more to the man than the posturings of a vulgar ambition.

He was born at Stoneleigh in Warwickshire, England, in 1815, the son of a small tenant farmer, and after a few years at school he took up manual work in Birmingham. In his late adolescence he served his apprenticeship as a bone and ivory turner. At the same time he began to take interest in the Chartist movement. After his marriage in 1836 he began a business on his own account, but failed so miserably that he decided in 1838 to emigrate to New South Wales. There he quickly established a reputation for success in public life and failure in business; by 1849 the man who spoke with passion on the convict system as a blot on the reputation of the colony was faced at home with bills he lacked the resources to meet. In 1850 he established a newspaper, the *Empire*, and in 1854 he was elected to the legislative council. In 1856 he was elected to the first legislative assembly in New South Wales, but by 1858 his financial difficulties became so acute that he was declared bankrupt, his assets then being 48,000 pounds and his liabilities 50,000. In 1870 he was in deeper water. This time his assets were 13,000 pounds and his liabilities 32,000 pounds, but he successfully outrode the storm of abuse and ridicule from all the respectable people, and two years later he became premier of New South Wales for the first time.

He was driven on by passions that were outside the ken of men who had been brought up in Melbourne provincial bourgeois rectitude. Parkes twice suffered the humiliation of bankruptcy in a society all too prone to judge a man by his solvency. His second wife had been snubbed at Government House in Sydney. He himself was often derided for his lower-class way of speaking. His passion for women was insatiable, and he was not relieved of the ravages or the pleasures of that 'fierce and savage monster' till he sank into the grave just before his eightieth birthday. Everything about the man was on a grand scale. His figure was huge, his eyes bulbous, his eyebrows bushy and ample; his white hair was carefully brushed back and across a commanding brow.

Parkes's ideas were conceived on an equally grandiose scale. As a young man he advocated political democracy with an almost religious ardour. In middle age he saw himself as the man to rid the minds of both Protestant and Catholic of the superstitions implanted by parsons and priests. In old age, when the prosaic were urging federation to make meat cheaper, Parkes spoke of it as a means to make Australia the mistress of the Pacific. Yet the man remained to the end a bundle of paradoxes. He was sustained by a belief in enlightenment, yet at times grovelled before parson and priest to cadge votes in elections. The man who gave generously of heart and mind sometimes had to go down on his knees before a bank manager beseeching him not to humiliate the premier of New South Wales by refusing to honour a cheque for some trifling amount. The man who had suffered all the humiliations of the low-born during ascent to high places was driven all his life to seek flattery and recognition from those English upper classes who had so poorly used him. Parkes epitomized all the contradictions found in men whose hopes of getting on in the world were not sustained by anything firmer than their own ambitions and a vision of humanity dedicated to enlightenment and material progress. The semi-tragedy of his

A schoolmaster collecting the school fees from pupils in 1874.

life sprang as much from the creed he expounded as the warring elements in his nature. It is possible, too, that the imaginative sweep of the man was smothered under the weight of debt and financial disaster. It is possible that such a fate transformed 'his vitalizing sap into a corrupting poison'. It is possible that financial pressures changed the man of principle into an opportunist.

Other politicians did not strut and fret on the stage of public life with the same tragic grandeur as Parkes. Each was influenced by his own upbringing and conviction. Catholic politicians were sensitive to the political opinions of their hierarchy, while some Protestants were obsessed with the objective of thwarting any increase in Catholic power. Some were tariff enthusiasts; some were for education; some were for immigration; some were content to squeeze a bridge or a road or a school out of a tight-fisted treasury. All, whether Catholic or Protestant, native-born or immigrant, born to great inheritance or local boys who had made good, believed in the bourgeois ideal of getting on, in equality of opportunity, and in material progress as the forerunner of spiritual and moral progress. It was when they turned their minds to the problem of how and what to teach their children that their society was almost split asunder.

By the late 1860s it was clear that the dual system of education in New South Wales, Victoria, Queensland, and Tasmania, the system where some schools were under a secular board of education and other schools were under a denominational board, had failed to provide adequate education for the children of the various colonies. The number of schools provided by either board had not kept pace with the growth of population, and the quality of the teaching in both types of schools left much to be desired. The bourgeoisie, the squatters, and the working classes believed in education as a means to ensure careers open to talent as well as on the principle that knowledge was both a foe to vice and a source of power. Where all previous generations had subscribed to the slogan that the world belongs to the brave, this generation believed that in an industrial civilization the world would belong to the well informed. So all but the lunatic fringe agreed that education should be free and compulsory.

The difficulty was how to achieve this within the dual system of the national boards and denominational boards. For the denominational system was dying on its feet. But if all children were to attend national board schools, would the priests and clergy of the various denominations be able to agree on a common curriculum? The hierarchy in all the colonies insisted that all Catholic children receive a religious education, by which they meant not an hour each day, or some such plan, but a system in which classes were conducted in rooms decorated with suitable religious symbols, in which the day began and ended with prayer, in which the entire program was God-centred.

The Anglicans were just as divided on this question as they had been on all questions since the reformation. The low-church faction was inclined to believe children could be taught all that was essential to salvation by studying the Bible under the guidance of either a lay teacher or a clergyman. To ask for the continuation of denominational schools was tantamount to using public money to subsidize error, to foster amongst them a 'system of Satanic delusion'. The high-church faction wanted to teach in their own schools, with their books and teachers, the doctrines of the Church of England, its glory and genius as a compromise between Catholic authority and the licence of dissent. The Presbyterians were equally divided, the Voluntarys supporting the movement towards secular education, and the conservatives wishing to preserve the denominational system as the one sure means of bringing up the young in the faith of their fathers. The Methodists, Baptists, Congregationalists, Independents, and others hastened to embrace secular education as their shield against popish and Anglican authoritarianism. In addition a small group cam-

An 1871 view of Aborigines stalking emus.

paigned for secular education as a means of bringing up the young with minds free from the superstitions, barbarous beliefs, and absurdities propagated by the various religious denominations.

By 1870 it was clear that not one of the interested groups commanded a majority. In the meantime public opinion in the colonies had been affected by the decline in religious belief as well as the undignified and grotesque behaviour of the parsons and the priests. Criticism of the Old Testament by scholars had undermined the Church's view of it as the inspired word of God, reducing it to a collection of manuscripts of unknown origin on the history of the Jewish people. The publication of *On the Origin of Species* by Charles Darwin in 1859 had thrown doubt on the biblical story of creation. The publication of Darwin's *The Descent of Man* in 1871 called into question the religious assumption of the uniqueness of man poised between the angels and the brutes. Scholars began to cast doubts on the Gospels as sources for the Virgin Birth, the Incarnation, the Resurrection and the Ascension. Others asserted that if God's purpose could only be achieved by an infinity of human suffering and the condemnation of a large proportion of humanity to eternal torments in hell, then they would not accept God's world.

To such criticism the churches replied with many voices. Some of the Protestants bravely if somewhat curiously refused to budge from the fundamentalist position that every word in the Bible was the inspired word of God. Others, bending before the scientific breeze, abandoned more and more of the teachings of their churches and took their stand on a vague deism, remaining discreetly silent about heaven and hell. Many continued to repeat the traditional justification for religion put forth by the Protestant clergy from the foundation of Australia in 1788 to their own day—namely, that morality was ineluctably connected with religious belief, that sensuality, frivolity, cupidity, and political

insubordination were always the close companions of atheism. Marcus Clarke, a supporter of a secular view of the world, in his *Civilization Without Delusion*, replied that since organized religion had demonstrably failed to lead men into the paths of duty and virtue, it was the task of the future to try morality without religion. The Anglican bishop of Melbourne asserted boldly in 1869 that the Bible had nothing to fear from science. Ten years later in Adelaide a dissenter contemplated with sadness how the church in her rashness and in her zeal for certain expressions of truth was waging a warfare against truth itself. To his regret the high Anglicans and the Catholics were 'retreating in timidity into the dark caves of Ritualism, tenanted by the owls and bats of mediaevalism, as though too weak to bear the sunlight of truth'. He urged his fellow-believers to stand with the sunlight of heaven in their souls, upheld by their faith in God, for then nothing could harm or affright them. For in response to science and Biblical criticism some dissenters tended to urge Christians to abandon most of their beliefs, to surrender the Virgin Birth, the God-Man, the Resurrection, the Ascension, miracles, and all the sacraments of the Church, and take their stand on belief in God and the teachings of the man Jesus.

In August 1883 Chief Justice George Higinbotham of Victoria told the congregation of Scots Church, Melbourne, that the salvation of the mind of Christendom depended upon the union amongst laymen of all churches who would cast out from their own minds and from the Christian churches the spectres of old and now discredited fallacies and withdraw from all the lower standpoints of thought to a high central platform of thought. He urged belief in God, which had been 'revealed anew to the intellect, and also to the responsive human heart, as the Father, the Friend, the Guide, and the Support of our race, and of every member of it, in the simple but profound philosophy, and also in the sublimest life, of Jesus of Nazareth, the Light of the World'.

Hunting kangaroos. Early settlers hunted some animals, such as the Tasmanian emu, to extinction.

By contrast the Church of Rome spoke with one voice and refused to abandon any of its beliefs. Believing passionately in its election by God as the divine instrument for the defence of religion, the Church surveyed the sad sight of the evils by which the human race was oppressed on every side, the widespread subversion of the primary truths on which society had been based, the obstinacy of mind that would not brook any authority, the endless disagreement, the civil strife, the insatiable craving for things perishable, and the complete forgetfulness of things eternal. She found the source of all these evils in the despising and setting aside of the holy and venerable authority of the Church. In the encyclical *Inscrutabili* or *On the Evils affecting Modern Society*, 21 April 1878, Leo XIII taught the faithful that this atrocious war against the authority of the Church, begun in the sixteenth century with the religious reformers, had as its purpose the subversion of the supernatural order and the enthroning of unaided reason. In the eyes of the Church of Rome, then, Luther and Calvin, rather than geologists, biblical scholars, Strauss, Renan, Bradlaugh, Darwin, Huxley, and Marcus Clarke, were the villains of the piece. Just as some Protestants viewed the Catholics, rather than the unbelievers and the rationalists, as the mortal enemies of the supernatural, so the Roman Church viewed the Protestants as their eternal enemies and the causes of the undermining of religious belief.

Part of the price for the madness and folly of such sectarian strife was the introduction of the secular clauses in the new education acts. While priest and parson held each other responsible for the decline of religious belief, and were unable to agree on what religion should be taught in the schools, the colonial parliaments passed legislation making education free, compulsory, and secular. The first of these laws was passed by the Victorian parliament in 1872. South Australia followed suit in 1875 with an act that directed the schools to give secular instruction during regular hours but permitted them to open in the morning one quarter of an hour before the fixed time for secular instruction, for the purpose of reading portions of scripture from the Authorized or Douay version, at which attendance was not compulsory. In the same year the Queensland parliament passed an act that made education free and compulsory and prescribed that in all the schools financed by the state (hence the name 'state schools') there should be four hours of secular instruction in every day. New South Wales introduced free and compulsory education in 1880, with the proviso that all teaching was to be non-sectarian, but the words 'secular instruction' were to be held to include general religious teaching as distinguished from dogmatical or polemical theology. In 1885 the Tasmanian parliament passed an act that made education free, compulsory, and secular, but instructed the state shools to set aside an hour each week in which the children could be instructed by the ministers of their own persuasion, with their parents' consent. In 1871 the parliament of Western Australia passed the Elementary Education Act, which prescribed that no religious catechism or religious doctrine that was distinctive of any particular denomination was to be taught in any government school. In 1895 the parliament of Western Australia passed an act to abolish government assistance to denominational schools.

The bishops of the Catholic Church objected to the use of Catholic funds—taxes paid out of Catholic pockets—for the establishment throughout the land of a system of education that not many Catholics could safely make use of, and that they fiercely believed was calculated to sap the foundations of Christianity. The faith of Catholic children educated in state schools was enfeebled; their manners became rough and irreverent; they had little sense of respect and genteelness; the playgrounds of the state schools were seedbeds of immorality and vice. The priests looked on the future of such wild, uncurbed children with misgivings. Such children, the bishops predicted, would plunge into darkness and make a shipwreck of the faith.

So the bishops campaigned for the renewal of state aid to each denomination, in the meantime raising money from their own congregations to build and equip schools. To assist in this work the bishops recruited members of the religious orders from Ireland. In the choice between the faith and possibly a substandard secular education, the bishops chose the faith. The Protestants remained as suspicious as ever of Catholic attempts to revive state aid to religious denominations. They campaigned in every colony for the teaching of the Bible in the state schools. But the bishops and priests of the Catholic Church warned the faithful that such a change would lead to a yet greater evil than unbelief, the Protestantizing of state education. So those fears and suspicions dividing Catholic and Protestant that had paved the way for the introduction of secular education also preserved secular education in succeeding generations.

After the introduction of free, compulsory, and secular education there were three types of schools in all the colonies. The Protestant schools educated the sons and daughters of the bourgeoisie in the cities, of the merchants, bankers, traders, manufacturers, publicans, and professional men, the sons and daughters of the squatters and the wealthy farmers, together with a few talented children whom they bought with scholarships. Their schools were modelled on the English public schools and designed for the education of boys and girls to serve God in church, state, and the professions—to produce that upright man who feared God and eschewed evil and at the same time was dedicated to the service of the worldly aspirations of the British people.

By contrast the Catholics provided only a few schools for the children of the bourgeoisie, the squatters, and the professional classes because their numbers came from the petty bourgeoisie and the working classes. To educate the children of those classes in Catholic schools the Church raised money from the faithful and used members of the religious orders as teachers. In such schools priests, brothers, nuns, and laymen presented a view of man and the meaning of his life, as well as a version of human history, quite different from what was taught in the Protestant schools. State schools taught a syllabus prescribed by the colonial department of education. The Protestant and the state school boy or girl grew up to believe in the contribution of the British to the freedom of men and the progress of the world; the Catholic child grew up nursing in his mind the melancholy history of the Irish people and a conviction that the British by great barbarity and cruelty had contributed to the oppression and degradation of the ancestors of his people in Ireland. The new education acts also continued the tendency to centralize the administration of the colonies. As neither party to the great debate on education was prepared to entrust the appointment of teachers, or the choice of syllabus and textbooks, to a local committee for fear of domination by one sect or another, control was vested in a department of education, responsible to the minister in the capital city of each colony. So the sectarian controversy contributed to both centralization and conformity. It also contributed to the timidity and that air of taboo that rapidly surrounded all controversial subjects, for as agreement between the contending groups was impossible, the education departments taught a history, an ethic, and a religion that were so vague and pallid as not to encourage the interest of the boys and girls in the great questions of life.

This shying away from the great questions of life occurred at a time when two quite different views of the nature of man and the meaning of life were taking shape. On such questions the children educated in those schools would be called on to make up their minds. On the one hand the rationalists were thundering against the hydra-headed monster of hypocrisy, bigotry, ignorance and intolerance that followed religious belief as night followed day. On the other hand the Pope was thundering against the evils of unbelief, which, he predicted, would subvert the primary truths on which society was based and promote endless sources of disagreement, which in turn would lead to civil strife, ruthless war, and that insatiable craving for things perishable and a complete forgetfulness of things eternal. The rationalists called on mankind to *Ecraser l'infâme*; the priests warned that without Christ mankind would be destroyed.

While Pope, priest, and parson were expatiating on the evils affecting modern society from the spread of unbelief, in 1878 the members of the Seamen's Union raised fundamental questions on the composition and organization of society in the Australian colonies. The union informed its members that the owners of the Australian Union Steamship Navigation Company had been quietly replacing European members of their crews with Chinese: 'In this what will be to them a gigantic struggle, they appeal confidently to their brother seamen to refuse most decidedly to ship Chinese in their places.' So on 18 November the seamen, cooks, and stewards walked off the ships of the Australian Union Steamship Navigation Company at Circular Quay, Sydney. The union was claiming a voice not only on wages and conditions of employment but on the composition of society. When the men agreed to return to work on 2 January, 1879, the company undertook to reduce the number of Chinese on their ships within three months of that date.

Four years later the colonies in eastern Australia were confronted with the problem of relations with the outside world. In April 1883, exasperated by the reluctance of the British government to take action to forestall a German annexation of eastern New Guinea, the Premier of Queensland, Sir Thomas McIlwraith, hoisted the British flag at Port Moresby. The action was disavowed by the Colonial Secretary, Lord Derby, who firmly declined to satisfy the greed of the Queensland sugar planters for cheap labour by increasing British commitments in the Pacific. At the same time the governments of Victoria and New South Wales were afraid that the French proposed to annex the New Hebrides. All these governments were also concerned with the havoc caused by convicts escaping from the French prison island in New Caledonia. To discuss these problems the premiers of the Australian colonies agreed to hold an intercolonial convention in Sydney in November 1883. At this convention, the new Premier of Queensland, Samuel Griffith, proposed that a federal Australasian council be created to deal with the marine defences of Australasia beyond territorial limits, as well as the relations of Australasia with the islands of the Pacific, the prevention of the influx of criminals, the regulation of quarantine, and such other matters of general Australasian interest. But the federal council was a dead letter from the start, partly because of its lack of administrative powers, but mainly because of the refusal of New South Wales to join. Just as the confrontation with the outside world was driving the colonies towards some form of union, the confrontation between the colonies was exacerbating the tendencies to a colonial provincialism. After James Service, the Premier of Victoria, returned to Melbourne from the intercolonial convention, he said at a banquet in his honour that he had noticed in Sydney the most intense jealousy in respect to Melbourne and the Melbourne people, and that Sydney had not forgiven Victoria or Queensland for running away from the mother colony. When this speech was reported in Sydney, feeling ran high. In the legislative assembly of New South Wales one man declared amidst cheers and hurrahs that New South Wales was as far above Victoria as heaven was above earth, while Sir John Robertson contemptuously described Victoria as a 'cabbage patch', and a Mr Cameron talked of the insult conveyed to the

Speaker, to the House, and to the people of New South Wales by the flippant and claptrap utterances of the gentleman who was for the time being premier of Victoria.

A month before the Australian seamen raised the question of coloured labour in Australia four policemen, Kennedy, Lonigan, Scanlon, and McIntyre, set out from Mansfield in north-eastern Victoria to arrest Ned Kelly, Joe Byrne, Dan Kelly, and Steve Hart, for horse and cattle stealing. On 26 October, 1878, when the police confronted the bushrangers on the Stringybark Creek, Ned Kelly shot and killed Kennedy, Lonigan, and Scanlon. McIntyre escaped to Mansfield to give the alarm. Immediately the colony was in an uproar. To the squatters, the bourgeoisie, and all the forces of law, order, and respectability, Kennedy, Lonigan, and Scanlon were three brave men who lost their lives while endeavouring to capture a band of armed criminals. But from the day of the outrage a legend began to grow amongst the cocky farmers, the fossickers for gold, the descendants of the convicts and the poverty-stricken Irish exiles, who, like Ned, had tried but failed to earn a living by lawful means in that hard and bitter country. It was said that Ned, like Robin Hood, was battling only to deprive the rich of their wealth and give it to the poor. So the man who killed the three constables in cold blood was apotheosized into a folk hero who would humble the proud, take the mighty from their seat, and send the rich empty away.

After Ned and his gang robbed the National Bank of Benalla in December 1878, and the Bank of New South Wales at Jerilderie, thirty miles on the New South Wales side of the Murray, he boasted that his men had never harmed a woman or robbed a poor man. But by one of those ironies in human affairs it was one of the little men whom he befriended who brought them down. In June 1880 the gang occupied the hotel at Glenrowan, near Wangaratta, in northern Victoria. Ned, puffed up with pride and insolence by his previous successes, had conceived the mad plan of destroying a train bringing the police and black-trackers to hunt for him. The gang tore up a stretch of track shortly before the train on which the police were travelling was due. While Ned and the other members of the gang were preparing a ghastly wake for their victims, a schoolteacher slipped out of the hotel and stopped the train in time. The police surrounded the hotel and set fire to it. Steve Hart, Dan Kelly and Joe Byrne were burnt to death, but Ned, mad as ever, put on his home-made armour and shot it out with the police till a bullet brought him down. He was brought to Melbourne, tried, and hanged on 11 November, 1880, when, according to legend, his last words were 'Such is life.'

The memory of him lived on. The squatters and the bourgeoisie attributed the Kellys and their outrages to the selection acts, which had afforded opportunities for people to take up land in remote districts where religious and educational influences could not penetrate. The result was a race of godless, lawless men and women, half bandits, half cattle-stealers, and wholly vicious. But to the dispossessed in both town and country Ned was a hero. In an age in which the gods of the old religions were toppling to their ruins, Ned, or the idea of Ned, was an image in which men could believe, because his life and death symbolized the experience of the native-born, their unwillingness to accept the morality of the English, and their groping for a new morality and a new way of life. Ned was hanged in Melbourne gaol on the eve of a period in which Australians fumbled towards a secular creed to replace the creeds of organized religion, towards a statement that would sum up their experience of just one hundred years of European civilization in Australia. That was the task to which the radicals and the nationalists addressed themselves in the period between 1883 and 1900.

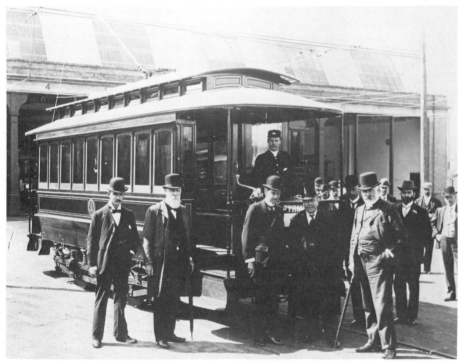

Far left above: A scene in Liverpool Street, Hobart, in 1879.

Far left centre: King William Street, Adelaide, 1879.

Far left below: A double-decker tram in Adelaide in 1883. 'The tramway system is the most complete in Australia,' wrote Richard Twopeny.

Above left: A horsedrawn cart, which was the home of an itinerant family in the north-west of New South Wales.

Above: A camel and sulky.

Centre: The opening of electric trams in Sydney. By 1900 there were 100 miles of steam and electric tramlines.

Left: Modern transport in about 1901.

CHAPTER NINE

RADICALS AND NATIONALISTS
1883–1901

ON THE MORNING of 14 June, 1883, a huge crowd gathered in Albury, a border town on the Murray River, to witness the connection between the railways of New South Wales and Victoria. The streets were gaily decorated with bunting; schoolchildren lined the streets to welcome the premiers of both colonies. That night a distinguished assembly sat down to a banquet at which the governor of New South Wales congratulated those present on the auspicious union of the two colonies by the iron rail. These Australian colonies, he went on, were peopled by the same race, spoke the same language, possessed the same traditions and aspirations. The iron link they had forged that day would be the emblem of union. He hoped this would be the dawn of a fresh era of happiness and prosperity. His colleague, the governor of Victoria, expressed his confidence that the inevitable result of the rail union would be the union of the colonies themselves.

Henry Lawson, short story writer and poet, and one of the creators of Australian identity.

Similar sentiments were expressed when the rail link between Victoria and South Australia was completed in January 1887, and between New South Wales and Queensland in January 1888. The delay in completing the link between South Australia and Western Australia (for the line between Port Augusta and Kalgoorlie was not finished until October 1917) helps to explain the strength of local sentiment in Australia's western third. Improvements in communication also provided the natural setting for the growth of the feeling of unity. Melbourne and Adelaide were linked by electric telegraph in July 1858; Sydney and Melbourne in October of the same year; Sydney and Brisbane in 1861; Sydney and Adelaide in 1867; Launceston and Melbourne briefly in 1859, and permanently in 1869; Port Augusta and Darwin in 1872; and Adelaide and Perth in 1877.

The first telephone exchange was opened in Melbourne in 1878, Brisbane in 1880, Sydney in 1881, Adelaide and Hobart in 1883, and Perth in 1887. Some were operated at first by private companies, but by the 1890s the colonial parliaments had placed ownership and control of telephone services under the colonial post offices.

At the same time native-born began to outnumber immigrants. In 1861 just over fifty per cent of the population had been born in the United Kingdom. By 1871 nearly sixty per cent had been born in the Australian colonies, by 1891 seventy-five per cent, and by 1901 eighty-two per cent. The increase in the proportion of the native-born provided a reading public for a national literature, in which the writers could illuminate the experience of the Australian and provide that cheek, wit, and confidence to bolster the morale of people whose talents, way of life, and achievements were belittled as 'colonial'. For nationalism was a comforter for the despised as well as a rebuke to those who fawned before everything English.

The first train crossing the Murray River at Echuca, Victoria.

The multiple switchboard in the switchroom of the Victorian Telephone Exchange Company, Melbourne, in 1886. Victoria was the first colony to install a telephone service, in 1878.

Over the same years the population was growing steadily. There were 2,306,736 in all the colonies in 1881—777,025 in New South Wales, 873,965 in Victoria, 221,849 in Queensland, 285,971 in South Australia, 30,156 in Western Australia, and 117,770 in Tasmania. There were 3,773,801 in all the colonies in 1901—1,354,846 in New South Wales, 1,201,070 in Victoria, 498,129 in Queensland, 363,157 in South Australia, 184,124 in Western Australia, and 172,475 in Tasmania.

At the same time the industries of Sydney and Melbourne began to look for markets for their goods outside the boundaries of their own colonies. The food-producing industries of Sydney were anxious to exploit the expanding market in Melbourne but found their way barred by the Victorian tariff. The farmers in the Riverina in New South Wales wanted to sell their wool and wheat in Melbourne but found the Victorian tariff prohibitive. The manufacturers in Melbourne and Geelong, especially in food and textiles, wanted to sell in Sydney and Adelaide but were priced out of the market by the special freight charges on Victorian goods using the New South Wales railways and by the South Australian tariff. Economic growth was thwarted by the dead hand of the past.

While the past divided Australia into six separate colonies whose boundaries were defined by historical accident rather than the facts of either geography or the production and exchange of goods, economic development, even though impeded by tariffs and other barriers, rushed ahead and brought the colonies closer and closer together. The business enterprises servicing the economy, the banks, the financial companies, the pastoral companies such as Dalgetys, Denys Lascelles, Elder Smith and Goldsbrough Mort, had branches in every colonial capital and in some of the country towns. In 1888 the Australian Federation of Employers was formed. Almost a decade earlier, in October 1879, the first intercolonial trades union congress had been held at Sydney, and the delegates had addressed themselves to such Australian issues as assisted and Chinese immigration. At the second intercolonial union congress in Melbourne in April 1884 the delegates discussed such common interests as amalgamation and legalization of trades unions, restriction of Chinese and coloured labour, and the direct representation of labour in parliament. Although attempts to unite the trades unions into a federal body failed at the Melbourne congress in 1884, Sydney in 1885, Adelaide in 1886, Brisbane in 1888, Hobart in 1889, Ballarat in 1891, and Adelaide in 1898, the annual congresses, interrupted by strikes and depression between 1891 and 1898, kept alive the idea that the workers of Australia, as distinct from any colony, had a community of interest in their attempts to achieve better wages, shorter hours, and better working conditions.

Between 1880 and 1900 the area under cultivation almost doubled from four and a half million acres to eight and three-quarter million acres. In this way agriculture in the Australian colonies responded to the Australian and world demand for goods caused in part by the increase in world population and in part by an improvement in the standard of living in many countries. A local cause for the increase in food production was the drift of population from the country districts to the capital cities of the various colonies. In 1871 the population of Sydney was 137,566 and the population of New South Wales 516,704. By 1901 the population of Sydney was 481,830 and the population of New South Wales approximately 1,400,000. In 1871 the population of Melbourne was 206,780 and Victoria 746,450, while by 1901 the population of Melbourne was 496,079 and Victoria approximately 1,200,000.

To meet this increase in demand the techniques of food production were improved in the 1870s by the invention of the stump-jump plough and the

A Queensland farmhouse. Building houses on stilts was a successful method of overcoming depredation by white ants, and was accidentally discovered in 1839 when four of the prefabricated buildings taken to Port Essington were raised eight feet high.

stripping and harvesting machine. To improve the yield per acre of wheat an agricultural scientist, William Farrer, experimented in breeding rust-resistant wheat and a wheat that could be grown in dry areas. These experiments were carried out successfully at Lambrigg near the present site of Canberra between 1885 and 1898. In 1886 the Chaffey brothers entered into an agreement with the Victorian government for 50,000 acres at Mildura with a further 200,000 acres on very favourable terms, on condition that they introduced irrigation in the area and subdivided the estate into small blocks of land, irrigated with water from the Murray River, on which fruits such as grapes, oranges, and pears were to be grown. Similar irrigation schemes began at Griffith and Leeton in New South Wales and Renmark in South Australia. The result was the creation of the dried-fruits industry and a big boost to the local production of wine.

In 1875 a factory for the refrigeration of meat for export overseas began operations in the Lithgow valley in New South Wales. Cattle and sheep were slaughtered, the carcasses were dressed on the most improved principles, and the meat was transported in refrigerated vans to Darling Harbour, Sydney, where it was frozen by a special process before being shipped to England or the United States in cooling chambers which ensured that the meat would remain frozen until it reached market. Since meat in England was four or five times the price of meat in Australia the exporters seemed assured of good sales, as well as the satisfaction of bringing meat to thousands for whom previously it had been an unattainable luxury. The first successful shipment of frozen meat was carried on the *Strathleven*, which sailed from Sydney in November 1879 and reached London in February 1880.

In the 1860s another experiment was successfully carried out in Queensland. In 1863 Captain Louis Hope planted twenty acres of sugarcane at Ormiston, near Brisbane, and reaped a rich harvest. At that time the clearing of the land, cultivation, planting, and harvesting were all performed by hand in a tropical climate, on land where the undergrowth was rank and luxuriant in the fertile river valleys of the coastal belt of Queensland. Such sugar had to compete with that grown by cheap 'black' labour in Fiji, Java, and South Africa. In a colony where the demand for labour exceeded the supply, it was impossible to employ Europeans on the canefields except for wages that would have made the 'white' sugar unsaleable. So the sugar planters began to import from the islands in the Pacific labour to clear, plant, and cut by hand. They came to be called 'kanakas', from the Hawaiian word for man. Between 1868 and 1876 just over 11,000 kanakas arrived in Queensland.

Queensland sugar planters imported from the islands in the Pacific cheap labour to work on the cane fields.

Immediately the missionaries, the philanthropists, the town dwellers and the workers accused the sugar planters of creating a system of slavery. In their view the kanakas were seduced from their island homes, or sold by their chiefs to white men, and then sold again on the wharves in Brisbane, Maryborough, Rockhampton, and Mackay. Kanakas, said the opposition, were merchandise. To prevent abuses, the Queensland parliament passed an act in 1868 to regulate and control the introduction and treatment of Polynesian labourers. Between 1868 and 1885 a series of Queensland and Imperial acts were passed to protect the kanakas against the greed and cruelty of the recruiter and the sugar planter.

By 1892 a majority in the Queensland parliament had come to the conclusion that the use of black labour was injurious to the best interests of the colony if it were to be regarded as a home for the British race. The Premier of Queensland, Samuel Griffith, summarized the arguments against black labour in this way:

1. It tended to encourage the creation of large landed estates, owned for the most part by absentees and worked by gang labour, and so discouraged actual settlement by small farmers working for themselves.
2. It led to field labour in tropical agriculture being looked down upon as degrading and unworthy of the white races.
3. The permanent existence of a large servile population not admitted to the franchise was not compatible with the continuance of free political institutions.

Griffith added that Queensland had been discredited by the abuses that prevailed for some years in the South Sea Island trade. For these reasons he proposed to abolish the use of black labour in the Queensland sugar fields.

But economic changes were removing the need to use black labour more effectively than all the arguments of the missionaries, the philanthropists, and the evangelists for British civilization. The conditions forced on the planters by the kanakas labour acts had raised the cost of black labour to the planters by more than fifty per cent between 1883 and 1889. New methods of production were gradually displacing manual labour. By 1895 machines were used for all field work except the cutting of cane. As the *Mackay Sugar Journal* put it in 1896: 'White men working for themselves and using the best labour saving implements are displacing the coloured workers rapidly. The large estates are rapidly becoming peopled with small farmers.' By 1895 the white man was easing the kanakas off the canefields in central and southern Queensland, but the kanakas outnumbered the white worker on northern fields such as Bundaberg by 2,612 to 304. If the Queensland sugar fields were to dispense with the use of black labour, it would be necessary for the state to protect the industry against competiton from the 'black' sugar of Fiji, Java, and South Africa.

Most of the planters in the north wanted to continue with coloured labour, but they realized that so long as the north remained part of the colony of Queensland their wishes and interests would be swept aside by the anti-black majority in the south of the colony. To preserve their plantations they were prepared to be separated from the south and made an independent colony. The majority in the south realized that if Queensland were to join with the other colonies to form a federation, that federation would be committed to a 'white' Australia. So Queensland could get white labour in return for a promise to protect its sugar industry against foreign competition. In this way the passions roused by the use of the kanakas converted the colonists in the south of Queensland into ardent supporters of federation. Once again economic developments had exposed the inadequacy of the existing political systems.

While ridding the colony of the 'leprous curse' of black labour, and proving the point in the quatrain:

Above: a cartoon illustrating equal opportunity for all in Queensland.

Above right: An impetus for federation of the colonies included the fear of coloured labour.

It's just as clear as figgers,
Sure as one and one make two,
Folks as make black slaves of niggers
Want to make white slaves of you

Queensland provincialism burgeoned into Australian patriotism. As the colonists saw it they were making sure that the deadly coloured alien biped never again lurked in the scrub with a cane knife waiting to butcher the first white man who came along. For such cruel fancies about the behaviour of other human beings poisoned their minds as they fumbled and groped towards ways and means of defending their way of life and their civilization. In this way the experiences on the sugar fields tainted their nationalism with racial prejudice.

All through the 1880s government and private enterprise expanded economic activity recklessly. The act of the Imperial Parliament in 1885 that created the federal council, the Colonial and Indian Exhibition held in London in 1886, and the Imperial Conference of 1887, attracted the attention of the British investor to the Australian colonies. The colonial governments raised loans in London in excess of their immediate requirements, and their ultimate capacity to pay, to build railways, roads, schools, and other public works. Investors advanced money to joint stock companies. Companies were formed in the wake of the boom in Melbourne to invest in real estate that was quickly forced up much beyond its real value. Others invested in the tin mines opened at Mount Bischoff in Tasmania in 1871, and the lead and zinc mines that began to be worked at Mt Zeehan in 1888.

In July and August 1890 a financial crash occurred in Argentina, which had been a centre of world speculation. In November Barings failed in London, and this in turn led to the rapid withdrawal of deposits from Australian financial institutions. Public works stopped, as did most private building. Government servants, contractors, the men in the building trades, bank clerks, and financial companies, were affected. In March 1892 one bank failed, another closed its doors in the following January, and in April and May thirteen banks in Victoria, New South Wales and Queensland closed.

In the country districts the farmer and the squatter were hard hit by falls of up to fifty per cent in the prices of their produce, especially since the high rates of interest charged by banks were not cut. The depreciation of land values brought further pressure on the mortgagees. After discharging their financial obligations, the farmers had little left to give them anything like an adequate return for their labour.

On Sunday, 19 November, 1893, three hundred unemployed in Sydney formed a procession led by an individual carrying a huge cross on which was nailed the effigy of a downtrodden man clad in tattered rags, his side besmeared by red paint, and on his back the words 'Murdered by the rich'. In general the clergy responded to the depression in the cities with sermons that mocked the destitute by attributing their misfortunes to improvidence, drinking, and gambling. The Anglican bishop of Melbourne reminded his flock in May 1893 that there was an intimate connection between sin and suffering and expressed his desire that his fellow-Anglicans should observe the following Sunday as a day of humiliation on account of suffering, accompanied by a penitent confession of sin and by that broken and contrite heart that God would not despise. The Presbyterian Assembly of Victoria also proclaimed a day of humiliation and prayer.

Not all were driven to beat their breasts and cry *Mea culpa, mea maxima culpa* to their Jehovah in the hope that He might resurrect the vanished boom. The *Bulletin* accused the parsons of making the church look ridiculous in the eyes

A soup kitchen in Sydney in the 1880s.

of the scoffer. The papers publishing a labour view of the depression asserted that the people had to choose between the capitalist plan, which was to reconstruct banks, and their labour plan, which was to reconstruct society. The *Brisbane Worker* wrote on 20 March, 1893:

The reconstructors of society join issue with the reconstructors of smashed banks and will fight to a finish to put an end to the present anarchy and oppose to the bitter end any attempt at its continuance by bolstering up an institution that has vampired the country dry.

The directors of the banks and financial companies drew quite different conclusions. They drew up plans for the reconstruction of the banks that had been obliged to close their doors. To avoid a repetition of the disasters of 1890-93 they urged the creation of a federal parliament with power to legislate on banking and currency. The depression had converted them into political nationalists. It had had a similar effect on the premiers of the colonies, who at a conference in Melbourne in May of 1893 resolved: 'That recent events prove that laws require to be enacted with respect to banking in all the colonies, and that the legislation should be uniform.' The bankers and the politicians were discovering federation as a servant to their material interests, which planted in the minds of some labour thinkers the dark suspicion that federation might become a means of preventing in perpetuity their cherished reconstruction of society.

A series of industrial strikes between 1890 and 1894 led to similar thinking by both capital and labour on the future of society. Before 1890 the causes of strikes had been attempts by unions to raise wages, to resist any increase in working hours, or to resist the dismissal of a man for holding a position in a trades union. In 1890 a series of strikes began in the eastern colonies that raised the question of the rights of unionism, and in so doing it led to a direct clash between capital and labour. When the employers in the shipping industry refused to allow the Marine Officers' Association to affiliate with the other

A shearer's hut at Seven Creeks Station near Longwood, Victoria.

labour organizations in the colonies, the men walked off the ships. In the same year the shearers came out in protest against the claim by the squatters for freedom of contract—their right to negotiate with union or non-union labour for a contract to shear their sheep. When the pastoralists began to employ non-union labour, or what the unions called 'black' or 'scab' labour, the wharf labourers in Sydney and Melbourne refused to handle wool shorn by non-union labour.

By August, Sydney, Melbourne, and Brisbane were in uproar. During disturbances in Melbourne the officer commanding the troops ordered his men to 'Fire low and lay them out—lay the disturbers of law and order out, so that the duty will not again have to be performed. Let it be a lesson to them.' In November, when bales of non-union wool were carted through the streets of Sydney by non-union labour under armed escort, the mob hooted, groaned, and cursed at the 'scab' workers, while the few outside the business premises near the Circular Quay—those monuments in stone and brick to bourgeois civilization—countered with demonstrations of encouragement, which provoked more outbursts of frantic yelling from the supporters of the unions. At the quay ten thousand people gathered and began to throw stones and other missiles. After the cheek of one of the constables had been laid open with a stone, the Riot Act was read and the crowd was dispersed by force. Later, outside the Wool Exchange, Captain Fisher thanked the troops and the police for upholding law and order.

At the same time anarchy and uproar held sway in the country districts. There were disturbances at Bourke early in 1891, and at the end of March there were armed skirmishes between the unions, the army, and the police at Barcaldine, in western Queensland. Without exception the governments of New South Wales, Victoria, and Queensland acted promptly to preserve law and order. In Queensland in June 1891 the Premier, Samuel Griffith, explained to the legislative assembly that for a time there 'appeared grave danger

Circular Quay, Sydney. In 1890, ten thousand people gathered at the quay to throw stones and other missiles during an industrial strike.

that the freedom of men to pursue their lawful avocations under the protection of the law would be seriously impaired'. Union leaders were arrested, charged with conspiracy, and sentenced to long terms in gaol. The leaders of the workers suspected that the government and the law courts were fighting to support capitalism, that the governments were committed to 'freedom of contract', rather than the suppression of lawlessness. The union leaders had been told in the liberal textbooks on political philosophy that the state was an umpire between contending groups; they had suspected that it was a committee for the management of the affairs of the bourgeoisie; now a few perceived that the state was an organization for the suppression of one class by another. The behaviour of the government of New South Wales during the strike of the silver, lead, and zinc miners at Broken Hill in 1892, and of the government of Queensland during the strike of the shearers and bush workers in 1893-94, confirmed these suspicions.

Others drew quite different conclusions from their experiences during the strikes. The Reverend Dr Watkin, a Methodist clergyman in Sydney, detected the hand of God in the great strikes. He saw the strike as a sign of God's vengeance for the desecration of the Lord's day in a multitude of ways by almost all classes. God, he suggested, used capital to smite labour and labour to smite capital, and labour and capital to smite the public. As his brother clergy had done when they contemplated the human suffering caused by the depression, the reverend doctor appealed for national humiliation and national atonement. To ward off such visitations he reminded his congregation that they must learn to keep God's Sabbath and to reverence God's sanctuaries. At the same time Cardinal Moran was looking to the day when there would be friendlier feelings between employer and employee. He suggested some compromise, some plan by which the shipowners would abandon ruinous competition among themselves and pay good wages to their workers and good dividends to themselves. But the cardinal was not able to indicate clearly how this could be achieved within the existing society.

As with the depression, the experiences during the strikes pushed the employers into support for federation. At the Pan-Australasian conference of employers at Sydney in September 1890 they reaffirmed their belief in freedom of contract and asserted that any infringement thereof was not only destructive of commerce but was also inimical to the best interests of the working classes. They also resolved to reply to force with force. Finally they encouraged all employers to join an employers' union for their mutual protection and defence and to form federal councils for each colony. That was in 1890. By 1893, after three more years of strikes and acute financial depression, the employers moved a stage further in their thinking and declared that their interests could be best served by a political federation of the Australian colonies.

At the same time experiences during the strikes had also converted the leaders of the workers to a belief in political action. Traditionally trade unionism was an instrument for improving the standard of living of the workers within capitalist society. The overthrow of that society, the workers argued, had not been part of their business. The strikes caused them to question that assumption. The trade unionists realized, as their leaders put it, that they had been travelling for many years in a blind alley the end of which was blocked by monopoly firmly cemented by the laws of the land. It was therefore their duty to ask themselves whether society should be changed, and if so, how. The trumpet note at the sound of which the barriers in society would fall, they argued, was essentially political. Once the workers perceived that the very basis of modern industry was antagonistic to their welfare, they had to set about the work of reform where it could be achieved—in parliament. There they were destined, amid all the hypocrisy of political life, to brighten the lot of their children—if not their own.

The idea was not new. In December 1874 Angus Cameron was elected to the Legislative Assembly of New South Wales as the member for West Sydney. To make it possible for a working man to sit in parliament the trades and labour council in Sydney paid him a salary. In 1880 N. Melville was elected for Northumberland and J. Garrard for Balmain, and in 1885 E. W. O'Sullivan was elected to represent Queanbeyan in the same assembly. These men did not see themselves as representatives of society. They saw themselves as men with a job to do, to put pennies on the pay and to take hours off the day.

This trade union conception of politics was one of many influences on Labour when they formed separate political parties. Labour electoral leagues were formed in New South Wales in 1891, and their candidates won thirty-five seats in the legislative assembly in the elections of that year. The Progressive Political Labour League won ten seats in Victoria in 1892. The Australian Labour Federation won fifteen seats in Queensland in 1893. In 1893 the United Labour Party in South Australia won eight seats in the legislative assembly, while representatives of Labour won six seats in Western Australia in 1901 and three seats in Tasmania in 1903.

In the beginning the trade unions were anxious to keep the Labour parties as their own. In South Australia, for example, in 1891, a trade union delegate moved at a conference of the United Labour Party that only those who were eligible to become members of a trade or labour society should be eligible to join the Political Labour League, but the motion was lost. By the end of 1893 the right of non-unionists to join was recognized in all the colonies. So Labour ceased to be an exclusively working-class party, a fact that probably gave it the opportunity to capture a majority in the parliaments of the colonies within the next fifteen years, though at the price of surrendering the ideal of the reconstruction of society. 'Labor' now became the accepted spelling for the party.

An Eight-Hour Day celebration in Melbourne in 1889.

From the beginning Labor's aim was to capture rather than destroy the institutions of the bourgeois state. Labor's aim was to make the bourgeois ideals of liberty and equality a reality for all members of society, not just for the privileged few. So in politics Labor was concerned to give everyone a voice in deciding the condition under which he lived. In their party they claimed the people made the policy. In the beginning they talked much about this political democracy—about the abolition of plural voting, the abolition of the legislative councils, the election of ministers, the right of recall, the redistribution of electorates to provide one man, one vote. They were political reformers rather than destroyers of the bourgeois state.

They were just as cautious in their attitude to bourgeois society. In the beginning they spoke and wrote with the enthusiasm and confidence of the righteous in the presence of great wickedness. In 1890 the *Brisbane Worker* told its readers that it was the mission of Labor 'to free the worker from wage-slavery, to reduce the world from shame and sorrow, to make men manly and women womanly and the little ones full of laughter and life full of love'. Or again in January 1890 the *Hummer* in Wagga told its readers that diseased, vicious, and evil conditions had bred infanticide and competition, each as bad as the other. 'Neither of them,' concluded the *Hummer*, 'are being mates!'

But when the first Labor political groups in New South Wales, Victoria, South Australia and Queensland came to put down on paper precisely what they would do to society, their ideas were just as reformist as their ideas on the institutions of the bourgeois state. The first platform of the Labour Electoral League in New South Wales in 1891 reflected the variety of influences on Labor's thinking. Plank 13, for example, was a summary of the opinions of the single-taxers:

The recognition in our legislative enactments of the natural and inalienable rights of the whole community to the land—upon which all must live and from which by labour all wealth is produced—by the taxation of that value which accrues to the land from the presence and needs of the community, irrespective of improvements effected by human exertion.

By 1889 there were fifteen branches of the single-tax league in New South Wales, and by 1890 there were branches in all the colonies. The single-taxers believed that by abolishing all taxation save that on land values they could raise wages, increase employment, abolish poverty, lessen crime, dignify menial tasks, purify government, and carry civilization to a still nobler height. Others believed that similar lofty aims could be fulfilled by a rigorous adoption of the principle of one man, one vote. Others again were influenced by the teachings of the utopian socialists—the ability of man to create a terrestrial happiness to replace that celestial happiness that had disappeared with the collapse of religious belief. Socialism, they believed, would make men brothers.

In the same movement there were men who learnt their ideas on the future of society from the encyclical *Rerum Novarum,* which was published in the foundation year of the Political Labour League in New South Wales. These men were taught by their religious leaders to be sceptical of all promises of happiness in this world. Cardinal Moran told the congregation at the requiem mass at St Mary's, Sydney, in 1890 for the repose of the soul of Cardinal Newman:

In many respects it is an age of ruins, and amid these ruins false scientists will set before us a phantom temple of socialistic atheism . . . in which selfishness and pride, the idols of a corrupt heart, demand our homage and worship. It is otherwise within the domain of the Catholic Church. She gathers her children around the altar of God to impart to them a divine life, to instruct them in heavenly wisdom, to unfold to them the secret of true happiness, and to lead them to their eternal destiny.

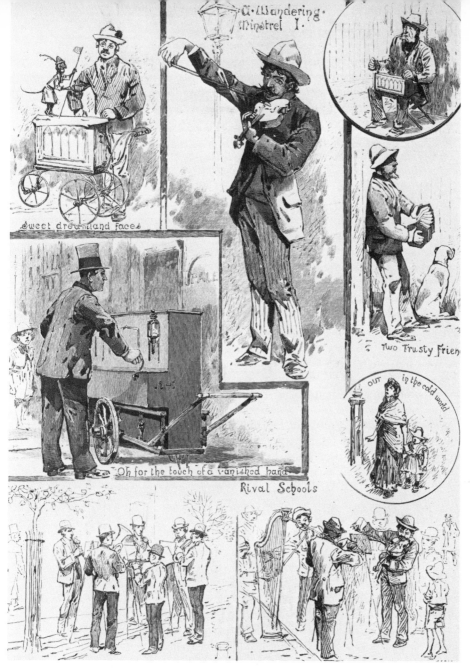

A Wandering Minstrel I.

Sweet dreamland faces

Oh for the touch of a vanished hand

Rival Schools

Two Trusty Friends

Out in the cold world

Street musicians in 1886.

When the Political Labour Leagues first ran candidates for the legislative assembly of New South Wales in 1891, thirty-five men were elected. Labor was jubilant. In the full flush of success one of their representatives, George Black, rose in the legislative assembly of New South Wales in 1891 and told the house '. . . we have come into this House to make and unmake social conditions'. But before the party could dedicate itself to this high purpose it was torn by faction fights; the free traders fought with the protectionists; the trade unionists wanted to capture the party for their own purposes; the single-taxers also tried to use the party for their own ends.

Above all the party was rent and torn by the introduction of 'the pledge'. In New South Wales, Queensland, South Australia, and Victoria, Labor became the third, or corner, party in parliament, and like all 'corner' parties offered support to one of the two others in return for concessions. Like all 'corner' parties they quickly perceived that their effectiveness depended on their solidarity in the house. Labor, too, believed that in their party the members made the policy. To achieve these objectives of solidarity and party democracy Labor administered a pledge to all members. The first draft of the pledge was made in New South Wales in 1891, and by 1893 all members had signed the following statement:

I hereby pledge myself not to oppose the selected candidate of this or any other branch of the Political Labour League. I also pledge myself, if returned to Parliament, on all occasions to do my utmost to ensure the carrying out of the principles embodied in the Labor Platform, and in all such questions, and especially in questions affecting the fate of a Government, to vote as a majority of the Labor Party may decide at a duly constituted caucus meeting.

In South Australia the pledge had been adopted in principle on the formation of the United Labour Party in 1891; in Queensland a pledge was included in the constitution of the Australian Labour Federation in 1890. Victoria adopted the pledge in 1894, Western Australia in 1902, and Tasmania in 1903.

Immediately the opponents of Labor howled to high heaven that the Labor members were the bond slaves of an outside body, that they were not responsible to their electors, and that the pledge infringed liberty of conscience and brought able and original minds under the tyranny of the majority. Some members within the party resigned as a grandiose and empty gesture for liberty rather than surrender their conscience to a party caucus. In this way Labor members were tricked into a defence of their political methods when they might well have spent their time working out what Labor would do once it achieved office.

Despite the enthusiasm of the tiny band of utopians within the movement, the shrewd judges of the contemporary scene summed up Labor as representing no serious threat to capitalist society. The Sydney *Daily Telegraph* wrote on 26 June, 1891: 'If the conduct of the Labor Party in Parliament is as rational as most of their legislative aims or as temperate as most of their husting utterances, capital will not be more troubled at what they will do than it now is at what they have done.' The immediate effect of Labor was more on the behaviour of the other parties. In New South Wales and Victoria by 1891, and in the other colonies by 1900, the advent of Labor marked the end of factionalism in politics, and with it the end of the 'faction' leader. In New South Wales and Victoria by 1891 the factions had been replaced by two political parties under recognized leaders. The days of such faction leaders as Parkes or Robertson or Gillies were over. In these two colonies the bourgeois parties were divided into free-traders and protectionists. Both were committed to material well-being for all, equality of opportunity, and the career open to talent. They differed in method rather than in fundamental aim.

The new men began to take over in politics. The politician educated by John Stuart Mill and de Tocqueville and the rough-and-tumble of colonial experience was giving way to the politician whose liberalism had been tempered by reading T. H. Green and Bosanquet and accounts of the legislation of the Gladstone government in England from 1868 to 1874. One of these men was endowed by nature with exceptional gifts. He was Alfred Deakin, who was born at Fitzroy, a suburb of Melbourne, in August 1856, and educated at Melbourne Grammar School and the University of Melbourne, where he studied law. At Melbourne Grammar he came under the influence of Dr Bromby, who had taken part in the great public debate on science and religion, which during Deakin's undergraduate days narrowed down to a discussion of the life of man without God. The liberalism Deakin embraced, the belief in progress, the pursuit of material well-being, the career open to talent, and political democracy, was in part a substitute for his lost celestial happiness. Despite the lavish gifts of nature, the commanding personal appearance and the superb oratory, the man seemed haunted by intimations that this world of affairs, this world of politics, of who's in and who's out, was not the real world at all; that a man ought to be laying up for himself treasures in heaven, that if God and the life of the world to come did not exist, then a man should achieve glory in the world of letters. Yet worldly glory came easy to him. He entered the legislative assembly of Victoria in 1879 as a member for West Bourke, and in 1883 took office in the Service-Berry government at the age of twenty-seven. In 1884 he went to America to study irrigation, and in 1887 he represented the colony of Victoria at the colonial conference in London, where he impressed the English with the dignity of his bearing and the flame of his political passion. On his return to the colony he dedicated all his energies to federation, and became the second Prime Minister of Australia in 1903.

From 1879 to 1900 he was the prime force in the Victorian parliament behind such liberal legislation as the factory acts, the abolition of plural voting, arbitration, and minimum wages. He was a superb orator, and while he was often the object of coarse and virulent attacks, he never answered vulgarity in kind or lowered the tone of his parliamentary life. His vision was noble and high-minded, yet tinged with sadness, with the melancholy of the deprived, as well as with faint intimations that this world of appearances was not all a man could know, that beyond it was the real world. So the inner man was tormented, while the outer man winced before the vulgar, as he proclaimed his faith in British institutions, the Protestant religion, and the British way of life as the greatest achievements of man. At heart Deakin remained a provincial, without an inkling of the wider loyalties made possible by the rapid developments in production, transport, and communication.

Sir George Reid, Lady Reid and family. Behind Reid's buffoonery and salacious stories there was a shrewd, talented and sensitive mind.

It was this sensitivity to the vulgar that explained his distaste for men such as Parkes and Reid. George Reid was a huge man, with a bloated face, a high-pitched, squeaky voice, and a taste for indecency that shocked the prude in Deakin. With the prig's lack of charity for the man whose conversation was suggestive and licentious and whose manners were coarse and uncouth, Deakin said Reid's earlier years were characterized chiefly by indolence and geniality. Reid was born in Scotland in 1845, migrated to Australia in 1852, became a civil servant, studied law part-time, and acquired some skill as a debater. With the cheek and confidence he was to display until the end of his days, he began his political career by standing against Sir Henry Parkes, and on nomination day he told the electors it was his ambition to be known for his services rather than the prizes he had won. The electors responded by placing him at the top of the poll.

In public Reid often behaved as a buffoon. Before huge audiences in town halls or in the open air his high-pitched voice, florid complexion, indolent stroking of his enormous stomach, and the vulgar ornaments on his watch-chain suggested that a successful larrikin had entered politics. Once, when he was speaking at the town hall in Melbourne, a heckler pointed to his belly and asked, 'What's it going to be George—a boy or a girl?' Reid replied, 'If you had anything to do with it, it would be a kangaroo.' The huge crowd roared its approval. On another occasion, in the Richmond town hall he told the crowd that the superiority of free trade over protection was demonstrated by the fewer lunatics per square mile in Sydney than in Melbourne.

The high-minded and the responsible winced at such vulgar posturings before the *demos*. But the buffoonery and the salacious stories were part of the mask behind which there lived a shrewd, talented, and sensitive mind. Like Deakin, Reid was a liberal who believed in the use of the state to secure material well-being for all and in a career open to talent. But, unlike Deakin, he believed in free trade rather than protection—which only meant that he had grown up intellectually in Sydney rather than Melbourne. Unlike Deakin he revelled in the hurly-burly of politics. A stranger to religious faith, utterly unresponsive to any promise of the life of the world to come, he believed that free trade, education, arbitration, minimum wages, factory legislation, and political democracy would in due season create liberty and happiness for everyone. On the way to that goal Reid was prepared to enjoy hugely the game of politics, to enjoy good food, good wine and conversation. The man had a faith in the goodness and dignity of mankind, and his passions never drove him to the humiliations Parkes had endured, nor did his mind or heart grope for those other satisfactions Deakin believed were lurking behind the facade of life.

Liberals with such principles, prodded and goaded into action by the Labor members of the parliaments, proceeded to make the political institutions of the colonies more democratic and to give the state a new role as the instrument and protector of the material well-being of its citizens. In 1870 Victoria introduced payment of members of the legislative assembly; Queensland followed in 1886, South Australia in 1887, New South Wales in 1889, Tasmania in 1890, and Western Australia in 1900. In 1893 New South Wales abolished plural voting for the legislative assembly; Victoria followed in 1899, Tasmania in 1901, Queensland in 1905, and Western Australia in 1907. South Australia had had single voting for the assembly since 1856 but had protected 'interests' against one man, one vote by gerrymandered electorates. South Australia introduced votes for women in 1894; Western Australia followed in 1899, New South Wales in 1902, Tasmania in 1903, Queensland in 1905, and Victoria in 1909. These changes went some way towards introducing political equality, or one man, one vote, for the legislative assemblies of the colonies.

The rights and privileges of 'interests' as distinct from population continued to be protected by the distribution of electorates that weighted the country vote against the city vote and by the legislative councils. Labor wanted the liberals to go further and abolish all remnants of political inequality such as gerrymandering and legislative councils, and such remnants of imperial control as colonial governors and the reserve and disallowance powers of the Imperial Parliament. A few conservatives predicted doom and disaster, or conjured up nightmares of a new age of men cowed and licked into uniformity by the new master—the majority. But the liberals and Labor retorted that the conservatives were protecting their material privileges rather than defending the liberty of the individual.

A Melbourne Cup party on the steps of Government House, Melbourne, in 1872.

The liberals, again after many promptings from Labor, also expanded the role of the state in economic life to provide material well-being for all. The Victorian parliament passed eight factory acts between 1885 and 1900, Tasmania passed a solitary one in 1884, and South Australia in 1894 and 1900. New South Wales passed an act in 1896 to provide for the supervision and regulation of factories, bake-houses, laundries, dye-works, and shops, in certain cases placing a limitation on the hours of working therein and extending the liability of employers for certain injuries suffered by employees. Queensland passed a factory act in 1896; Western Australia in 1899 passed an act to require that seats be supplied for shop assistants and in 1904 passed its first comprehensive factory act. The conservatives denied the right of any parliament under the sun to fix the hours of labour; the liberals and Labor were not bothered by problems of abstract right but were concerned with how to protect the working classes against Chinese competition, the evils of sweating, and the evils of free competition.

To achieve such objectives the parliament of Victoria passed an act in 1896 that empowered the government to appoint a wages board to determine the lowest rate that might be paid to any person engaged in manufacturing in a factory or workroom. Again the conservatives preached their jeremiads about a society that to their mind was wantonly transgressing the laws of freedom of contract, but the liberals and Labor used their majority to put the idea on the statute book. Before the strike of 1890-94 press and pulpit propagated the idea of collaboration between capital and labour. A typical cartoon represented capital as a businessman with mutton-chop whiskers dressed in frockcoat, butterfly collar, and top-hat, clasping warmly by the hand a clean-shaven worker dressed in dungarees, a worker's shirt, and ample braces, in every way the epitome of clean living. After the strikes some wondered whether antagonism rather than collaboration would henceforth characterize the relations between capital and labour. The pessimists amongst the employers began to talk of coercion, or to weave fantasies about a golden age in the past before the days of trade unions when their 'hands' were docile, content with their penury, and lay down each night exhausted after the hard day's toil with sentiments of gratitude to their employers in their hearts. A few of the Labor leaders maintained that antagonism between capital and labour would survive so long as the means of production, distribution, and exchange were privately owned.

The liberals from the bourgeois parties and the reformists from Labor put forward arbitration and conciliation as the solution to such antagonism. 'It is frankly admitted,' wrote the royal commission on strikes in New South Wales in 1891, 'that a great many disputes originate in ignorance, in mutual misunderstanding, in unfounded suspicions, in exaggerated alarms, and that very much is gained if all these disturbing accessories can be got rid of, and the controversy can be narrowed to its simple issue.' To dispel these mists the parliaments in Victoria and New South Wales introduced voluntary arbitration in 1891 and 1892, South Australia in 1894; and in 1901 the parliament of New South Wales introduced compulsory arbitration in industrial disputes. Again the conservatives took their stand on the moral evils of compulsion, but this time the confrontation between capital and labour was temporarily lost sight of in the excitement and enthusiasm of the creation of the Commonwealth of Australia.

The federation movement intruded more and more on the political life of the colonies in the last twenty years of the century. It was a movement with a long history. As early as 1842, when the agitation to divide the old New South Wales into two or three separate colonies first got under way, the far-sighted presented the case for some central government on the grounds of convenience; but their counsel fell on the deaf ears of men bent on the tri-section of New South Wales, or those even deafer ears in South Australia that confounded all central government or federation proposals with domination by New South Wales. Again when Earl Grey advised the colonists in 1846-50 to ponder the dangers of separate parliaments legislating on such subjects of common interest as railway gauges, posts and telegraphs, quarantine, and defence, the warning was rudely pushed aside by men who believed their future lay in self-government and responsible government, but not in any unitary or federal government. The price for colonial folly was that New South Wales adopted the standard railway gauge, Victoria the five feet three inches, and Queensland, South Australia and Western Australia the three feet six inches.

The colonial parliaments imposed customs duties on the goods of other colonies, or discriminated against them with differential rail rates. In New South Wales there was a vested interest in free trade; in Victoria there was a vested interest in protection. New South Wales was a convict colony; South Australia was not. New South Wales and Queensland played Rugby football; the other colonies played Australian Rules. So all proposals for federation between 1850 and 1881 foundered on the rocks of intercolonial rivalry and the absence of sufficiently powerful motives for entertaining wider horizons than the provincial and the petty.

Overleaf: Sir Henry Parkes, an innovator in the New South Wales legislative scene and the Father of Federation.

Defence, fears of coloured labour, and economic interest, strengthened the motives for union over the last twenty years of the century. In 1889 Major-General Edwards informed the colonial governments that if the colonies had to rely on their own defence resources their position would be dangerous. It was, the major-general believed, quite impossible to put the defence forces on a proper footing without a federation of the forces of the different colonies. It was this question of defence, in the opinion of Parkes, that brought the colonies 'face to face with the imperative necessity for a Federal Government'. The informed and tiny group of men who took interest in the world outside were afraid of German aggression in New Guinea, of the French in the New Hebrides, or, more vaguely, of Russian and American economic imperialism in the Pacific. Indeed, every war scare in the Pacific, every real and imagined threat from the time of the Crimean War to Major-General Edwards's report, led to talk about federation.

After reading the Edwards report Parkes suggested a federal conference, to consist of delegates from the six colonies and New Zealand elected by their parliaments. At the conference, which met in Melbourne from 6 to 14 February, 1890, five colonies and New Zealand sent two delegates, and Western Australia sent one. The conference began with an oration from Parkes on the lofty significance of their work, and after speeches by other delegates in which the vision of a united Australia was often lost in sordid and petty colonial jealousy and human vanity, they agreed to summon a convention to Sydney in 1891 to draft a federal constitution. When the delegates presented the constitution drafted at this Sydney convention to their own parliaments, New South Wales rejected it: not only because the proposed constitution was unfair to that colony, but because federation was part of the political game, and as such had to be judged by its effect on the power of the main political parties. Federation had become a political football. The motive to combine for defence was not sufficiently powerful to persuade Australians to transcend colonial interests.

Other motives—the fear of coloured labour, economic interest, and the chauvinism of the 1890s—provided the impetus needed for federation. Between 1880 and 1900 the fear of coloured labour degenerated into hysteria in the eastern colonies. The workers in Queensland, New South Wales, and Victoria feared a lowering of their living standard from competition between white and coloured labour. In Queensland the workers were afraid lest 'niggers' and Chinese reduce all white workers, if not to slavery, than at least to a lower standard of living. The bourgeoisie feared competition from Chinese importers and furniture manufacturers. They were obsessed with the evils of miscegenation and with the problem of permitting Chinese, Japanese, Pacific Islanders, or Indians to live in Australia when they did not share the political tradition of bourgeois or liberal democracy. As Deakin put it in 1901, the question touched

... the profoundest instinct of individual or nation—the instinct of self-preservation—for it is nothing less than the national manhood, the national character, and the national future that are at stake. ... No motive power operated more universally ... and more powerfully in dissolving the technical and arbitrary political divisions which previously separated us than did the desire that we should be one people and remain one people without the admixture of other races.

Economic development in the last quarter of the century strengthened this feeling of being one people with one destiny. From 1880 on the manufacturers in Australia chafed and fretted at the reputation of colonial goods as second-

VOTE FOR SIR HE

Federation, Local Govern

TRIUMPHANT RETU

(From THE AUSTRAL.

RY PARKES.

t and General Prosperity.

OF SIR HENRY PARKES.

TAR, of Saturday, July 20th.) *1895*

rate or shoddy. 'Colonial wine,' it was said, 'was sour; Colonial ale was watery; Colonial cheese was rancid; Colonial preserved fruits were pulpy.' No bishop could be manufactured in the colonies, no professor, no judge—or so the nationalists maintained. But that fallacy would be exploded, the manufacturers believed, that slur on the native force would be exposed, and their opportunity to get to the top would be assured by the creation of a united Australia.

The events of 1890 to 1894 convinced sections of the bourgeoisie that federation would promote their material interests. Not all argued with the crudity of the Tasmanian who said: '. . . we shall create a glorious nation and meat will be cheaper.' The manufacturers wanted to abolish intercolonial tariffs and differential freight charges; some employers believed a strong federal state would prevent a recurrence of the strikes of 1890-93; the farmers and graziers in border districts such as the Riverina, New England, the Wimmera, the Mallee, and the Darling Downs clamoured for the end of colonial tariffs; some bankers and financiers believed a federal government might prevent a repetition of the financial depression of 1890-93.

The 'border' interests began the final attempt at federation. The delegates from the Corowa conference of 1893, where the delegates came from the Australian Natives Association, the Chamber of Commerce and the Chamber of Manufactures in Melbourne, Progress Associations, and Commercial Travellers Associations, resolved:

That in the opinion of this Conference . . . the present and future interests of the Australian colonies will be promoted by their early union under the Crown, and that such colonies have now increased in population, wealth, and discovery of resources, and in self-governing capacity to an extent which justifies their union under one Legislative and Executive Government on principles just to the several colonies.

In 1894 George Reid, as premier of New South Wales, sent telegrams to the other five premiers suggesting they confer at Hobart. At the ensuing Premiers' Conference in Hobart in January 1895 the premiers resolved that a convention, consisting of ten representatives directly chosen by the electors, be charged with the duty of framing a federal constitution. In March 1897 elections to choose ten delegates were held in Victoria, New South Wales, South Australia, and Tasmania. The Western Australian delegates were elected by their parliament. Queensland did not send delegates, partly because of the argument between the legislative assembly and legislative council on the method of election, partly because federation became tangled up with the move for the separation of North Queensland.

So fifty delegates, some of whom weighed over twenty stone, met in hot sticky weather dressed in serge suits, starched shirts and collars, for sessions in Adelaide from March to April 1897, in Sydney in September 1897, and in Melbourne from January to March in 1898, to draft a federal constitution. There were many lions in the path. The Political Labour League was very suspicious. Of the fifty delegates only one represented their point of view, and he with such lack of zeal that he left the movement a few months after the Melbourne convention. The rest represented to Labor the bourgeois conspiracy. The fathers of federation, as they saw them, were the men who had given the orders to fire on the strikers in Melbourne and Barcaldine in the troubles of 1890-93. Some entertained the darker suspicion that the bourgeois parties were creating a federation in the hope that it would overwhelm the Labor Party. Labor, said the hot-heads, should be on guard against the federal conspiracy. Others within the labour movement, believing federation to be inevitable, argued that it was their task to make the federal constitution conform as closely as possible to their slogan, 'one man, one vote'.

At the conventions of 1897-98 all the delegates agreed there should be a federation, but they were dismayed by the difficulties. If the federal parliament were empowered to levy customs duties, what sources of revenue would be left to the colonial parliaments? If the federal government had a surplus revenue, on what principles would that surplus be divided between the six colonial governments? Would it be by population, or by area, or by financial need? A federation was a series of contracts between two parties—the individual colonial parliaments and the federal parliament. If the two parties to the contract were equal in power, then the minority could dictate to the majority; if on the other hand they were not equal in power, then the federal principle would be subordinate to the principle of responsible government.

After months of argument the delegates arrived at a compromise decision to gloss over the differences between the conservatives and liberals, between the state's-righters and those for a strong federal parliament and government. The new federation was to be called the Commonwealth of Australia; the six colonies were to be known as States. There was to be a House of Representatives elected on universal franchise, a Senate consisting of six representatives from each State chosen by the electors of that State, and a High Court consisting of judges appointed by the Commonwealth parliament whose function was to hear cases on conflicting jurisdiction between the Commonwealth and the States. Power to legislate on subjects such as trade and commerce with other countries and among the States, taxation, posts and telegraphs, banking, marriage, divorce and matrimonial causes, invalid and old-age pensions, immigration and emigration, external affairs, and conciliation and arbitration for the prevention and settlement of industrial disputes extending beyond the limits of any one State, was given to the Commonwealth Parliament; they were called the 'specific' powers. The 'residual' powers, such as education, health, and railways, remained with the State parliaments.

This constitution was submitted to a referendum of the people entitled to vote in the various colonies. But in the interval between the Melbourne session and the referendum the Reid government in New South Wales passed a bill through the New South Wales parliament that required the 'Yes' vote to exceed 80,000. When that figure was not reached in the referendum of June 1898, the premiers of the colonies agreed to meet in Melbourne to consider amendments. At that meeting in January to February 1899 proposals on deadlocks, the distribution of the surplus revenue, amendments of the constitution, and the powers of the Senate, were amended to meet the criticism that the first draft was too conservative and too weighted in favour of the less populous States. Also, to soothe the pride of New South Wales without affronting Melbourne unduly, it was agreed that the federal capital would be in New South Wales, a reasonable distance from the city of Sydney. When the amended constitution was submitted to a second referendum, New South Wales, Victoria, South Australia, Tasmania, and Queensland turned in 'Yes' majorities, though only forty per cent of those entitled to vote supported it and approximately sixteen per cent of those entitled to vote rejected it.

Western Australia still held out. In that colony the electors in the goldfields at Coolgardie and Kalgoorlie were clamouring for federation as a stick with which to beat the conservatives and provincials of Perth. The government of Western Australia, dominated as it was by a large fish in a small pond, John Forrest, was plagued with anxiety about goldfields radicalism and about government revenues after the loss of the right to impose customs, which in 1898 comprised nearly ninety per cent of the revenue of the colony. So they bargained with the eastern colonies and with London, and they were offered the right to levy customs for five years after the creation of the Commonwealth, and promised that the Commonwealth would build a railway from Kalgoorlie to Port Augusta in South Australia if Western Australia became an original member. On 31 July, 1900, they held their referendum at which forty-six per cent of the electors on the rolls voted 'Yes' and just over twenty per cent voted 'No'. This was the highest proportion for 'Yes' in all the colonies.

In the meantime delegates from New South Wales, Victoria, South Australia, Queensland, and Tasmania were discussing the text of the constitution with the Secretary of State for the Colonies, Joseph Chamberlain. Chamberlain was not happy about the absence of a right to appeal from the High Court to the Privy Council, partly for sentimental reasons and partly because he wanted to encourage British capitalists to go on investing in Australia. To meet the British point the delegates swallowed their rather aggressive nationalism and agreed to meet Chamberlain halfway with a compromise that permitted appeals from the High Court to the Privy Council on the limits *inter se* of the constitutional powers of the Commonwealth and those of any State or States if the High Court decided the question was one that ought to be determined by the Queen in Council. When the delegates heard that Chamberlain had accepted, they rejoiced.

So by 21 May, 1900, all was in readiness for Chamberlain to introduce the bill in the House of Commons, where he proclaimed that in sanctioning the union of Australia they had in no way impaired or weakened the unity of the empire. The British, he believed, could contemplate the consummation of this great achievement without the slightest drawback to the pride they felt in the wisdom and patriotism of their Australian kinsmen. In July Queen Victoria signed the bill, but within a year the Queen died, and one year later the first open-hearth steel was poured in New South Wales. When the Japanese destroyed the Russian fleet in 1904-05, the days of European domination in Asia seemed numbered. The old order was dying at the moment when bourgeois statesmanship and civilization reached their apogee in Australia.

Yet at the moment when changes in methods of production and revolutions in transport and communication were destroying the uniqueness of the bushman and his isolation from the world, some Australians went on noisily proclaiming their uniqueness and their opportunity to build a new society free from the old-world evils of class, poverty, and war. What the English or the European observed in the Australians was their Britishness. Francis Adams, an English man of letters who lived in Melbourne, Sydney, and Brisbane between 1884 and 1889, wrote in 1886:

The first thing that struck me on walking about Sydney one afternoon . . . was the appalling strength of the British civilization. . . . Everywhere are the thumbmarks and the great toe marks of the six fingered six-toed giant, Mr Arnold's life-long foe, the British Philistine! . . the Jehovah (or shall we say the Moloch?) of Puritanism, of Calvinism, is the same in Sydney as in London, in Melbourne as in Edinburgh! . . . These people in Sydney have clung not only to the faith but to the very raiment of their giant. The same flowing dresses, cumbrous on the women, hideous on the men, that we see in England! . . . the same food, the same overeating, and overdrinking, and (observe how careful we are) at the same hours!

This was precisely what the nationalists were protesting against—the Australians being confounded with the British. The manufacturer resented the slurs when his own goods were compared with the goods of the 'old country'; the writer resented the cringe, the bowing down, and stooping to the works of the British and the sneers for his own; the entertainers wanted more of the bowyang, the boomerang, and the sliprail in the music hall songs, and less of the Wee Doch-an-doris and Mother Machree. The question was, if the Australians were not British, what were they? Perhaps the most memorable attempt to answer this question was in the short stories of Henry Lawson.

Lawson was born in a tent on the Grenfell goldfields in New South Wales in 1867, the son of a Norwegian seaman turned gold prospector and an Australian mother with aspirations for a life of culture rather than the rough-and-tumble of the diggings. He was educated at Eurunderee State School, and at the age of sixteen he moved to Sydney with his mother when she left her husband. There an innate inability to deal with the things of everyday life gave him a taste of city poverty to supplement the rural poverty and squalor of his days at Grenfell and Eurunderee. He began to write stories and poetry for the *Bulletin* in Sydney in 1887. He married unsuccessfully in 1896, drank unwisely, for drink was poison to a man of his temperament, went to London in 1900 on a disastrous search for recognition, and received snubs and hurts that he nursed and cosseted till the end of his days. To add to his worldly difficulties he became progressively deaf.

The man had in him a vision of mateship as a comforter against a harsh, indifferent environment, and possibly as a consolation for the loss of that life of the world to come, as well as for all the slights and humiliations to which his wayward, sensitive soul had exposed him. But the provincial setting in which he raised his voice warped his vision. He wrote with simplicity and fire on mateship and the dignity of man. He wrote with compassion on the lives of the men and women in the bush who fought heroically and courageously against the soil, the weather, the market, and the evils of the capitalist system. He put down on paper the character of the native-born and of the colonial. He created his Mitchell, the cheeky, irreverent, roguish man, a cheat and a liar in his dealing with his opponents but the soul of honour and the repository of all the virtues in his dealings with his mates.

Lawson was concerned only with the problems of provincials, thus failing to deal with the universal problems of man in a capitalist society deprived of the consolations of religion. In darker moments he held up to ridicule Chinese, effeminate Englishmen, and culture. For Lawson applauded the same philistine qualities observers had criticized in British middle-class society, and left to posterity no clear directions on the way forward. That was the task of men such as Furphy and Brennan, who, at a time when some Australians were intoxicated by the nationalist jingles, began to address themselves with patience and dignity to the deeper problems of mankind.

Below left: A Government House At Home.

Below: Novelist Joseph Furphy ('Tom Collins') published his novel Such is Life *in 1903.*

CHAPTER TEN

THE AGE OF THE OPTIMISTS 1901—1919

FROM EARLY MORNING on 1 January, 1901, trains, trams, and ferries carried thousands of people to the great city of Sydney. The sun burst through the overhanging clouds at ten in the morning, and an invigorating southerly breeze tempered the terrible heat. At eleven a procession set out from the Domain to march to Centennial Park. Led by the shearers and followed by floats illustrating aspects of Australian life, the procession wound its way through the streets past crowds of cheering people and under arches bearing slogans that breathed the spirit of unity and brotherhood. Swarthy Maoris sat on great, lean horses like statues; Indians paraded in gorgeous costumes; gay dragoons and lancers swept past to thunderous applause from the crowd; the heads of all religious bodies, except the leaders of the' Roman Catholic Church, contributed a note of solemnity and dignity. But in general, according to an eyewitness, the people laughed and cheered and kept on cheering, while some wiped away tears that began to flow freely in the general excess of patriotism, loyalty, and kindly feeling.

At Centennial Park, in the presence of seven thousand invited guests, the imperial troops, a choir of fifteen thousand voices, and sixty thousand spectators, a slight and interesting figure, Lord Hopetoun, came on to the arena to loud and sustained applause. After the choir sang 'O God Our Help in Ages Past', and the Anglican primate recited the prayers set down for the occasion, E. G. Blackmore, who had been clerk to the federal convention of 1897-98, administered the oaths of office as Governor-General of the Commonwealth of Australia to Lord Hopetoun. The choir sang a Te Deum, which because of the terrible heat wafted fitfully around the arena; the flag of the new Commonwealth was hoisted, and the artillery thundered as cheer after cheer ran round the great arena. Then in loud, clear tones Lord Hopetoun read messages of congratulations and hope from the Queen and from the British government. Again cheers resounded round the arena, only to be drowned by the playing of the national anthem, after which the official party retired. So ended the 'bright and brilliant' inauguration of the Commonwealth of Australia.

The day before, Lord Hopetoun had commissioned Edmund Barton, a Liberal Protectionist whose political experience had been gained in the legislative assembly of New South Wales, to form the first government of the new Commonwealth. The bourgeois press used the occasion to express their optimism and their confidence. It was a matter of good omen for the cause of Australian industry, wrote the Melbourne *Age*, not only that there was a thoroughly protectionist ministry in power, but that it was to be confronted by a free-trade leader whose ragged reputation handicapped his party in advance. For, the *Age* went on, in spite of some ability of a certain kind, Mr Reid stood hopelessly

A wounded soldier's reunion with his family at Randwick Military Hospital, Sydney.

The Earl of Hopetoun, the first Governor-General of the Commonwealth of Australia (1901–03), taking the oath at Centennial Park pavilion, Sydney, on 1 January 1901.

Novelist Henry Handel Richardson, the author of The Fortunes of Richard Mahony *and many other works.*

discredited by political trickery and deceit. So Melbourne, the seat of government till the move to Canberra in 1927, began to impose its rectitude, its uprightness, and its philistinism on the new Commonwealth.

Labor opinion was equally optimistic, though for a different reason. The Commonwealth of Australia, as the Brisbane *Worker* saw it, sprang up free of most of the superstitions, traditions, class distinctions, and sanctified fables and fallacies of the older nations. Australia stood on the threshold of the future with its fate in its own hands. On the other hand the more extreme nationalists and radicals were not happy about the events on inauguration day. The foreign troops, the *Bulletin* noted, marched into the reserved enclosure; the Australian troops remained outside. A few trade-union representatives were admitted inside the arena, while thousands of 'society people', the privileged classes, and the sycophants were seated near the pavilion of ceremony. To them the Governor-General looked puny and wan, as if in his own person he figured the wan and puny basis of the idea of monarchy. To an Australian, the *Bulletin* added, it was appropriate that the British representative should come at the tail, because he was the least necessary and the most insignificant of all the procession's components.

After the festivities the political parties prepared for the first elections to parliament. Broadly, three parties entered the field. The Conservative Free-Traders were distinguished by what they opposed rather than by what they affirmed. They were committed to such political commonplaces of the day as a White Australia and material well-being for all, but were opposed to any use of the state that might infringe the liberty of the subject. As free-traders they were committed to a policy of laissez-faire. So they spent their campaign dis-

Edmund Barton, left, the first Prime Minister of Australia (1901–03) and Alfred Deakin, who succeeded Barton in 1903 and was Prime Minister three times.

sociating themselves from the proposed methods of their opponents rather than stating how they proposed to achieve their aims. They drew their support from the pastoral areas, traditionally devoted to free trade, the more opulent suburbs in the capital cities, the chambers of commerce, and the large importing firms.

The other bourgeois party, the Liberal Protectionists, were also committed to a White Australia, the career open to talent, and material well-being for all, but were prepared to use the state to ensure a minimum standard of living and to protect the weak against the strong. They differed from the Labor Party both in the extent to which they were prepared to use the state, drawing in their propaganda a vague distinction between state capitalism and state socialism. To the Liberal Protectionists the Labor pledge violated liberty of conscience and destroyed the responsibility of a member to his constituents by forcing the members to obey the commands of the annual conference of the party. From the beginning there were two groups within the Liberal Protectionist Party, a conservative group, supported by the chambers of manufactures and the professional classes, and a radical group, supported by the petty bourgeoisie and the working classes in the towns. In time the party lost the former to the conservatives and the latter to Labor, but from 1901 to 1909 the interests of manufacturers and liberal idealists seemed to harmonize in Australia as they did in Great Britain and France.

In the beginning, Labor was a reformist rather than a radical or revolutionary party. Putting itself forward as the party of the working classes it was careful to include in its program points that appealed to other classes in the community, while at the same time eschewing any general revolutionary aim that would drive the moderates into the arms of the Liberal Protectionists. When the Federal Parliamentary Labor Party was formed in 1902, it was committed to a series of 'planks'. Then at the 1905 federal conference of the party, when the radicals clamoured for a socialist aim and the reformists fearfully opposed any such radical declaration, the decision was for this compromise:

1. Securing of all results of their industry to all producers by collective ownership of monopolies and the extension of the industrial and economic functions of the state and municipality;
2. Cultivation of an Australian sentiment based upon the maintenance of racial

At the opening of the first national Parliament on 9 May, 1901.

purity and the development in Australia of an enlightened and self-reliant community.

This summed up neatly the aspirations of the main articulate groups within the party: the Catholics, influenced by the publication in 1891 of the papal encyclical *Rerum Novarum,* the radical secular humanists, and the nationalists. It was this claim by Labor to be the nationalist party that persuaded the economic nationalist, the local manufacturer competing against imported goods from England, Europe, America, and Japan, to support Labor, thus widening its electoral appeal and diluting the power of its radical fringe.

The Catholic influence was equally moderating. From 1891 to 1905 a series of pronouncements by members of the Catholic hierarchy in Australia had distinguished between European socialism—which proposed to overturn the present order of society, concentrate men's aims on their earthly welfare alone, and leave heaven to the angels and the sparrows—and those who sought to redress the wrongs and to alleviate the miseries of the labouring classes from motives of Christian charity. Christ himself, the bishops reminded the faithful in a pastoral letter in 1905, said in the wilderness to the hungry thousands about him, 'I have compassion on the multitude.' In so far as these were the motives of the Labor Party in Australia, the bishops could see no reason why a Catholic should not vote Labor.

By 1905 circumstances had pushed the Catholic voter into the arms of the Labor party. There were many reasons for this. As the *Freeman's Journal,* a Catholic weekly published in Sydney, pointed out on 8 November, 1902, a party that aimed at the material elevation of the masses could not be antagonistic to a church that aimed at the spiritual elevation of the masses. In the eyes of the Catholic hierarchy the Conservative Free-Traders and Liberal Protectionists were Protestant parties, deeply committed to the secularization of Australian public life, and in their eyes secularization always followed the Protestantizing of society. The Catholic leaders had supported federation because increasing the strength of Australia would reduce English domination, and anything that upset the English from the seat of the mighty appealed strongly to the Irish Catholics. So from 1902 on the Catholic press urged their readers to join a branch of the Labor Party. The capture of the party by the Church had begun, and with it the voice of the radical within the party was weakened.

The first leader of the Australian Labor Party was J. C. Watson, who was born in Chile in 1867 and educated in New Zealand, where in the printing trade he began to hear of the hope of better things for man, and of the virtues of moderation and reformism. The moderation of Labor, and the progressive liberalism of men such as Barton, Deakin, and Kingston, made possible a working association between Labor and the Liberal Protectionists.

The state of the parties in the first Commonwealth Parliament made such agreement inevitable. Indeed, from 1901 to 1910 none of the three parties was able to win an absolute majority in the House of Representatives. In the first election in 1901 the Liberal Protectionists won thirty-two seats, the Conservative Free-Traders twenty-seven, and Labor sixteen. In the Senate the Liberal Protectionists won eleven, the Conservative Free-Traders seventeen, and Labor eight. With promise of Labor support the Barton government had a working majority in both houses to carry out its policy of White Australia, protection, arbitration, and social service legislation.

On the policy of White Australia the members of all parties, except two doctrinaire free-traders in the Senate, were in agreement. This wish to preserve a predominantly European society in Australia by prohibiting the immigration of Asiatics and Pacific Islanders, deporting the kanaka labourers on the sugar fields of Queensland, and discriminating against Asiatics and Pacific Islanders

Station hands play a quiet game.

(including Maoris) resident in Australia, had a long history. The idea was first tossed up in response to the squatters' attempt to use coolies to replace convicts in the 1840s, and appeared again as a result of the antagonism between the Europeans and the Chinese on the goldfields. Experiences between 1860 and 1900 strengthened the demand for exclusion and discrimination. The American Civil War seemed to prove the folly and evils of using slave or semi-slave coloured labour. Political equality and the career open to talent were incompatible with a plantation economy in which the base of the social pyramid always consisted of one class. European domination in Asia was taken to illustrate the teaching of Darwin on the survival of the fittest. The Asians and the Pacific Islanders, it was argued, were doomed for the wall, while the Europeans must avoid the fate of Humpty Dumpty. The workers were convinced that the use of coloured labour threatened their standard of living and their privileges. The middle classes were afraid of the threat to European civilization and to British political institutions, as well as of the evils of miscegenation.

So the Immigration Restriction Bill was introduced into the House of Representatives in 1901 by Deakin, a good bourgeois liberal, upright and high-minded, who spoke with dignity of how the national manhood, the national character, and the national future were at stake. The heritage of political freedom must be passed on to their children and the generations after them undiminished. Watson, the Labor leader, spoke with dignity of White Australia as a necessary condition of a high standard of living for the working classes. Outside the House restraint and discretion were thrown to the winds. The Brisbane *Worker* wrote:

Australia is to be saved from the coloured curse, to be relieved from strikes, to be famous for having no paupers or poor houses, to be a government of, by, and for the people. Or else to be a mongrel nation torn with racial dissension, blighted by industrial war, permeated with pauperism, and governed by cliques of lawyers and bankers and commercial and financial adventurers.

The *Bulletin* wrote later of Australia as the only pure white nation to be found outside Europe. Australia, they wrote, proposed to show the world for the first time since the days of the primeval ape a whole continent under one flag, one people, and one government. A few feared the long-term consequences of insulting the people of Asia and wondered whether Australia would have the power to survive should the children of future generations have to resist retribution for the sins of the fathers. But the believers in the brotherhood of man and the equality of all in the sight of God were silent. So the men who believed that the unity of labour was the hope of the world united with the apostles of Christian civilization to preserve Australia for the white man.

The method was simple. Under Section 3 of the Immigration Restriction Act of 1901, any person who failed to pass a dictation test of fifty words in a European language could be declared a prohibited immigrant. Any immigrant resident for less than five years could also be given the test and, on failure, be deported. By an amending act in 1905 the words 'prescribed language' were substituted for the word 'European' to avoid giving offence to Japan and India. In the same year students, tourists, and businessmen from India and Japan were permitted to enter for a maximum period of five years, and in 1912 this concession was extended to the Chinese. Under the Pacific Island Labourers Act passed in 1901 all Pacific Island labourers who had migrated to Queensland were to be deported by 1905. An amending act in that year allowed those in a few categories to remain on compassionate grounds, or to avoid the death to which they would be sentenced should they return to their native island.

In addition both Commonwealth and State legislation discriminated against Asiatics, Pacific Islanders, and Aborigines. By Section 16 of the Commonwealth Posts and Telegraph Act of 1901 no contract or arrangement for the carriage of mails was to be entered into on behalf of the Commonwealth unless it contained a condition that only white labour was employed in such carriage. Under Section 4 of the Commonwealth Franchise Act of 1902 no aboriginal native of Australia, Asia, Africa, or the islands of the Pacific except New Zealand was entitled to have his name placed on the electoral roll unless so entitled by Section 41 of the constitution, which conferred the Commonwealth franchise on all entitled to be enrolled in their State. Section 16 of the Invalid and Old Age Pensioners Act of 1908 excluded Asiatics (except those born in Australia) and Aboriginal natives of Australia, Africa, or the islands of the Pacific from a pension. Under the New South Wales Shearers' Accommodation Act of 1901 the Chinese were to use different living quarters from the whites. The constitution of the Australian Workers' Union excluded Asiatics, Aborigines, and half-castes from membership. So by immigration restrictions, deportation, and discrimination the aim of Australia for the white man was to be achieved.

The governments that held office between 1901 and 1909 were determined to raise the white man to a high level of material civilization. Protection was but one means to that end. The motives of the first tariff were as much to raise revenue as to protect native industry against European, American, and Asiatic competition. But in the second tariff the motives were to promote regular employment, to furnish security for the investment of capital, to render stable the conditions of labour, and to prevent the standard of living of workers in industry from being depressed to the level of foreign standards. That was the 'old' protection. In 1908 the Liberal Protectionists, prodded and encouraged by Labor, introduced the 'new' protection, by which the manufacturer was guaranteed exemption from outside competition to enable him to pay fair and reasonable wages, provided the industry was not impaired and its capacity to supply the local market not reduced. The High Court, which had been created by the Judiciary Act of 1902, declared that parliament had no power under the constitution to legislate for wages, let alone fair and reasonable wages. So the 'new' protection lapsed for want of constitutional power, but the 'old' protection, the protection of native industries, remained and became an article of faith for radicals and nationalists and a source of profit for manufacturers.

At the same time the idea of 'fair and reasonable' wages was not lost sight of. By an Act of 1903 parliament created a Commonwealth Court of Conciliation and Arbitration, one of whose tasks was to conciliate and arbitrate in industrial disputes extending beyond the borders of a State. When H. V. McKay, on behalf of Sunshine Harvester Company, brought the attention of the court to a dispute between his company and the union over the minimum wage in 1906, the chief judge of the court, H. B. Higgins, a Deakinite liberal who had had the courage to say in public that the British behaviour in South Africa was morally indefensible, declared that the task for the court was to decide what were the normal needs of the average employee. He proceeded to answer his own question by saying that parliament meant to secure to the workers something they could not get by the ordinary system of individual bargaining with employers, namely, a wage sufficient to provide them with proper food and water, proper shelter and rest, proper clothing, and a condition of frugal comfort estimated by current human standards. Higgins confined himself to figures for a family's rent, groceries, bread, milk, fuel, vegetables and fruit, and did not include expenditure on savings, benefit societies, insurance, fares, school requisites, amusements, holidays, intoxicating liquors, tobacco, unusual contingencies, religion, or charity. As he saw it, all those were outside the minimum needs of a civilized human being.

For the Liberal Protectionists and Labor were more concerned about protecting the weak against the strong than about creating a new civilization. In a sense White Australia was one gigantic act of protection. Old age and invalid pensions were a similar manifestation of the same impulse on a smaller scale. Under the Invalid and Old Age Pensions Act of 1908 old age pensions were payable to all native-born and naturalized British subjects who reached the age of sixty-five years, provided the latter had resided in the country for a stipulated number of years. All native-born and naturalized British subjects who were invalids were also entitled to a pension on proof of their disability. To the Liberals and Labor both pensions were evidence not of their desire to take down the mighty from their seats, or to cut off the heads of tall poppies, let alone redistribute wealth, but rather to improve the lot of labouring people and to make Australia a civilized nation able to occupy a high place among the nations of the world and fulfil the great promise envisaged by its founders. But again the promise and the material well-being were reserved for the white man, since Asiatics, and aborigines of Australia, Africa, and the islands of the Pacific were specifically excluded from the right to receive a pension, while the residential qualifications were then such that only 'Dinkum Aussies'. not 'Pommies', or 'Dagos', or 'Huns' could qualify.

By the end of 1908 the fundamental ideas of the Liberals and Labor had been written into the statute book. Australia, as they saw it, was to be a liberal, bourgeois society in which the materially weak, the aged, the halt, the lame and the blind were to be protected against the laws of supply and demand by a benevolent though austere and frugal state. By that time the Liberal Protectionists believed they had moved as far as their principles would allow in the use of the state to warm the icy spots in capitalist society. They were uneasy, too, at the loss of their vote to Labor candidates in the industrial suburbs, which were developing rapidly in response to the Liberal and Labor policy of protection. In 1908, for example, the electorate of Corio, with its centre in the rising industrial town of Geelong, was lost by the Liberal Protectionists to Labor. At the same time the more conservative wing of the party, who either had a vested interest in protection, or felt indifferent to the vision that sustained Deakin, were becoming more and more alarmed at the long-term implications of the 'monopolies' declaration by the Labor Party. Another cause for anxiety was the political instability caused by the fact that there were three major parties, so that between 1901 and the election of 1908 no party was able to command a majority in the House of Representatives.

In this state of alarm caused by their declining popular vote, the fear of the radicals within the Labor Party, the instability of the three-party system, and some immediate if rather ephemeral anxieties about Labor's proposals for defence and the distribution of the surplus revenue of the Commonwealth, Deakin entered into negotiations with the leaders of the Conservative Free-Traders for a union of the two parties. The result was a fusion of the two into the Liberal Party with Deakin as leader in May 1909. The objective was the union of all liberals throughout the Commonwealth, to secure in parliament liberal legislation for the development of Australia on a democratic basis. In the platform there was reference to their intention to uphold the federal union, to maintain the policy of effective protection, to establish a White Australia, to develop the Australian naval and military forces by means of universal training, to achieve the assumption by the Commonwealth of the public debts of the States, to promote economy in the public expenditure and efficiency in the public services, and to assert the principle that all representatives of the people should be directly and solely responsible to the people for their votes and actions. Liberalism had abandoned its role as a pioneer in social reform and committed itself to the defence of the *status quo*.

The bourgeois press hailed the agreement with enthusiasm. 'Standing as it does,' wrote the Melbourne *Age,* 'midway between the extremes of Conservatism and Labor, the Liberal party has a vitally important duty to perform.' The Labor press was sour and scurrilous: 'Office is his vice,' wrote the *Australian Worker* about Deakin's role in the fusion, 'and is as indispensable to him as opium to the Chow, and grog to the drunkard.' When Deakin walked into the House of Representatives in Melbourne in May 1909, a few days after the announcement of the fusion, some cried Judas, and Hughes on the Labor side, who knew in his heart all the wretchedness of treachery and dishonour, jeered that Judas at least had had the decency to go outside and hang himself. To his dismay, Deakin found that all those with whom he had laboured to lay the foundations of a liberal, bourgeois state were on the opposite side of the House, while his erstwhile opponents had become his political friends.

By an odd irony the immediate political result of the fusion was an election in which one party obtained a majority for the first time in the House of Representatives. But it was the Labor Party and not Deakin's new Liberal Party that achieved this distinction. For in the general election of 13 April, 1910, Labor won forty-one seats to thirty-one for the Liberal Party in the House of Representatives, while after the election Labor had twenty-two in the Senate and the Liberals fourteen. So on 29 April Deakin resigned, and the leader of the Labor Party, Andrew Fisher, became Prime Minister of Australia. Deakin's fears of Labor extremism were not fulfilled by Labor's use of its power, for the new government behaved with the restraint and respect for vested interests of a reformist rather than a radical party.

With the firmness befitting its claim to be the party of Australian national sentiment, it proceeded to choose Canberra, a pastoral centre one hundred and ninety miles south-west of Sydney, as the site for the national capital. Despite the suggestions by its more self-conscious devotees of culture to call the capital Shakespeare, the majority in the government stood firmly for the Aboriginal name. So out of the sordid rivalry between Sydney and Melbourne and a chance swing of the political pendulum, Australia acquired a capital in a district of great natural beauty. Fortune, too, continued to smile on the building of that city, for in a world-wide competition for a city plan, the winning entry was submitted by Walter Burley Griffin, an American architect with an eye for beauty of design and a rebel against the messiness and ugliness of late-Victorian architecture. That was in 1911. In the same year, the Labor gov-

Above: Early morning at Albury during a tour of parliamentarians to federal capital sites.

Right: A cartoon by 'Hop' (Livingston Hopkins) on royal visits.

Right: Pomp and circumstance surrounded the naming of Canberra on 12 March, 1913.

ernment announced that no 'stagger juices' would be sold in the Australian Capital Territory, for Labor was puritanical and more committed to making the bourgeoisie behave, and making the working classes respectable, than to the making and unmaking of social conditions.

Their contribution to social welfare legislation between 1910 and 1913 was meagre. They passed an act to create the Commonwealth Bank that, after the froth and bubble talk of a people's bank had been skimmed off, was the old pale brew. The existing system of banking was to be made more efficient by introducing competition between private and state enterprise. The Land Tax Act of 1910, with its aim of forcing landowners either to use or to dispose of large tracts of unused land, sprang from their belief that breaking monopolies rather than attacking the inner citadel of economic privilege was the road to social progress. They found themselves virtually unable to legislate on such social and economic subjects as wages, prices, and the ownership of the means of production because of constitutional limitations, and so they turned some of their energies towards amending the constitution. When their leaders spoke or wrote in public to justify such proposals, their words had the vagueness and woolliness of men who were bankrupt of theory if not of principle. When Hughes published *The Case for Labour* articles in the *Daily Telegraph* in 1910, Louis Esson wrote in the *International Socialist* that Hughes had not written *The Case for Labour*, but for the Labor Party. 'In the matter of the book,' Esson wrote, 'we find no statement of principle—no economics, no philosophy—we find no suggestion of any far off diverse event to which Mr Hughes and his followers are supposed to move.'

In its first term in office with a majority, then, Labor was distinguished for its selection and planning of the national capital, and the creation of a national army and navy, rather than for its ideas and actions on the shape and future of Australian society. After the election of May 1913 the Liberal Party had a majority of one in the House of Representatives and was in a minority in the Senate. Their new leader, Joseph Cook, formed a government that survived till June 1914, when the Governor-General dissolved both houses after the Labor majority in the Senate twice rejected the Government Preference Prohibition Bill. But by the end of July the provincial issues in Australian politics had been swept into the maelstrom of world affairs. On 28 June the Archduke Franz Ferdinand had been murdered at Sarajevo. All through July Australians took up themes that had touched them deeply in their history. Dr Mannix, the

Dr Daniel Mannix, the Roman Catholic Archbishop of Melbourne from 1917 to 1963.

new Catholic Coadjutor Archbishop of Melbourne, rejoiced that the opening of Newman College at the University of Melbourne would fit Catholics to fill the higher places in the public, professional, and commercial walks of Australian life. The first airmail flight between Melbourne and Sydney was made; and Melbourne shivered in the rain and sleet of its late July weather. But on 28 July the report of the terms of the Austrian ultimatum to Serbia shocked them out of their provincial complacency.

When the press announced on 30 July that Austria, Hungary and Russia had mobilized, Mr Fisher, speaking for the Australian Labor Party at Colac, Victoria, on 31 July said: 'But should the worst happen after everything has been done that honour will permit, Australians will stand beside our own to help and defend her to our last man and our last shilling.' Thunderous applause greeted his remarks. On 3 August the Prime Minister, Joseph Cook, announced the government's decision to place Australian vessels under the control of the British Admiralty and to offer the imperial government an expeditionary force of 20,000. On the last Sunday before the war, priests and clergy asked their congregations to pray for peace, while in one Labor paper one writer said, 'If Europe is to get drunk with blood, there is all the greater reason why Labor should keep a clear head.' But when Great Britain declared war on Germany at midnight on 4 August, crowds sang the national anthem in the streets, bands played 'Rule Britannia' in the cafes, and crowds cheered and sang in the theatres. A mob got out of hand in Melbourne and raided the Chinese quarter of Little Bourke Street, and at the University of Melbourne on the following day the students sang 'God Save the King' at the end of lectures.

All through August the Cook government went on with preparations for war and for elections. At these elections, which were held on 5 September, the Labor Party won forty-two seats in the House of Representatives and the Liberal Party thirty-one, with one independent, while in the Senate the Labor Party won thirty-one and the Liberal Party five. Andrew Fisher again became Prime Minister of Australia, while Hughes took the portfolio of attorney-general and soon began to dominate cabinet and caucus by the force of his personality. William Morris Hughes was born of Welsh parents in London in 1862 and educated partly in Wales and London for the profession of schoolmaster; but in 1884 he decided to emigrate to Australia. After turning down an offer to teach at a Queensland school back of beyond, he took various positions as

A 1914-18 recruiting poster.

stone-breaker, boundary-rider, drover, and seaman. He then moved to Sydney, where he worked as a pantryman and actor in Shakespeare, bought a bookshop, and began to study the history of society and labour conditions with an ardour that drove him into the affairs of the Waterside Workers' Union, the Political Labour League of New South Wales, and the legislative assembly of that State, which he entered in 1894. In 1901 he was elected to represent West Sydney in the first Commonwealth parliament.

It may be doubted whether he loved any man. Endowed by nature with a short, almost dwarfish frame, and made deaf by his harsh experiences in the western lands of Queensland, his affections for his fellow-man were deadened by the pitilessness he had experienced in his own struggle for survival. He brought to politics the cunning and the determination of a man who had graduated in a hard school. His early political career in Sydney was concerned with tricks with ballot-boxes, absconding from howling mobs, and mixing it on the waterfront, rather than with schemes for the future of mankind. For the man had no faith in human beings. Humanity, he believed, was too mean-spirited to work for any but selfish ends. Although from 1890 to 1910 he was tempted to believe that some of the human vileness from which he suffered was the product of the capitalist system, he did not carry his inquiry to its logical conclusion. His first marriage (his wife died in 1906 after bearing four children) had further soured him against mankind. So Hughes became a pessimist about human nature. While giving the appearance of wanting to take down the mighty from their seat and send the rich empty away, he was utterly devoid of any view of what to put in their place. The experiences during the war were to uncover dramatically his role as the servant of the bourgeoisie rather than of the working classes.

All through August and September the Cook government first, and then the Fisher government, prepared for war. On instructions from the imperial government small expeditionary forces from Australia and New Zealand occupied the German colonies in New Guinea, the Solomons, and Samoa. At the same time the government called for volunteers to make up the expeditionary force of twenty thousand men promised to Great Britain. Wagons, harness, and uniforms were manufactured, ships were refitted to carry troops, food was requisitioned, and medical equipment was prepared, while the volunteers trained at Liverpool, near Sydney, and Broadmeadows, near Melbourne. By

The Prime Minister, William Morris Hughes, presenting a cheque to the aviator Ross Smith in 1919, after Smith and his brother Keith made the first England to Australia flight.

the end of October twenty-six Australian and ten New Zealand transports had gathered in the deep waters of King George's Sound on the south coast of Western Australia, and on 1 November, under an escort of British and Australian warships, the convoy steamed out on to the high seas bound for the Middle East. En route the Australian cruiser *Sydney* engaged and sank the German raider *Emden* at the Cocos Islands.

By December the British General Staff had conceived the plan of weakening Turkey by forcing a passage through the Dardanelles and bombarding Constantinople. This would also relieve Turkish and German pressure on the Russians on the eastern front, who were by then suffering from the defeat at Tannenberg. It was a plan for romantics, a plan for those who believed a rich prize outweighed the suffering, cruelty and losses. For the heights of Gallipoli were steep, and defended by a well-equipped and heroic force trained to a fighting edge by the German military adviser to Turkey, Liman von Sanders. In the meantime the Australian and New Zealand expeditionary force trained for war at their camp near Cairo, or relaxed and pursued pleasure in the cafes and low dives of Cairo, unaware of the ordeal being planned for them by the men in black in London.

On 1 April, 1915, the Australians and New Zealanders were informed that all leave had been cancelled. On 3 April the force entrained from Cairo to Alexandria, where they boarded the convoy bound for the Dardanelles. Before dawn on 25 April the advance party rowed for the shore in small boats. But nature was as unkind to them as that chance of fate that had first made them the sport or playthings in a design of such grandeur. The current swept their boats away from the bay where the incline on the cliff was gradual, to a bay where the incline was as steep and forbidding as on the cliffs off the south coast of Australia. When the men scaled the heights, they were met by merciless fire from Turkish guns. But they hung on, dug their trenches, and prepared to attack, while their fellow Australians, New Zealanders, and British and French troops began their part in the assault on the Dardanelles, and naval guns pounded the Turkish lines.

From April to December the allied forces held on till the order came from London for the withdrawal. On 19 December the Australians and New Zealanders embarked on the ships of a convoy instructed to take them to Egypt. By then 7,600 Australians and nearly 2,500 New Zealanders had been killed; 19,000 Australians and 5,000 New Zealanders were wounded. The French casualties were as high as those of the ANZACS, the name adopted for the Australian and New Zealand Army Corps, and the British lost nearly three times as many. The grand design of a swift end to the war in the Middle East ended in a military disaster. The soldiers, if not the people to whom they belonged, were in part apotheosized by the ashes of defeat, for from that year the landing at Gallipoli became Anzac Day. For some it symbolized the noblest aspirations of the people. For others it was the bond of those who had been through the fiery furnace and been uplifted by it, not beyond good and evil, but beyond the mean, the petty, the trivial and the unworthy.

Early in 1916 the General Staff in London decided to move the Anzacs from Egypt to the western front in France. By 19 March the first troops arrived in Marseilles, where to the tune of the 'Marseillaise' from the regimental bands, tin whistles, shouts, cheers, and profanities and obscenities, the troops entrained for the western front. To the relief of their officers, who had expected pandemonium to break loose when the Australians landed on French soil, the behaviour was exemplary. 'Not a single case of misbehaviour or lack of discipline has been brought to our notice,' wrote the British commandant at Marseilles. This was a record. By May the troops had taken up their positions near

Armentières on the western front to prepare for the blood-baths, the mud, and the privations soldiers of all the armies had suffered since the madness began on 4 August, 1914.

In the meantime the government in Australia geared the economy to serve the war, which greatly increased the role of the state in economic life and the power of the Commonwealth in relation to the States. Prices were fixed, and when a baker named Farey in Glenferrie, a suburb of Melbourne, questioned the power of the Commonwealth to fix prices, the High Court in 1916 ruled against him. The government created systems for state control of the marketing of wool, wheat, and other primary products, and bought ships to supplement the small numbers available for the English-Australian trade. The war speeded up the development of secondary industry, too, as the demand for foodstuffs, clothing, boots, weapons and ammunition gathered momentum. To meet this demand, as well as to replace British products, the iron and steel works of Broken Hill Proprietary Limited were opened at Newcastle in April 1915. So by an odd coincidence the war not only contributed to the deepening of the Australian tradition at Gallipoli, but provided the economic setting for the development of an industry that in time would carry the industrialization of Australia to a point where its uniqueness and its bush lore disappeared. The iron rails tethered the bush to the world.

The war was also destined to end the vision that had sustained the high-minded amongst the Liberals and Labor at the end of the century. In October 1915 Fisher accepted the position of High Commissioner in London, and Hughes became Prime Minister. As British casualties in France rose towards the million mark and German submarine warfare cut supplies from overseas to England, the British government looked to the colonies and dominions for

Supporting troops of the First Division on a duck-board track near Hooge in the Ypres sector in Belgium in 1917 as they moved towards the front line to relieve their comrades.

replacements. To examine the plight of the mother country at first hand, Hughes accepted the invitation of the British government to visit England early in 1916. In the heat and passions aroused by a country at bay, Hughes put himself at the service of those who shared his own craving for an eye for an eye and a tooth for a tooth. He stormed up and down England shouting to audiences caught up in the hysteria of war, 'Wake up England.'

As the standards of civilized behaviour were crumbling around him, Hughes jeered at Asquith, Grey, and Haldane, who had been the models of English liberalism. Intoxicated by his success as a mob orator and feted everywhere by the men who had prospered from the war, Hughes went on in triumph to the western front, where the soldiers hailed him affectionately as the 'Little Digger'. By then he was convinced that Australia must increase its supply of men, munitions and food. He was also convinced that the only way Australia could provide the 16,500 soldiers per month—the figure set by the Imperial General Staff—was to introduce conscription for service overseas. In return the British promised Australia a voice at the peace table when the victors carved up the spoils of war.

But Hughes was the leader of a party pledged to oppose conscription for overseas service and deeply suspicious of all imperialist wars. From the moment he landed at Adelaide in August 1916 the crisis over conscription began to split the country into two opposing camps. At every station on the train journey from Adelaide to Melbourne crowds gathered to sing 'Home Sweet Home' and the national anthem to the 'Little Digger'. At Melbourne crowds cheered or shouted 'Hullo, Billy', and when Hughes told them he hoped later to say some words on a serious matter, a soldier warmly grasped his hand and called on the crowd to give three cheers for conscription. But within his own party Hughes was received with that iciness and hostility that men reserve for traitors to a cause. The Political Labour Leagues of New South Wales and Victoria reaffirmed their opposition to conscription. When Hughes announced his intention of holding a referendum of the people on the question, the Sydney Political Labour League expelled him from the Australian Labor Party.

During the campaign for the referendum feeling ran high. Hughes took his stand on the facts. 'We,' he wrote in his manifesto to the electors, 'boasting our freedom, are called upon to prove ourselves worthy to be free.' To do that Australia must supply 16,500 men each month to the army. This the voluntary system had failed to do. With an appeal to solidarity with the soldiers who, Hughes asserted, were calling to them to come and stand by them, he adjured every man and woman in the Commonwealth in the name of democracy to vote 'Yes' on 28 October. A section of the Labor Party had their doubts. They urged their fellow-Australians to vote 'No' to keep Australia a white man's country, because the voluntary system was supplying enough recruits, because conscription, if applied in Australia, should be applied to the whole of Australia, because no man should decide the fate of another, because conscription threatened unionism, and because conscription had been rejected by every Labor organization and a vast majority of unionists. So Labor Party propaganda raised the bogy of White Australia and class solidarity.

Sectarian loyalties were also roused. The Anglican synod in Melbourne declared that the war was a religious war and that the voices of the allies were being used by God to vindicate the rights of the weak and to maintain the moral order of the world. They passed without discussion a resolution in favour of conscription and, in an outbreak of rectitude and patriotic fervour, rose to their feet and sang 'God Save the King'. Bishop Mannix saw it in quite a different light. The war was, he believed, a sordid trade war and, though he believed it would be desirable for the allies to win, Australia had made sufficient sac-

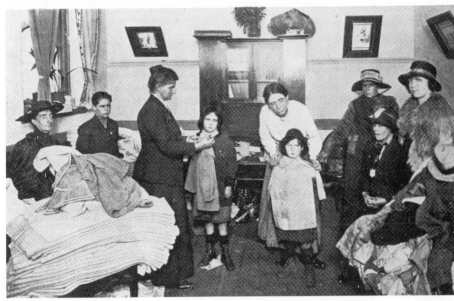

Clothing being distributed at the Trades Hall, Melbourne, in 1919.

rifices. It was possible to do their duty and to do it nobly without conscription. The pulpit, he added, was not the place for a priest to become a recruiting agent. At the close of his speeches the crowd sometimes rose and sang 'God Save Ireland'.

On 28 October, 1916, the electors were asked to answer the question: 'Are you in favour of the Government having, in this grave emergency, the same compulsory powers over citizens in regard to requiring their military service, for the term of this war, outside the Commonwealth, as it now has in regard to military service within the Commonwealth?' 'Yes', voted 1,087,557, and 1,160,037 voted 'No'. From the voting figures by electorates, the voting was in the main on party lines—despite the sectarian sound and fury and the savagery of the propaganda by both sides. The Labor Party then turned to deal with Hughes as a man who had broken the pledge, for by one of those ironies the man who had so wittily and brilliantly defended the pledge in *The Case for Labour* was about to become one of its most memorable victims.

On 10 October Hughes had boasted in a speech at Ballarat, Victoria, that '. . . in a little while we shall separate the wheat from the chaff. We shall prove how much of the labour movement is worthy to survive—how much must go.' Cheers greeted these words, but it was a hollow victory, for it was not given to Hughes to determine the future of the labour movement. When the parliamentary members of the party met in the party room at Parliament House, Melbourne, Mr Finlayson moved: 'That the Prime Minister [Mr Hughes] no longer possesses the confidence of the Party as Leader, and the office of Chairman be and is hereby declared vacant.' In a rage, Hughes asked his supporters to follow him from the room. Four ministers and twenty-six of the rank and file walked out of that room with him. 'Labor,' said the Melbourne *Argus*, 'had blown out its brains.'

But the surviving Labor members saw it in quite a different light: They had removed the chief of the conscriptionists from the leadership of an anti-conscriptionist movement. They had purged their ranks of traitors. The split so weakened the Labor Party that it remained in the political wilderness for thirteen years. It strengthened the Irish Catholic influence in the party. The weakness of the political wing of the movement, breached as it had been by the chauvinism of Hughes and his followers, provided the occasion for the militants to capture the unions. So from 1918 on the Industrial Workers of the World, the Syndicalists, and the One Big Union movement influenced the attitude of the unions to strikes, to co-operation with the employers, and to the tactics of the labour movement.

After his dramatic walk-out in Melbourne, Hughes immediately began negotiations for the formation of a national government. The new Labor leader, Frank Tudor, snubbed the offer, but the leader of the Liberal party, Joseph Cook, responded to the overtures. The result was not only the formation of a national government (from November to January Hughes headed a government with Liberal support) in January 1917, but the formation of the Nationalist Party, which was a fusion of the Hughes group with the old Liberal Party. They pledged themselves to victory, democracy, and White Australia, but abandoned all pretence of the liberal idealism or the radical sentiments that had been held by their predecessors.

Against a background of news of further blood-baths on the western front, Hughes decided to hold a second referendum on conscription on 20 December, 1917, when the voters were asked: 'Are you in favour of the proposal of the Commonwealth Government for reinforcing the Australian Imperial Forces overseas?' This time feeling ran high. Dr Mannix in a speech at the Exhibition Building in Melbourne called Hughes a 'little Czar'. Hughes retaliated with talk of deporting the Archbishop; eggs and tomatoes were thrown at the Prime Minister when he arrived at Warwick in Queensland; Hughes retaliated by having pages of the Queensland *Hansard* in which the Irish Catholic Premier Ryan had denounced Hughes as a trickster and a liar expunged from the book. While Australia was torn in two by sectarian and provincial rivalries, the Bolshevik party stormed the Winter Palace in Petrograd. On 7 November Lenin told his followers in the Smolny building in that city: 'Today has begun a new era in the history of mankind.' On that day workers in Queensland were pelting Hughes with rotten eggs, while mobs sang 'God Save the King' or 'God Save Ireland'. On 20 December 1,015,159 voted 'Yes', and 1,181,747 voted 'No'.

In the meantime the war on the western front was approaching a critical phase. The troops were chafing under the strain of heavy casualties, sniping, gas warfare, new and terrible weapons such as tanks and bombs delivered by aeroplanes, and rumours of an impending German offensive. The news of the successful revolution in Russia, and the Bolshevik slogans of peace, bread and land contrasted sharply with the imperialist slogans of a war to the finish. The Germans struck in March 1918 and at one point penetrated to within thirty-five miles of Paris, but the allied armies, now reinforced by the American army, contained the threat, and then drove them back till the German retreat degenerated into a rout. Austria-Hungary sued for a separate peace on 28 October. The German navy mutinied at Kiel a day later. Early in November an almost bloodless revolution occurred in Germany. The Kaiser abdicated, and a social democrat, Ebert, became chancellor in time to accept the armistice terms offered by Foch on behalf of the victorious allies. At 11 a.m. on 11 November the firing ceased. When the news of the armistice was announced in Australia, flags were unfurled, the bells of the churches tolled, bands played, and people embraced in the streets.

Of the 416,809 who entered the services during the war, 331,781 had taken the field. Of these, 59,342 were killed, 152,171 were wounded. The cost of the war between 1914 and 1919 was assessed at 364 million pounds; and between 1919 and the outbreak of World War II in 1939 the consequential cost in pensions, repatriation, care of the wounded, interest on war debts, and aids to returned soldiers was about another 270 million pounds.

With the tenacity and flamboyancy that had characterized his whole political career, and his passionate conviction that the weak go to the wall, Hughes arrived in London and announced publicly that Australia would not be bound by the idealism in Wilson's Fourteen Points.

When the peace negotiations opened at Versailles in January 1919, Hughes resisted pugnaciously the proposal of the Big Five to hand over the German colonies to be administered under a mandate that would permit freedom of migration. Under these provisions, Hughes realized, the Japanese would be able to migrate to New Guinea. Here was one of those battles for survival that he relished. As he said later, 'The soldiers died for the safety of Australia. Australia is safe.' He meant that Australia, by his efforts, was saved from the Japanese, for under the compromise suggested by a member of the Australian delegation at Versailles, the nation to whom the territory of New Guinea was mandated could apply its own immigration laws to the area. Hughes was just as pugnacious and effective in ensuring that the covenant of the League of Nations did not contain a clause that would bind all members to promise equality of treatment to all other members. From such behaviour the delegates might have inferred that the aim of the war was to keep Australia white rather than to achieve those high-minded aspirations summed up in the Fourteen Points. Hughes was just as rapacious in his handling of the reparations question. He wanted a large war indemnity: he wanted the Germans to pay towards the 364 million pounds Australia had spent on the war. But this time the 'Little Digger' had to settle for half and turn for home.

When Hughes stepped out of the train at Melbourne on 31 August, the soldiers greeted him with deafening cheers. Someone clapped a digger's hat upon his head and swathed him in an Australian ensign. As his car wended its way slowly from the Spencer Street railway station to the town hall, there were similar scenes of enthusiasm. At the hall the diggers seized him bodily from his car and carried him up the stairs, while the crowds cheered and shouted 'You beauty' and 'Little Digger'. Some wept for joy in that moment of victory and achievement. When Hughes spoke the following night at Bendigo, he spent most of his time jeering at the visionaries who were deluding the people that there was some short cut to paradise. When he rose to his feet in the House of Representatives on 10 September, he spoke with emotion of how Australia had passed through the valley of the shadow of death, how they could lift up their voices and thank God that through the sacrifices of their soldiers they had been brought safely into the green pastures of peace. 'There is,' he added, 'no way of salvation save by the gospel of work. Those who endeavour to set class against class, or to destroy wealth, are counsellors of destruction.'

When the Prime Minister, 'Billy' Hughes, returned from peace negotiations in Europe in 1919, soldiers in Melbourne greeted him with deafening cheers, shouting 'You beauty' and 'Little Digger'.

CHAPTER ELEVEN

THE SURVIVORS
1919—1941

WHEN HUGHES SPOKE in the House of Representatives on 10 September, 1919, he told the members:

We went into this conflict for our own national safety, in order to insure our national integrity, which was in dire peril, to safeguard our liberties, and those free institutions of government which, whatever may be our political opinions, are essential to our national life, and to maintain those ideals which we have nailed to the very topmost of our flagpoles—White Australia, and those other aspirations of this young Democracy.

He went on to pose the question, 'Now, what have we got?' To which he supplied the answer: simply, national safety, White Australia, and freedom from communism. 'Australia,' said Hughes, 'is safe.' The age of the survivors had begun.

The main political parties accepted this definition of aim, though they differed in emphasis and methods. The Nationalist Party was deeply committed to the promotion of capitalist society and the fight against communism, but many members were somewhat embarrassed by the virulence and fanaticism with which Hughes flogged the ideal of White Australia. The Nationalist Party was committed, too, to maintain the Australian standard of living by the traditional methods of protection to native industry and by arbitration. The one cloud on the political horizon was not the challenge from Labor, for Labor had not recovered from the split of 1916–17, but the rise of the Country Party.

Until 1917 the country interests had exercised influence by their own sectional organizations, such as the pastoralists' associations or the farmers' and settlers' associations. Between 1917 and 1920, however, the country interests, the wool growers, the wheat farmers, dairy farmers, orchardists, and professional men in country towns formed their own parties in all States and the Commonwealth. One wing of this party was composed of pastoralists and successful farmers, who were deeply conservative and fanatically opposed to radicalism, IWW-ism, socialism, communism and bolshevism, and even branded democracy as a poison because one man, one vote meant the domination of the hard-working pastoralist or farmer by the city 'gas-pipe loafer'. The other wing, composed of the small farmers, farm labourers, petty bourgeoisie, and working classes of the country towns, was a radical group within the party that clamoured for the cutting up of the large estates and toyed with the single tax and similar radical ideas. At the same time they supported the country myth about the city—that through city influence the farmer and the country town dweller lived in squalor; that the high basic wage was encouraging the spread of prickly pear and other pests over the Australian countryside; and that the wealth of Australia was not brought about by hard labour, but by borrowing from overseas.

By 1933 nearly one-third of bread-winners were unemployed. After photographing these unemployed men during the 1930s depression the photographer gave each a ten-shilling note, which they spent at a pub.

The entry of the Country Party into the politics of the Commonwealth in 1920 meant a return not only to three political parties, but to the probability that the Nationalists would lose their majority in parliament and would thus depend on the Country Party to remain in office. It was this role of the corner party, the ability to squeeze concessions for country interests in return for support, that the leaders of the Country Party exploited with great skill over the next forty years. They employed the tactic of supporting protection for secondary industry in return for the protection of country interests. For they, too, saw themselves as survivors and as such entitled to a share in the high standard of living.

Labor, too, wanted the workers to have a just share of the cake, though they were bitterly divided on how this could be achieved. From the beginning of the Russian Revolution in November 1917 until 1920 the radicals, the militants, and the doctrinaire socialists continued their uneasy association with the Labor Party, or joined more extreme movements such as the Victorian Socialist Party. With the formation of the Australian Communist Party in October 1920 these groups broke finally with the Australian Labor Party, the members of which thundered against the wickedness of the Bolsheviks with as much zeal as the leaders of the bourgeois parties. The New South Wales Labor leader, J. Storey, said in March 1919:

We stand for the cultivation of an Australian sentiment based upon the maintenance of racial purity, and the development in Australia of an enlightened and self-reliant community, the securing of monopolies, and the extension of the industrial and economic function of the state and the municipality.

Labor remained safe for reformism and its share of the cake.

At the Brisbane conference of the Australian Labor Party in October 1921 the majority voted in favour of a new objective: 'The Socialisation of Industry, Production, Distribution and Exchange.' This meant different things to different members of the party. To the radicals the new objective would release the workers from 'the bonds of wage slavery', and release Labor in power from the farce of administering 'the capitalistic system'. Others within the party confessed they did not know what it meant, while others said that it meant the

A poster used for agricultural shows and lectures.

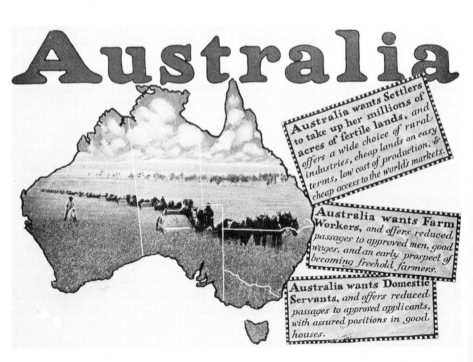

eventual control of industry by the state, and that the change must be evolutionary, not revolutionary.

For the decade 1919-29 political power remained with the Nationalist Party and the new Country Party. In the election of 9 December, 1919, the Nationalists won thirty-five seats, the Labor Party twenty-six, and the Country Party ten; independents won four, all but one generally voting with Labor. In the Senate the Nationalists had thirty-five members and Labor one. Hughes again formed a government pledged to tariff protection, White Australia, the preservation of the Australian standard of living, and the suppression of the Communists. The Tariff, Arbitration, and the Immigration Restriction Acts remained the instruments for such purposes. To reward those who had brought Australians safely into the green pastures of peace, the Hughes government passed acts to enable returned soldiers to buy blocks of farmland at low prices and reasonable mortgages, so that they might reasonably be expected to make a good living should prices and seasons be propitious.

The suppression of the Communists was pursued with the same zeal as the exclusion of Asians. Hughes brought down amendments to the Immigration Restriction Act that empowered the Commonwealth to declare as prohibited immigrants or to deport any persons who advocated the overthrow of the existing government of the Commonwealth by violence. The Crimes Act passed in 1920 also contained a clause declaring any person who advocated the overthrow of the existing government of the Commonwealth by violence to be guilty of a crime punishable by imprisonment. The Hughes government proposed to withhold the Australian standard of living and the Australian way of life from Asians and Communists.

Hughes did not continue for long to lead Australians into the green pastures of peace. After the election of December 1922 the Labor Party had thirty seats, the Nationalists twenty-eight, the Country Party fourteen, the Liberals two, with one independent, while in the Senate Labor had twelve, the Nationalists twenty-three, and the Country Party one. The Nationalists could not form a government without some sort of understanding with the Country Party. By that time Hughes had alienated members of his own government and party by his overbearing pride and arrogance, which had swollen to monstrous proportions after his social successes in London in 1916 and his gaining a reputation as a world figure by his wit, tenacity, and victory at Versailles in 1919. With the passage of time he had become somewhat careless in concealing his contempt for the low calibre of other members of his cabinet. So, despite the public tributes to his achievements in London and at Versailles, other leaders of the Nationalist Party began to plot with the leaders of the Country Party to bring down Hughes.

When Earle Page, a doctor from Grafton in northern New South Wales who had become leader of the Country Party in April 1921, revealed that his party would not work with Hughes but was prepared to work with another leader, Hughes resigned in February 1923. Page then immediately negotiated with Stanley Melbourne Bruce to form a coalition government.

Bruce was born in Melbourne in 1883 into a patrician family and was educated at Melbourne Grammar School in the classics, which strengthened his natural tendencies of temperament to believe in the government of society by a benevolent and high-minded elite. From Melbourne Grammar he went straight to Cambridge. He entered the bar in 1907, and on the outbreak of war took a commission in the Worcester regiment, in which he served with distinction till wounded while fighting with the British army at Suvla. He was invalided back to Australia in 1917, entered the family business of Paterson, Laing and Bruce, and was elected to the House of Representatives as member for Flinders in 1918. Not by birth, education, or temperament did he ever feel any sympathy with the bush myth of mateship and equality, or the larrikin tradition of the towns. Naturally aloof by inclination, he advertised his difference from the democratic tradition by the Englishness of his clothing (he wore spats), by his English rather than Australian accent, and by his English manners of speech when speaking to the working classes (he always addressed a member of the Labor Party in the lobbies of the House by his last name only). So in 1923 an urbane patrician, a fine flower of transplanted English civilization in Australia, formed a coalition with a shrewd country doctor for the government of the Commonwealth of Australia.

Their aims were the same as those of Hughes. They wanted to maintain the White Australia policy, to preserve the Australian standard of living, and to ensure the national safety. Their policies differed from those of Hughes in their conception of how this could be achieved. Bruce, with support from the chambers of manufactures and commerce, believed in more protection for native industry, in incentives to English investment, in increase in population, and in the search for markets for Australia's surplus produce. Page, with support from the pastoralists' associations, the farmers' and settlers' organizations, and the dairy farmers, saw the solution in schemes of protection in primary industry and in improvements to country life that would bring the creature comforts of electric light, more entertainment, and better roads. Both agreed that communists, bolsheviks, anarchists, militants, and the survivors of the IWW movement must be removed to places where they could not do harm.

Below: A solitary Aborigine demanded to see 'the whole plurry show' at the opening of Parliament in Canberra on 9 May 1927.

Below right: Opera singer Nellie Melba as Violetta in Traviata.

Between 1923 and 1928 the government administered its stimulants to production and distribution. A retail price for sugar was fixed by the government, and the producer was protected from foreign competition. A bounty was paid to grape-growers when the price fell below a certain amount. The canned-fruits industry was given a subsidy to enable it to compete in overseas markets. The home consumption price of butter was raised, and the difference between the agreed price and the natural price was used to pay a bounty again to enable the exporters to sell in London in competition with New Zealand, European, and American dairy farmers. To encourage immigration, special assistance was offered to immigrants from Britain, for Bruce and Page, like Fielding's Tom Jones, were men of heroic ingredients who confounded the future of

civilization with the welfare of the Protestant religion and British institutions. Between 1921 and 1929, just over two hundred and twelve thousand migrants arrived in Australia. To encourage their settlement in the country as well as to ease the rural slump, the Bruce-Page government made extensive grants to the State governments for the building of roads. To make possible a more equitable and efficient distribution of government revenues between the Commonwealth and State governments, Page persuaded parliament and people to endorse a financial agreement between Commonwealth and States in 1927.

In the meantime, as part of the policy of encouragement to public works and development, the government pushed on with the building of Canberra. By 9 May, 1927, all was in readiness for the opening of parliament in Canberra by the Duke of York. On that day thirty to forty thousand people gathered outside Parliament House in that small city of undulating plain and open sky to watch the arrival of the Duke and Duchess. As they stood on the steps of the new white building, Dame Nellie Melba sang 'God Save the King'. A solitary Aborigine demanded to see the 'whole plurry show', but as he was deemed to be inadequately clad for the occasion, a policeman led him away. From the steps the Duke urged the people to listen to the voices of the noble army of the dead and march in step with them towards a glorious destiny. At the official lunch to celebrate the occasion only one toast was drunk—to His Majesty—and that in fruit cup. No intoxicants were served, and speeches were taboo. Again Labor leaders were suspicious of the junketings and the worship of social class. 'The Canberra turn-out,' wrote the *Labor Call* in Melbourne, 'seems to have been a bit of a frost.'

The government was preparing plans to come to the aid of those who were in any way afflicted or distressed in mind, body, or estate. Even before he became Prime Minister, Bruce had moved for the appointment of a royal commission to inquire into national insurance as a means of making provision for casual sickness, permanent invalidism, old age, and unemployment. In its first report in 1925 the commission reported in favour of sickness, invalid, and maternity payments, and in its second report recommended a scheme of national insurance for unemployment. In 1928 Bruce brought down a national insurance bill for a first reading, but before the House could discuss it adequately the government itself suffered shipwreck through its handling of what

Stanley Melbourne Bruce, Prime Minister from 1923 to 1929, Mrs Bruce and Sir John Butters.

it believed to be another sickness of capitalist society—the activities of the militants and Communists.

In 1925 and 1926 seamen and waterside workers brought the waterfront to a standstill by a series of strikes. Believing the unionists to be the dupes of Communist agitators such as Walsh and Johnson, Bruce amended both the Navigation Act and the Immigration Restriction Act to give the government the power to break strikes in shipping or to deport the extremists amongst the union leaders. In this way White Australia became the instrument for a politically pure and respectable Australia. But the scheme misfired; for at the end of 1925 the High Court quashed the attempt to deport Walsh and Johnson, while the repressive legislation and the casual remarks dropped in the heat of controversy made the moderates and the rank and file of the Labor Party suspect that Bruce was aiming to grind the workers into the dust.

Bruce rather hastily decided that the source of some of this industrial unrest lay in the overlapping and conflicting jurisdictions of the Commonwealth and State arbitration systems, and he submitted proposals for reform to the electors in November 1928. The coalition of Nationalists and Country Party won forty-two seats, but Labor increased its representation by eight seats to thirty-one, with two independents, while in the Senate the Nationalists had twenty-four, the Country Party four, and the Labor Party seven. Bruce unwisely interpreted this as approval for his measures of repression. In August 1929 he introduced the Maritime Industries Bill, which in effect abandoned the field of industrial regulation to the States. Hughes, who had been waiting for an opportunity to revenge himself on Bruce for the treachery of 1923, accused Bruce of proceeding 'from stunt to stunt', and then in the committee stage of the bill brought a motion that toppled the government by one vote. Exultant, Hughes waited for the call from Labor and a reconciliation with his old 'mates', but such was not to be. The only satisfaction for Hughes was the empty one of the defeat of the Bruce-Page government in the election of 1929, and the defeat of Bruce in the electorate of Flinders. When James Scullin formed his government, there was no suggestion of a reconciliation with the 'Little Digger'. The policy of undying hostility to political traitors was followed implacably, and Hughes remained in the political wilderness, known to Labor as the man who had split the party asunder, and to the Nationalists as the man who had brought down the Bruce-Page government.

But Labor in 1929 had little more to offer than the ability of its members to administer the bourgeois state. Torn by faction fights all through the 1920s, the tiny band of idealists who had proudly announced their intention in 1891 to enter parliament to make and unmake social conditions had developed into a group more and more concerned with the means of capturing political power and less and less concerned with how to use it. Labor had held office in Queensland from 1915 to 1929, and in New South Wales from 1910 to 1916, 1925 to 1927, 1930 to 1932. There was little to distinguish a Labor from a non-Labor administration, except the emphasis on social welfare and the creation of state enterprises. In Queensland the government owned and controlled sheep stations, butcher shops, a fishery, a cannery, a hotel, cokeworks, smelters and mines. They had abolished the legislative council in 1922. The government of New South Wales had shipyards, brickworks, metal quarries, pipe and reinforced concrete works, and coal mines. The motive was state control of capitalism rather than the use of the state to build a new society. For the purpose of these enterprises was to promote competition between the state and private enterprise, to increase the quality and quantity of goods available, and to keep prices down rather than destroy private enterprise. In their administration of the education system of the States Labor governments were reformist rather than revolutionary. Labor used its power to reward its followers with the key positions in the civil service and the judiciary.

The mantle of radicalism had fallen on the shoulders of the Communist Party, which was pledged to the destruction of the bourgeois state and the creation of the dictatorship of the proletariat. In other ways, too, the Communists were more radical than Labor. Although the Labor Party had adopted the slogan 'The Unity of Labor is the Hope of the World', on White Australia it remained loyal to its race rather than its class. At the third meeting of the Pan-Pacific Secretariat at Vladivostok in 1929, the Australian delegates accepted the proposition that White Australia was a theory based not only on the fear of economic competition from lower paid labour, but also on the false doctrine of the superiority of the white race, a doctrine that was deliberately being fostered by the imperialists in their own interests, and in preparation for coming imperialist wars. The leaders of the Labor Party were furious. The *Australian Worker* in January 1929 denounced the earlier Shanghai conference of the Pan-Pacific Secretariat as a meeting where 'coloured gentlemen' decided that the Australian labour movement must be 'undermined and wrecked with the object of upraising the communist party on the debris'.

Yet the Communists failed to gain a following amongst the working classes. Their leaders were drawn from the petty bourgeois intelligentsia and renegades

Sir Isaac Isaacs, the first native-born Governor-General of Australia (1931–36).

from the Catholic Church, while the rank and file of the party were drawn as much from the middle-class intellectuals as from the working classes. It was as difficult for the Communists in Australia to convert people to the overthrow of the existing society as it was for the missionaries in Tahiti to convince the natives of original sin. Their upright if stiff-necked loyalty to the doctrine of increasing misery did not help them to convince the masses that they knew how to remove the causes of human conflict and create material well-being for all. Their loyalty to all the changes of tactics and policies in Moscow exposed them to the charge that they were not masters in their own house.

The Scullin Labor government then, sworn in at Canberra in October 1929, differed from its predecessor in degree rather than kind. The minority in the Labor Party who thought of the socialization pledge as a commitment to a new society were frustrated by their lack of support in the party, by the absence of constitutional power, and by the lack of a majority in the Senate. But Labor was the party of Australian nationalist sentiment as well as of social reform. When Lord Stonehaven retired as Governor-General, Scullin put forward the name of Isaac Isaacs, a cultivated Jew with a political past as a Deakinite liberal, and a long and distinguished career as a judge of the High Court. George V was not impressed. He asked rather sharply through his secretary, 'Who is Isaac Isaacs?' Scullin stood firm, and George V had no alternative but to announce with as good grace as possible the appointment of the first native-born Australian as Governor-General of the Commonwealth.

Scullin, however, was firmer in his nationalism than in his social and economic policy. Immediately after his assumption of office in October 1929 he was faced with a budget crisis for the six State governments as well as for the Commonwealth. Early in 1929 sharp falls in the prices of wool and wheat, the withdrawal of English capital, and the fall in export prices by fifty per cent, began a severe financial crisis. Between the financial years of 1928-29 and 1929-30 the national income declined from 640 million to 560 million pounds. Unemployment increased sharply: by 1933 nearly one-third of the bread-winners were unemployed. In all the capital cities the unemployed clamoured for work or relief; the conservatives preached hard work and sacrifice; the financial cranks preached Douglas Credit; the priests and the clergy mumbled in their pulpits and prayer-desks that the depression was a sign of Divine displeasure at their

John Lang, Premier of New South Wales from 1925 to 1927 and 1930 to 1932.

sins; one clergyman shouted they were dancing their way to damnation; the Communists sardonically predicted that the crisis of capitalist society would grow graver daily.

The Labor government had no firm answer to the crisis. Within the government were men such as Scullin and J. A. Lyons who were influenced by Catholic social teaching and the melancholy history of the Irish, men such as E. G. Theodore who were flirting with financial credit, and men such as Frank Anstey who were tempted to believe the depression was the work of wicked capitalists driven on by their greed and their class hatred to grind the faces of the poor. Scullin rather tamely accepted the arguments for retrenchment at the first Premiers' Conference to discuss solutions in October 1929. Early in 1930, with national income figures and prices still falling and the number of unemployed swollen, Scullin invited Sir Otto Niemeyer of the Bank of England to Australia to meet the premiers. Niemeyer arrived in June and by August was ready to present his analysis of the Australian situation to the premiers.

Niemeyer recommended further retrenchment. As he saw it, the Australian policy of protection of native industry and heavy borrowing abroad had created a standard of living that bore little relation to the Australian level of production. This was to call in question the fundamental assumptions of Australian political and social life. What concerned Sir Otto was the absence of any firm foundation for the high standard of living. He was not concerned with Australia's moral right to, or the expediency of, such a high standard while her neighbours in Asia lived in squalor and wretchedness. Under the influence of Niemeyer the premiers undertook to balance their budgets, and not to use borrowed money for unproductive purposes.

Then the leader of the Labor Party in New South Wales, J. T. Lang, began a campaign in his newspaper, the *Labor Daily*, in which he represented Niemeyer as a malevolent tool of the English bondholders who were determined to squeeze the last penny out of the simple-minded, hard-working Australians. Again the Englishman was represented as sinister, complex and corrupting, while the Australian was represented as the paragon of those new-world virtues of simplicity and innocence. Lang's campaign showed the effects of his years in party machine politics in New South Wales. Born in 1876 in Sydney, he worked first in an accountant's office and then established an estate agency in Sydney; he entered the legislative assembly of New South Wales in 1913, and was elected leader of the Labor Party in 1923. In his first term of office as premier from 1925 to 1927 he had put on the statute book the Labor reformist conception of the shape and direction of New South Wales society. He created public enterprises to force private enterprises to be more efficient and just, he brought order and efficiency out of the chaos and inefficiency of public transport in Sydney, he introduced measures of relief for the sick and needy.

Somewhere between his first assumption of office in 1925 and the State elections in the middle of 1930, however, the man who had proved that Labor could provide as efficient a team as the bourgeoisie to run the State became corrupted by the power he wielded within the party. He began to demand blind obedience to his will in a party that prided itself on being the voice of the people in the making of its policy. He became a demagogue; street hoardings proclaimed 'Lang is right', or 'Lang is greater than Lenin'; at huge public meetings in the Sydney Domain crowds cheered to the echo as he ranted against the English bondholder. But of policy, or political doctrine, or plans for the future of society the man was completely bankrupt. All that he could say was that the chief exponents of socialism were imported politicians. 'Australian-born members of the movement,' he wrote later, 'have never been socialists. We are far too practical for empty theories.' In October 1930 he became pre-

Above: Joseph and Enid Lyons and family at The Lodge, Canberra. Mr Lyons was Prime Minister from 1932 to 1939 and Dame Enid became the first woman member of the Commonwealth House of Representatives in 1943.

Above right: A United Australia Party pamphlet for the 1932 elections.

mier of New South Wales for the second time after the victory of the Labor Party in the State elections.

In the meantime faction fighting was leading the Scullin government to its destruction. Lyons and J. E. Fenton had been shocked at the charges against E. G. Theodore of corruption in the Mungana goldmining case, and were dismayed when this man, as soon as the flush of scandal faded from his cheeks, began to advocate a policy of repudiation of overseas debts. Joseph Aloysius Lyons was born in Tasmania in 1879 into a family of staunch Irish Catholics. In his early days as a schoolteacher in Tasmania he was moved by a desire to win a career for the members of his own group as well as that infinite merit before the most high God. On the surface he had all the virtues of a simple country boy, and that benevolence and affection for all men of which the Galilean had spoken with such passion before the fateful journey to Jerusalem. At a deeper level he had the cunning and the skill of a people who for hundreds of years had been striving for survival against a more powerful foe.

After entering the Tasmanian house of assembly in 1909 Lyons quickly won a reputation for efficiency, which gave him office in the Labor government of 1914-16 and the office of premier of the State in 1923. In 1929 he was elected to the House of Representatives, where he came into contact with men who were concerned not just with making things work, or rectifying an ancient wrong while they waited for the resurrection of the dead, but with the reconstruction of capitalist society. Lyons was horrified. He resigned from the Scullin government and toyed with the idea of talking things over with the leaders of the opposition. One night in May 1931 he went to the Canberra railway station and boarded a train for Melbourne. A friend in the Labor Party ran alongside the train as it gathered speed and called out, 'For God's sake, Joe, don't do it.' But he did do it, and in Melbourne he formed, with the Nationalist Party, the United Australia Party, pledged to decency, honesty, respectability, and the slogan 'All for Australia and the Empire'.

The UAP promised to restore credit and enterprise by restoring confidence in the integrity and honest administration of government finance; to honour national obligations; to reduce governmental and other public expenditure; to introduce a sound tariff policy with preference to Australia's best customer— Great Britain; to re-employ people by encouraging active enterprise; to give a fair deal to every section of the community; to suppress communistic and seditious organizations and all publications that advocated the disturbance of industrial or civil peace; to wipe out communism by the only method it under-stood—vigorous abolition; and to maintain preference to returned soldiers. The *Australian Worker* described the actions of Lyons and those who followed him out of Labor's camp as one of the most cynical betrayals of the working class in Australia's history. The United Australia Party, they went on, the Country Party, the financial institutions, the federated employers, the capitalist press, and the numerous secret agents in the service of Big Business, were planning to deliver a combined attack upon the labour movement.

In March 1931 the Lang faction within the Labor Party had resigned from the Scullin government. With his government and party crumbling at the edges, Scullin met the premiers in Melbourne in June. The result was a Premiers' Plan by which the Commonwealth and the States undertook to reduce gov-ernment expenditure by twenty per cent, to convert the internal debts of the governments by reducing interest rates, to reduce bank rates of interest on deposits and advances, and to increase taxation. Lang accepted the plan, though with that sullen resentment with which the man who has talked big generally submits to the measurers and the economists. When Theodore introduced into the House in November a scheme to provide Christmas relief for the unem-ployed, the government was defeated. In the ensuing elections in December there was a landslide against Labor. After the elections the United Australia Party had thirty-seven seats in the House of Representatives, the Country Party had seventeen, and Labor sixteen, while in the Senate the United Australia Party had twenty-two, the Country Party four, the Labor Party eight, and the Lang group two.

Lyons was sworn in as Prime Minister and Treasurer of the Commonwealth of Australia. It seemed as though the forces of conservatism and respectability had won a resounding victory. At the Victorian State elections of April 1932 the Anglican archbishop of Melbourne published a letter in the *Church of Eng-land Messenger* in which he told upright and Protestant Melbourne that they had an opportunity to save the rest of Australia from financial collapse if they, as Christians and churchmen, displayed their stand for honesty by voting for the United Australia Party. By then tempers were running high. In January Lang had defaulted in his payments to the London bondholders. To the con-servatives, Labor, or a section of Labor, represented lying, repudiation, and disloyalty.

On 19 March, 1932, over 750,000 people gathered in the streets of Sydney to watch the ceremonial opening of the bridge across the harbour. Represen-tatives of the churches blessed the new bridge, though not together as might have been appropriate. A ribbon was stretched across the bridge at its southern end, but before Lang could cut the ribbon Captain de Groot of the New Guard, mounted on a horse, charged the ribbon at a gallop, hacked it with his sword, and declared the bridge open on behalf of the decent and respectable citizens

The two parts of the huge span of Sydney Harbour Bridge nearly meet. At the opening of the bridge on 19 March 1932, Captain F. E. de Groot rode up and slashed the ribbon with a sword while thousands of people were waiting for the Premier, John Lang, to do the task. De Groot received 2500 congratulatory letters and telegrams.

of New South Wales. As he put it later, this was to show Lang and his mob that decent and respectable people could not be pushed around. After the ribbon was hastily retied, Lang cut it on behalf of the people of New South Wales.

From that day events moved swiftly. The Lyons government rushed through two acts to force Lang to honour his promises under the Premiers' Plan. When Lang refused to pay, the Governor of New South Wales, Sir Philip Game, dismissed Lang for breaking the law. Crowds gathered in an angry mood at Parliament House in Macquarie Street, but Lang, who had incited the people by his inflammatory language and his irresponsible talk about bondholders and the rapacious English bankers, did not appeal directly to the people against the forces of law, order, and respectability that were arrayed against him. Lang went as quietly as did the Commonwealth Labor government. With the victory of the UAP in the elections in Victoria and New South Wales, the conservatives had temporarily won their battle for survival. But it was a hollow victory, for in the world outside Australia events had happened that robbed them of any chance of enjoying that victory in peace and security.

In the years 1932 to 1937 the Lyons government concentrated on the objectives of financial stability, reduction of unemployment, and the destruction of the Communist movement. Budgets were balanced, imperial preference, as defined in the Ottawa Agreement of 1932, was continued, and Communists and fellow-travellers were hounded by what their supporters called the six acts against civil liberty. Once again, as so often in human affairs, some politicians who were afraid of political radicalism, sensing that the corruption of conventional morality prepared the mind for conversion to communism, attempted to prohibit the importing of all books, pamphlets and newspapers that were likely to deprave or corrupt. So works of stature such as Joyce's *Ulysses* and Lawrence's *Lady Chatterley's Lover* were banned, while comics glorifying violence and pulp magazines guaranteed to rouse the passions of the icy were not banned. In the zeal to defend an old order the government was beginning to lose its way.

In the meantime the urbanization and industrialization of Australia were proceeding rapidly. In 1906, 35.49 per cent of the population lived in the capital cities; in 1921, 43.01 per cent; and in 1940, 47.5 per cent. For despite the croaks and promises of disaster from the moralizers the movement of population to the cities continued. Bad railways, bad roads, bad education, the absence of creature comforts in the home, and lack of entertainment in the country towns, were part of the reason for the migration. The most powerful cause, however, was the growth of secondary industry. In 1901 just over 26 per cent of the work force was employed in industry, and 32.5 per cent in primary production. By 1933 just over 27 per cent was employed in industry,

Below: The Paradise Theatre, on the Esplanade at St Kilda, Melbourne, in 1915. 'Perfect pictures' were 'perfectly projected' in this theatre, whose roof was 'that Inverted Bowl they call the sky'.

Below right: An early broadcast of the popular radio serial, 'Dad and Dave'.

and nearly 17.5 per cent in primary production. By 1947 over 33 per cent was employed in industry, and nearly 14.5 per cent in primary production. On the eve of the depression in 1929, 56 per cent of employees in Australia belonged to unions, a percentage that fell to 43.5 per cent by 1934, and climbed back to nearly 50 per cent at the beginning of the war with Japan in 1941.

With urbanization, mass entertainment and mass information came to influence more and more Australians. The silent films had almost driven such earlier forms of entertainment as the minstrel show and the variety concert from both city and country by 1930. In 1928 the first talking picture was shown in Sydney and Melbourne, and though the defenders of the old order sneered at the American accent as 'nauseating, nasal, and inane', very soon the 'hits' of the talkies were to be heard in every dance hall in the country, as young and old urged each other 'Don't bring a frown to old Broadway, for you must clown on Broadway'. This spread of mass culture was speeded on by the development of radio broadcasting. The first regular broadcasts began in 1923, and from 1924 till 1932 licences to broadcast were let to private companies by the Post-master-General's Department. In July 1932 the Commonwealth government created the Australian Broadcasting Commission, which was instructed to create national broadcasting stations that would transmit 'adequate and comprehensive programmes . . . in the interests of the community'. They were also instructed to form 'groups of musicians for the rendition of orchestral, church and band music of high quality'. So a public corporation was given the responsibility of raising public taste in music, drama, and education.

A still from a classic film of enduring popularity, The Sentimental Bloke, *based on a C. J. Dennis poem. The poem was dramatized and twice filmed.*

At the same time the Postmaster-General's Department continued to grant licences to commercial stations from which by day and by night the ears of listeners were flattered by advertisements at one moment, and at the next by Rudy Vallee's voice reassuring them that 'Life is just a bowl of cherries. Don't take it serious, it's too mysterious'. The portable gramophone and the sale of cheap gramophone records also strengthened the spread of this culture. So by 1939 the beaches of Melbourne, Sydney, Adelaide, Perth, Brisbane and Hobart, and the lovely hinterland of those cities, began to hear Charlie Kunz play Irving Berlin's 'What'll I do?' The more esoteric people sipped brandy crusters at Palm Beach or Portsea to Duke Ellington's 'Solitude' or Louis Armstrong's 'Shine'. As a supplement to the talking pictures, the wireless and the gramophone, American musical comedies dominated the commercial stage from 1920 to the beginning of the war with Japan. In the first of the decades 'No, No, Nanette', 'The Desert Song' and 'The Student Prince' had their first runs, while the second decade was devoted to revivals. So songs such as 'Lucky in Love' and 'Deep in My Heart' for the sentimental, or 'Tea for Two' for the brittle and the frivolous, were added to mass culture, while the local artists, playwrights, scriptwriters, and musicians complained that cheap canned American culture was sucking the lifeblood out of the local culture. One man of comic genius, Roy Rene or Mo, kept alive in vaudeville shows the image of the Australian as the innocent exposed to the corrupting influences of the English and the Americans. During the same decades the Australians continued to receive their news of the outside world from English sources. Overseas news reports from places as far apart as Tokyo and New York were funnelled through London. So the motor car, the aeroplane, the cable, the wireless, the talking pictures, the gramophone, and the mass-circulation newspaper brought all hearts and minds under the same influences. This was happening in a country whose past had already imposed certain uniformities and conformities of behaviour on its people.

In the nineteenth century Protestant Christianity and Irish Catholicism had strengthened the grip of the puritan and the philistine on local culture. Industrialization added a habit of conformity and uniformity. The intellectuals were provoked by this strength of the puritan and the philistine. Responses differed from group to group and indeed from city to city. In Sydney, the financial and social centre of the pastoral interest, as well as the capital for the 'ancient nobility of New South Wales', one group—Christopher Brennan, a poet, Norman Lindsay, an artist, and John Anderson, professor of philosophy at the University of Sydney—under the influence of Nietzsche, preached culture for the 'great souls' as their antidote to the puritanism and philistinism of the many. As one of their followers wrote in the first number of the journal *Vision*, which began publication in May 1923:

We would bring the Goddess to Poetry, Music and Art. Here is the eternal search of spiritual youth, and if we can sing a few songs fragrant with this desire we shall have proved our youth and freedom as no chants about bullocks and droughts can prove it. That febrile disintegration of mind called Primitivism must disappear before the first laughter of the gods. In Gaiety and Beauty the gods descend to earth, and those who build that bridge have done more for their countrymen than any ballad monger or realist can do.

By contrast other groups, mainly centred in Melbourne, were less concerned with killing the twin giants of Australian puritanism and Australian philistinism than with providing happiness, culture, and material well-being for all. They saw themselves as the inheritors of what they termed those democratic traditions of the Australian people: the mateship and equality for which their predecessors had paid in blood at Eureka in 1854, at Barcaldine in 1893, and in the Kalgoorlie goldfields at the turn of the century. They agreed with the poet Bernard O'Dowd, who wrote:

> That culture, joy and goodliness
> Be th' equal right of all:
> That greed no more shall those oppress
> Who by the wayside fall.
>
> That each shall share what all men sow:
> That colour, caste's a lie:
> That man is God, however low—
> Is man, however high.

They agreed, too, with Joseph Furphy's confession of faith in *Such is Life,* which was first published in 1902, though it was not until the 1920s and the 1930s that his vision was absorbed by the 'future of humanity' men: 'Collective humanity holds the key to that kingdom of God on earth, which clear-sighted prophets of all ages have pictured in colours that never fade. The kingdom of God is within us; our all-embracing duty is to give it form and effect, a local habitation and a name.' The group did not despair of their power to build this 'kingdom' in their 'local habitation'. Daunted neither by the reports in the capitalist press of brutalities and murders committed in Russia to manure the soil for the future harmony of mankind, nor by the atrocities committed by both sides in the Spanish Civil War, they clung tenaciously to their belief that bad conditions rather than innate depravity were the cause of human evil. Their one disagreement was on the methods to be used to achieve their goal: some, perhaps the majority, looked to the day when the Labor Party, purged of its careerists and opportunists, would proceed to build the 'kingdom'; others, certainly the minority, believing Labor to be ineluctably reformist and corrupt, looked to the Communist Party to destroy the institutions of the bourgeois state and establish a dictatorship of the proletariat to guide mankind into the 'kingdom'. But by 1937 those who cocked an occasional ear or eye toward Europe or Asia knew that the old dream of creating a 'millennial Eden' in Australia, where men were free from the corrupting influence of old civilization, had gone beyond recall. For by then this debate on the future of humanity between the defenders of an old order and the advocates of a new was swallowed up in a new struggle for survival.

The storm clouds came from both Asia and Europe. Since the days of the defeat of the Russians by the Japanese in 1905, a few in Australia had predicted that the day would come when the Japanese would threaten the survival of European civilization in Australia. Before 1914 that day seemed far off, or even avoidable by encouraging the Japanese to expand westwards into the mainland of China. The behaviour of the Japanese during World War I and at Versailles confirmed the darkest fears of their future expansion into the South Seas. The Tanaka memorial of 1927, which put Australia on the list of areas to be conquered by Japan, the Japanese attack on Manchuria in 1931, and the police incidents at Shanghai in 1937, kept these fears alive. In 1936, when the Australian government adopted a trade diversion policy that discriminated against the Japanese to protect British textile interests in the Australian market, the discerning predicted that such policies might convert the Japanese from economic to military expansion.

The main political parties differed in their opinion on how to resist Japan. The United Australia Party believed it was impossible for the Australians by their own forces to defend themselves against a determined aggressor. Australians, as they saw it, in the last resort depended on the British fleet at Singapore. Australia could not maintain its White Australia policy through its own strength. Besides, they argued, Australia did more than half its trade with Britain, and so had a community of interest as well as being materially dependent on Great Britain. For that reason they saw themselves as imperialists as well as Australians. The Country Party agreed with this sentiment, though the increase in wool and other primary produce exports to Japan made them anxious not to offend their new customers. By contrast the Labor Party was suspicious of all imperialist actions, whether by Britain, America, or the Japanese, and was opposed to conscription for military service overseas. Where the United Australia Party looked to the Singapore naval base as their bastion against the Japanese, the Labor Party proposed to build a strong air force to defend against the warships of an invader. The Federal Labor Party adopted this new defence policy at their conference in Canberra in 1937.

At the same time both parties addressed more and more of their attention to the gathering storm in Europe. Like all conservative parties, the United Australia Party was divided in its attitude to the Nazi government of Germany. Frightened on the one hand by the noisy talk of wars of revenge against France and England, and angered by the bestial persecution of the Jews, yet attracted on the other hand by the promise to defend western civilization against communism, the United Australia Party confined itself to promises of support should the Nazis attack Great Britain. On that score sentiment and material interest were stronger than any vague hopes that the old order in Europe could be propped up by the whip, the concentration camp, and the gun. Labor, too, had its agonies. For while the Party taught that Fascism and Nazism menaced the trade unions and the labour movement, the Catholic and moderate elements within the Party were reluctant to push the argument too far lest they be driven into the arms of the Communist Party.

These anxieties and divided loyalties were epitomized in the way of life and the values of the new leaders of the two main political parties. When Lyons died in April 1939, Robert Gordon Menzies was elected leader of the United Australia Party. Menzies was then just forty-four years old. He was born in 1894 in Jeparit, a small country town in the wheat belt of north-western Victoria, the son of an erstwhile member of the Victorian parliament with radical leanings, and the grandson of a president of the miners' union in that colony. He was educated at state schools in the country, where he early displayed his great intellectual promise by heading the scholarship examination for the whole State. Later at Wesley College in Melbourne, to which he won a scholarship, and at Melbourne University where he studied law, prizes and honours were conferred on him for his learning, his wit and his oratory. He entered the Victorian bar in 1918, where again success in the world came easily to him, though, as at the university, he was not quite so successful in getting on with the world. For this he was tempted to blame the envy of *demos* for the men of distinction, while the victims of his brilliant mockery pointed to the overweening pride and arrogance of the man. After ten years at the bar he entered politics in 1928 as a member of the Legislative Council of Victoria, then transferred to the Legislative Assembly in 1929, where he quickly rose to prominence as minister for railways and deputy premier. In 1934 he was elected as member for Kooyong to the House of Representatives in Canberra, and took office as Attorney-General in the Lyons government, a post he held till March 1939, when he became Prime Minister.

The man was driven by three consuming passions. One was that spur to fame that had taken him so quickly to the top in his home country; during this rise to power, incidentally, he conceived such contempt and disdain for his associates that he alienated himself from most of the people with whom he worked. More and more he felt the need to be surrounded by men and women who came to admire and laugh when he paraded his great gift as a raconteur.

The second ruling passion of his life was the veneration—indeed, almost superstitious respect—he developed for British institutions, something he probably acquired as a student of Professor Harrison Moore, the dean of the faculty of law at the University of Melbourne. He believed passionately that the British had created the highest civilization and greatest degree of liberty known to man. It was this sense of mission and high purpose that conferred a dignity and stature on his life. That stature was impaired by the use of his great powers for the defence of an order doomed to decay.

The third ruling passion of his life was to ridicule all who offered a way forward, who wanted 'progress'. He wanted the grandeur, the pomp, the cere-mony, the wit and the urbanity of the London of the Edwardian age at a time when that great achievement of humanity was crumbling to its ruin. The inner man searched feverishly not only for the snows of yesteryear, but also possibly for the innocence of his years at Jeparit. This quest conferred a tenderness and a loneliness which roused sympathy and won the affection of those who were privileged to peer behind the mask of worldly success and glory. But in 1939 he believed passionately that all was not lost—that British institutions and the British way of life were synonymous with civilization. All who did not share this view were the deluded victims of a superstitious barbarism.

By contrast the new leader of the Labor Party was a man who had once entertained a vision of a way forward for humanity. He was John Joseph Curtin, who was born in Creswick, Victoria, in 1885, the son of a police sergeant from Ireland. As a youth, under the influence of the rationalists and the socialists, Curtin abandoned his Catholic hopes in the resurrection of the dead and substituted instead the utopian socialist dream of the perfection of man on earth. He joined the Socialist League in Victoria. He also took a leading part in the campaign against conscription, in which loyalty to his own people and an acquired hatred of imperialism were happily combined. In 1916 he accepted the editorship of the *Westralian Worker* and moved to Perth. From that year until 1928, when he entered parliament as member for Fremantle, the years of labour in the political wilderness, and his own struggles with alcohol, so soured him that a bitter droop formed at the two extremes of the mouth that a decade earlier had responded so enthusiastically to the hope of better things for mankind promised by the Russian revolution of 1917. Then in 1935, when his victory over alcohol was complete, he was elected leader of the Australian Labor Party. So a man who was by birth and conviction suspicious of all policies pursued by British governments, and who believed that men should love and comfort one another for the loss of eternal life, but who was vague and muddled on how this was to be achieved, confronted from March 1939 in parliament a man who believed the British to be the paragons of civilization, a man who looked with a lofty disdain on those comforters that had sustained Curtin in childhood, youth, and middle age.

This difference was underlined in their responses to the outbreak of war with Germany on 3 September, 1939. Menzies spoke with dignity of his mel-ancholy duty to inform Australians officially that as Germany had persisted in her invasion of Poland, Australia was now at war. Truth, he concluded, was with us in the battle and that truth must win. 'May God in his Mercy and compassion grant that the world may soon be delivered from this agony.' For him the war began because the German chancellor had lied, broken promises, and not behaved as an upright man. He did not touch on the crimes of the

Nazis against democracy and human dignity. By contrast, Curtin stated simply
that the Labor Party could be relied upon to do the right thing in the defence
of Australia and of the integrity of the British Commonwealth of Nations.

Menzies then turned to prepare Australia for war. As he saw it, Australia's
duty was to assist the mother country, which she could best do by sending
supplies and foodstuffs to Great Britain, by maintaining the lifelines of the
British Commonwealth, and by suppressing all Communists, fellow-travellers,
and saboteurs of the war effort. The government immediately took steps to
increase the production of war equipment and to raise, train and equip an
army to serve with the British army overseas. Lieutenant-General Sir Thomas
Blamey was appointed to command the Sixth Division, which was recruited
for service either at home or abroad. In November the government introduced
compulsory military training for home service. At the end of the year the
government sent the Sixth Division to Palestine to be trained before joining
the British expeditionary force in France. In April the Seventh Division was
recruited and dispatched to the Middle East for training. But the entry of Italy
into the war in June 1940, and the collapse of France in the same month, made
it necessary to step up training.

From September 1940 to July 1941 Australian forces went into action to
resist an Italian and later a German attack on Suez along the north coast of
Africa. In April 1941 Australian forces tried in vain to halt the German advance
into Greece; then came their heroic but doomed defence of Crete in May 1941,
where some of the flower of Melbourne youth were drowned. In June and
July of 1941 the Seventh Division fought a successful though costly campaign
in Syria against the Vichy-controlled local forces. In the intervals between these
campaigns the men relaxed in the houses of entertainment in Egypt and Palestine, much as their fathers had done in 1915-18. While a few walked in awe
over the ground on which the holy feet had trod, some roared with laughter
when one of their number shouted in a cafe in Jerusalem: 'I'm so hungry I
could eat Christ's shinbones.'

While Moscow radio was informing the whole world in its short-wave language broadcasts that the crisis of capitalism was becoming graver every day,
Menzies saw it all as a threat to what he held most precious—British civilization.
All through June 1941 there were rumours of German troop concentrations
on the Russian frontier. On 21 June the Melbourne *Age* informed its readers
that the riddle of Russia remained unsolved and that Stalin was living up to
his reputation as 'Inscrutable Joe'. At 4 a.m. on the morning of Sunday, 22
June, the German army invaded Russia. At 5.45 a.m. Dr Goebbels announced
on the German radio that German planes had bombed Kiev, Sebastopol, and
Kaunas. Later that morning Hitler informed the German people—and the
world—that since Jewish Bolsheviks wanted to set the whole world on fire, and
since the Jews with their centre in Moscow wanted to spread their domination,
he had ordered the German forces to oppose this menace with all the might
at their disposal. The German people, he went on, were fully aware that they
were called on not only to save their native land, but to save the entire civilized
world from the deadly danger of Bolshevism, thus clearing the way for true
social progress in Europe. So the madman spoke, and the German armies
marched to their destruction.

In London Churchill declared, 'We are resolved to destroy Hitler and every
vestige of his Nazi regime.' It followed therefore that Britain would help Russia
and the Russian people. But for Churchill this was a gesture of expediency:
for him the Nazi regime was indistinguishable from the worst features of communism. In Australia the German attack on Russia provoked similar reactions.
In Catholic churches the faithful offered up Novenas for a just peace; in the

Anglican Cathedral in Melbourne a bishop lamented the spiritual power of the followers of anti-God. The political Left hailed the event as an opportunity to convert the war from a conflict between empires into a people's war of liberation from oppression.

Menzies would have none of this. For him this was another example of Germany breaking her most solemn obligations. 'If any additional proof were needed,' he added, 'of the fact that to Germany a treaty is a mere piece of paper, and, no sense a contract, here it is.' History seemed to be passing him by. By then Menzies was too engrossed in provincial politics to perceive the universal significance of what had happened. Ever since the election of 1940 his government had had to work with a slender majority in the House of Representatives. Within the government and amongst the members of the two government parties in both houses of parliament there was dissatisfaction with Menzies as a leader. He never had suffered fools gladly, and in the heat and passion of war and party politics the numbers who had been wounded by his tongue increased.

At a cabinet meeting in Canberra on the night of 28 August the dissidents persuaded him to resign. The man who had seen himself as a vessel for the salvation of British civilization walked out of Parliament House despised and defeated. But with the dignity and courage he always could muster in the hours of adversity, he prepared the way for the recovery of his reputation and his honour. The next day he had the satisfaction to read a statement by Mr Arthur Coles, the member for Henty in Melbourne, that 'those wretched people' had brought down a great man. For on the previous evening, disgusted by the treachery and place hunting, Coles had walked out of the party room of the United Australia Party, declaring he was resigning from the party from that moment.

This meant that Arthur Fadden, the leader of the Country Party, whom the anti-Menzies faction had chosen as the next Prime Minister, had to depend on the support of two independents, Coles and Wilson, to remain in office. When the budget was brought down in October, first Coles and then Wilson announced his intention to vote against the government. The Labor Party took over the government. In a moment of enthusiasm the Labor members milled around their leader, John Curtin, in the party room in Parliament House and sang the words: 'The workers' flag is deepest red. . . .' So John Joseph Curtin, ex-Catholic, erstwhile socialist, a man who had once had in his heart the vision of that day when men would neither hurt nor destroy, became the Prime Minister of the Commonwealth of Australia.

He had with him other men who had lived through the days of unleavened bread, the bitter days of the depression, and the anguish of the hopes roused by 1917 bearing the bitter fruit of the treason trials in Moscow. He had with him Joseph Benedict Chifley, who like Curtin had been brought up to believe in the Nicene creed and *Rerum Novarum;* Herbert Vere Evatt, an intellectual, who thought of Labor as the means to the fulfilment of the Enlightenment; and Jack Beasley, who had learnt his politics in the rough-and-tumble of the trades hall of New South Wales, and who was a stranger to that 'light on the hill' that beckoned to Curtin and Chifley. These men were just as determined that the depression and all the suffering it entailed to the working classes should not return as that Australia should win the war. But before their plans could mature the Japanese attacked Pearl Harbour on 7 December, 1941. By that time the German army was outside the gates of Moscow. Labor had first to win the battle for national survival before committing itself to the deeper question of whether to patch up the old order, or return to its dream of building a new.

CHAPTER TWELVE

BETWEEN TWO WORLDS 1941—1969

IN THE BEGINNING of the war the Australians, the Indians, the British, and the Americans were as chaff before the Japanese wind. The Fifteenth Japanese Army landed at Kota Bharu in northern Malaya on 7 December, 1941. Three days later Japanese planes sank the British capital ships, the *Prince of Wales* and the *Repulse*, off the east coast of Malaya. Two bastions of Australia's defence were rotting, useless, at the bottom of the sea. On the same day the Japanese occupied Guam; on 23 December they occupied Wake Island; and on 26 December the British and Canadian garrison at Hong Kong surrendered. The Japanese army was advancing so swiftly down the peninsula of Malaya that by the end of December they had reached the province of Johore and were preparing to cross over to the island of Singapore.

Far left: Sir Robert Menzies, Prime Minister from 1939 to 1941 and from 1949 to 1966, at a reception for Queen Elizabeth at Parliament House, Canberra.

Left: John Curtin, Prime Minister from 1941 to 1945.

In the meantime the mood of the Australians changed from complacency to anxiety and, in some cases, panic. Rumours spread in the cities of Japanese plans to land on the Australian coast. On 29 December Prime Minister Curtin told Australians in a New Year message:

Without any inhibitions of any kind, I make it quite clear that Australia looks to America, free of any pangs as to our traditional links or kinship with the United Kingdom. . . . We know . . . that Australia can go and Britain can still hold on. We are, therefore, determined that Australia shall not go, and we shall exert all our energies towards the shaping of a plan, with the United States as its key-stone, which will give our country some confidence of being able to hold out until the tide of battle swings against the enemy.

The Australian government's policy, he added, was based on two facts: first, the war with Japan was not a part of the struggle with the Axis powers, but was a new war; second, Australia must go on to a war footing. The stature of Curtin began to grow as he confronted the crisis. But others were not so swift to discard the traditional patterns of thought. Hughes, who had taken over the leadership of the United Australia Party from Menzies, said it was suicidal and false for Australia to think of Britain's support as of less importance than that of other countries. The British navy, he added, was the most powerful and most potent of all navies.

While the party politicians wrangled, darker news was reported from the war fronts. On 23 and 24 January, 1942, the Japanese began their advance on Rabaul, New Britain; Kendari, Celebes; and Balikpapan, Borneo. On 15 February, 1942, the British forces on Singapore formally surrendered to the Japanese; 15,384 Australian troops became prisoners of war, while 1,789 died as a result of the campaign and 1,306 were wounded. On 19 February Japanese planes bombed Darwin in the Northern Territory and Broome in Western Australia. Just over a fortnight earlier, when surrender seemed inevitable in

Malaya, Curtin told a meeting of people at the Fremantle Town Hall that he was too busy now to consider any '. . . blue print of a new social order after the war. We have to concentrate on the one supreme task which the enemy has imposed on us—we have to defeat him or die.' It is no use, he added, preaching the precepts of the Apostles to the enemy—the whine of bullets was the only epistle the enemy would understand.

By that time the whine of bullets was coming closer and closer to the Australian mainland. On 3 February the Japanese bombed Port Moresby on the south coast of New Guinea. On 17 February the Australian war cabinet rejected the request of the Pacific War Council in London that the Seventh Australian Division, now sailing towards the Pacific, should serve in Burma. Both Churchill and Roosevelt urged Curtin to reconsider the decision, but Curtin refused. So on 22 February Churchill replied with some heat: 'We could not contemplate that you would refuse our request, and that of the President of the United States, for the diversion of the leading Australian Division to save the situation in Burma.' But still Curtin stood firm: 'Australia's outer defences are now quickly vanishing and our vulnerability is completely exposed.' So Churchill, grumpy and irritable, instructed the convoy for the Seventh Division to proceed to Australia. On 8 March the Japanese landed at Lae and Salamaua on the east coast of New Guinea and began to advance overland along the Kokoda Trail towards Port Moresby. In the following month Japanese expeditionary forces sailed under naval cover from Truk in the Solomons, intending to make a landing at Port Moresby. On the night of 7 May Curtin, his face deathly pale, interrupted a debate in the House in Canberra to tell members that the Australian and American planes based on the Queensland coast had intercepted this force in the Coral Sea. A day later, after an indecisive engagement later known as the Battle of the Coral Sea, the Japanese force returned to its base. South New Guinea and the east coast of Australia had escaped the ravages of an invader.

Meanwhile Japanese land forces had moved swiftly over the mountain barrier dividing north from south New Guinea, and by July were within striking distance of Port Moresby. But from that month Australian forces, which had landed near Lae and Salamaua, harassed the Japanese bases, while at Milne Bay, to the east of Port Moresby, Australian forces inflicted a crushing defeat on the Japanese. The fear of invasion and of the destruction of European civilization in Australia began to give way to the long agony of driving the Japanese out of the conquered territory in New Guinea, the Solomons, the Indonesian archipelago, Malaya, Borneo, Guam, Wake Island, the Philippines, and Hong Kong.

At the same time the war in Europe and Africa moved through a similar sequence of events. All through 1942 German armed forces penetrated deep into Soviet territory, reaching the outskirts of Leningrad in the north, and coming close to Moscow in the centre and to Stalingrad in the south. In Stalingrad at the end of 1942 several hundred thousand men, the flower of the German invading army, were trapped by the Soviet army and forced to surrender. Just as the Coral Sea, the Kokoda Trail, Milne Bay, and Wake Island opened the way for the defeat of the Japanese, so Stalingrad changed the war in Europe from a desperate fight for survival into a struggle for total victory.

The Australians, as their government saw it, could make three contributions to that victory. They could act as a granary for countries in the front lines such as the British Isles; they could help drive German and Italian forces from the north coast of Africa; they could help to drive the Japanese from conquered territories in the Pacific. At the end of December 1941 the Australian forces succeeded in raising the siege of Tobruk after two hundred and forty-two days.

But in the first six months of 1942 disaster overcame the British forces in Africa as swiftly as the disasters in the other theatres of the war. The outbreak of war with Japan had, of course, weakened the allied forces in Africa: supplies intended for the Middle East were diverted to the Pacific.

In the first six months of 1942 German and Italian forces drove the depleted allied forces back to El Alamein, where in June the opposing forces were locked in a series of indecisive battles. All through July and August Rommel's forces struggled to break through to the Nile delta. In the meantime the allied Eighth Army under the command of Montgomery, which included the Ninth Australian Division, began a decisive engagement with the Germans and the Italians at El Alamein, which rumbled on through October and November till the Axis forces fell back towards Tripoli with the Eighth army hot in pursuit. In this engagement 4,863 Australians were killed or wounded and 946 taken prisoner. On 13 November the allied army reoccupied Tobruk; on 23 January, 1943, they entered Tripoli, and on 12-13 May all axis forces remaining in Africa surrendered to the allies.

The Australian forces were contributing to the expulsion of the Japanese from the conquered territories in the Pacific. But this was a slow business, for during 1942 the allied commanders had adopted a policy of containing the Japanese until such time as the war in Europe had been won. The Australian government was not entirely happy with this policy, and no one less so than the Minister for External Affairs, Dr Herbert Vere Evatt. By birth and conviction he belonged to that legal intelligentsia that had played a greater part in shaping British Labour than Australian Labor politics, for in Australia Labor was traditionally suspicious of the intellectuals as representatives of the class enemy. Evatt was born in 1894, educated in state schools in Sydney and the University of Sydney, where he became a child of the Enlightenment rather than a believer in the Kingdom of God. Under the influence of John Stuart Mill, who taught him the right of the individual to decide for himself, of Dicey, who taught him the might, majesty, and power of the law, and of the socialists, who inspired him with their dream of a day when man was liberated from his oppressors and gaolers, Evatt became not only a believer in the perfection of mankind, but a man with a creed. He believed in individual liberty, in the day

Below left: Dr Herbert Vere Evatt, the Minister for External Affairs during World War II.

Below: Ben Chifley, 1ime Minister from 1946 to 1949, laying the foundation stone of the Australia National University, Canberra, in 1949.

when human minds would be freed from priestcraft and superstition, in international rather than national or provincial loyalties, and in culture as a comforter for mankind. He saw evil as the result of an unfavourable environment, for he accepted the view held by the radical intelligentsia that just as bad conditions were the cause of evil, good conditions would make men good.

Yet the gods or chance had so fashioned his clay that under strain he behaved in ways quite different from the vision that sustained him. After a brilliant university course in arts and law, in which prizes were showered on him, he entered the bar in Sydney, became secretary to W. A. Holman, another bourgeois intellectual who became an early Labor premier of New South Wales, had a brief spell in the Legislative Assembly of New South Wales, and became a judge of the High Court in 1930, from which position he resigned in 1940 to enter the House of Representatives. When Labor formed a government in October 1941, the caucus elected him to the cabinet and Curtin offered him the portfolios of Attorney-General and External Affairs.

While other ministers were concerned with the day-to-day administration of their departments and the problems of war, Evatt was engaging in that never-ending quest of the intellectual to detect a pattern in the chaos. With the assistance of some gifted Australians who were graduates of the London School of Economics and who shared his faith that material well-being and happiness for all could be produced by economic planning, Evatt gradually worked on a plan for the future. His first move was to persuade men in high places in Washington that more aid for the war against Japan was not incompatible with their policy of winning the war in Europe. In 1942-43 he led the Australian missions to Washington and London. He was not successful, for he ran into the problem of all provincials when confronted by metropolitans. All through 1943 and 1944 the war in the Pacific remained a war of attrition, while the Soviet armies gradually drove back the Germans. When the Soviets pursued the retreating German army out of Russia and Poland, and the Western allies landed in Normandy in June 1944 to open up the second front, anxious if not strident voices of alarm and prophecy began to be raised again in Australia about the threat of communism to western civilization.

No such anxieties crossed the minds of the Labor leaders as they worked on their plan for the future of Australia. As they saw it, the task of government was to prevent the repetition of the two evils of unemployment and Japanese expansionism. Their answer to the former was the welfare state. Until 1943 lack of political strength and the grave state of the war had forced them to hold their hand. But a landslide victory in the elections of 1943, in which they won forty-nine out of seventy-five seats in the House of Representatives, and a more favourable war situation, gave them their opportunity. Child endowment, hospital benefits, invalid and old age pensions, maternity allowances, unemployment and sickness benefits, and widows' pensions were either improved or begun. Able sons and daughters of necessitous parents were given scholarships to enable them to take a university or technical college degree. In 1946, when doubts were raised of the constitutional power of the Commonwealth to legislate for social services in peacetime, the Labor government held a referendum to amend the constitution accordingly.

To give Australia permanent security against Japan, the Labor government signed an agreement with New Zealand in January 1944. This was known as the ANZAAC pact. With that gift for discerning the historical significance of all he was doing, Dr Evatt compared the signing ceremony in Canberra with other meetings of allied leaders. His enemies snorted and raged at the theatricality of the occasion and the absurdity of the claim, but missed the tragedy of a man whom chance had swept into a moment of prominence only to expose his party's limited vision on the issues of the day. For when Evatt justified the pact to parliament, he spoke with pride of how a screen of islands would protect Australia and New Zealand, and how a program of welfare for the people to the north of Australia would so strengthen their material power that never again would the Japanese scatter the friends of European civilization in the south Pacific as chaff before the wind. By consultation between Australia and New Zealand, Evatt argued, the two would ensure that their voices were not only heard but heeded in London and Washington. With even less insight into the issues of the day, the opposition leaders sneered at the histrionics of Evatt, or warned about the dangers of offending America and Great Britain. This was not the time, the opposition declared, for Australia and New Zealand to be inventing their own Monroe Doctrine for the Pacific. The pact, they said, reeked of isolationism. For they, too, were unaware that events in China and eastern Europe would ever give them the chance to resume their role as the defenders of western civilization against the Communists.

The war in Europe was drawing to a close. Government and opposition leaders hailed the Soviet and allied victories with enthusiasm. A minority in Australia, writing at that time in such periodicals as the Sydney *Bulletin* or the Catholic *Advocate* in Melbourne, raised the cry that civilization was in danger from communism. But in the flush of final victory in Europe in May 1945 they were forced to bide their time. The one dark incident in that hour of victory was the death of Curtin in Canberra in July, at a time when his party's policies on defence and welfare seemed to be sweeping all before them.

On 6 August an American plane dropped an atomic bomb on Hiroshima, and on 9 August another American plane dropped a second atomic bomb at Nagasaki. In Australia the comment on the occasion was confined to an estimate of the immediate consequences. The new Prime Minister, Joseph Benedict Chifley, predicted the war would last for another twelve months. Despite the use of atomic bombs, he said, time passed rapidly in war. The president of the Australian Council of Churches was pleased that Americans rather than the Germans or Japanese were able to use the terrible weapon first. Unless the righteous powers, he believed, retained control, an evil power could extinguish humanity. In Europe the Vatican sounded warnings to posterity; the Archbishop of Canterbury had the courage to speak of the defilement of those who had used a weapon with a potency to take one million lives. But the leaders of opinion in Australia kept off the wider horizons.

At nine on the morning of Saturday, 15 August, 1945, the Prime Minister announced that the war with Japan was over. Sydney plunged headlong and full-throated into celebration; people shouted and shrieked and sang and danced in the streets; sirens wailed; bands played 'Rule Britannia' or 'Roll Out the Barrel'. In Melbourne the wistful, the joyous, the sad and the sorrowful sang and shouted their relief that the war was over. Amid a great din of sirens, bells, whistles and voices, the city of 'sodden rectitude' burst into 'whoops of joy'. The next day over 200,000 attended a thanksgiving service at the Shrine of Remembrance to celebrate the victory for the democratic cause. In Canberra smaller groups gathered in Civic Centre to celebrate the occasion.

With the high-mindedness and industry they had displayed through the dark days of the struggle, the Labor ministers turned their energies to prove that peace had its victories no less renowned than war. In the fighting against Germany and Italy, 9,572 were killed or died as prisoners of war; 17,501 were lost in the fighting against the Japanese. Of the 22,000-odd in the army, navy, and air force who had been taken prisoner by the Japanese, 7,964 did not survive the terrible privations and humiliations to which they were subjected: the emaciated bodies and tortured eyes of those prisoners who returned to their native land told a tale to which neither tongue nor pen could do justice. At the same time other men in the services were demobilized and trained at the expense of the government for their re-entry into civilian life. Some were subsidized to enable them to study at a university; others completed trade courses or received instruction in farming to equip them to take up a block of land under the soldiers' settlement scheme.

It was the age of the planner, and in the flush of victory over Germany, Italy and Japan a note of confidence and enthusiasm was in the air. At the universities of Melbourne and Sydney the students, leavened by returning servicemen, caught on to the prevailing faith that by political action it would be possible to remove the causes of human evil and suffering. High-minded, hard-working and dedicated secular humanists and Fabians worked together for a common end. The heroic achievements of the Red Army, the imminent victory of the Communists in the Chinese civil war, the defeat of reaction and obscurantism in eastern Europe, and the victory of Labour in the British general elections of 1945, fed their elation and hope for the future. So despite the warnings of the priests that human beings could not achieve happiness on earth, despite the sneers of liberals and conservatives at those who talked of a 'light on the hill' for humanity, the whole labour movement, large sections of the intelligentsia, and religious groups at the universities were caught up in this optimistic and forward-looking mood.

By a great stroke of fortune Prime Minister Chifley was endowed with the power to win the affection of those with whom he worked and the respect of the idealistic. His life, personality, and tastes seemed to sum up the history and aspirations of radicalism in Australia. He was born in 1885 at Bathurst, New South Wales, into one of those Irish Catholic families that had placed their stamp on radicalism in Australia. He was educated briefly at a Patrician Brothers' school in Bathurst, where he imbibed the teaching of the Church on man and society. At seventeen he joined the railways, where he rose to be a first-class locomotive driver at twenty-four. He also succeeded in union politics. During those years he added some of the hopes of the secular humanists to his view of the world. From that time his faith in the future of humanity was expressed in images that appealed to both the religious and secular-minded in his party. Both groups saw their own hopes fulfilled in Chifley's 'light on the hill'. He was also endowed by nature with a toughness that enabled him to survive the Tammany Hall flavour of Labor Party politics in New South Wales in the 1920s and 1930s without losing either his reputation for integrity or the affection of the idealists. In 1928 he won the Macquarie seat in the House of Representatives, lost it in 1931, and then fought a campaign against the Lang faction. In 1940 he was elected again for Macquarie, and in October 1941 he became treasurer in the Curtin government. By the time of his election as leader of the Labor Party he had endeared himself more firmly to the minds and hearts of the labour movement by his lovable behaviour. He fought shy of the pomp and ceremonies of bourgeois society: when etiquette demanded dress clothes, he wore a plain suit or stayed away. He was frugal by nature, if not tinged with the puritanism that pervaded Irish Catholicism and, through it, the Labor Party.

For a period Chifley and other leaders in the Labor government conceived schemes to match their vision. In 1946 and 1947 the government announced plans to encourage migration from Europe. They decided to offer assistance not only to British migrants but also to displaced persons from eastern Europe who were idling in refugee camps in Germany. At times this scheme was defended for its contribution to the economic and defence needs of Australia. At times, too, the minister responsible, Arthur Calwell, was careful to remind the House that for every foreign migrant the government proposed to bring out ten from the United Kingdom, so as to protect the British predominance as well as to shield the foreigner from the veiled hostility of the native-born. But at other times the minister spoke of Australia's duty to the victims of religious, racial, and political persecution. For his part he would not turn away anyone who had the will to become a good Australian citizen. For it was never doubted that anyone who came to this country would become a 'dinkum Aussie'.

All through the debate the survival theme peeped through both the high-mindedness and the provincialism. 'We have not,' said Calwell in November 1947, 'unlimited time to build our strength or plan our future. Our decisions now must be the right ones, else our Australian nation might not survive beyond the lives of the children of this generation.' Between June 1947 and June 1959 assisted British migrants numbered 360,156 and the other European migrants 341,685. Between June 1959 and December 1968 British migrants numbered 658,236 and the European 468,275, to which Italians, Greeks, Dutch, Germans, and Yugoslavs were the main contributors.

By 1967 the estimated population was 11,928,889. Of these, at the preceding census 3,877,473 classified themselves as members of the Church of England, 1,103,969 as Roman Catholic, 1,932,161 as Catholic, 1,124,310 as Methodist, and 1,043,570 as Presbyterian, while 1,138,900 exercised their right to give no reply, and 94,091 said they had no religion. The members of religions other than the Christian or the Jewish numbered 13,112.

By 1969 the European minorities were influencing not only the eating and drinking habits, but also the mental horizons, of the 'dinkum Aussie'. In 1947 Immigration Minister Calwell said: 'The days of isolation are over.' Perhaps he was expressing a hope rather than making an observation. By the 1960s the migrants from Europe, and the revolution in communications, had broken down the cultural isolation, left the bush culture as a historic survival, liberated some from the dead hand of their puritan past, and prepared Australians to confront the universal problem of man in the age of plastics, chromium, and the bomb.

The developments in civil aviation produced the greatest of the revolutions in transport and communication. Before the Second World War civil aviation had been developed by private enterprise. In 1929 C. E. Kingsford Smith and C. T. P. Ulm, both pioneers in aviation in Australia, formed a company to fly regular services between Sydney, Brisbane, Melbourne, and Tasmania. After the company ran into financial difficulties in 1931 the Holyman brothers started in a modest way with a service between Launceston and Flinders Island and succeeded so well that in 1936 they registered the new company as Australian National Airways in Melbourne, and began to drive other interstate companies out of business. By 1939 they were running services between all the State capitals.

In 1945 the Chifley government introduced legislation to nationalize all civil airlines and to create the Australian National Airlines Commission, which was empowered to provide for the establishment and operation of national airline services by the Commonwealth. But when the private airline companies brought a case before the High Court, the court ruled that the Commonwealth did not have the power to establish a monopoly. So Trans Australia Airlines, the trading name of the Australian National Airlines Commission, began its first flight on 9 September, 1946, between Sydney and Melbourne in competition with the private airline companies, especially Australian National Airways. By the end of 1946 Trans Australia Airlines was operating services between all the States.

No sooner had Australian National Airlines escaped expropriation by government than it faced a takeover by another company. R. M. Ansett had begun in business with a passenger car service between Hamilton and Horsham, Victoria. By 1936 he had accumulated a fortune from his fleet of passenger bus services and ancillary hotels. In that year he formed Ansett Airways. With the profits from a prosperous tourist industry in the post-war boom, Ansett began to make inroads on both intrastate and interstate air traffic. In 1958 the company took over Australian National Airways and flew under the name of Ansett-ANA. By 1962 passengers, freights, and mail were shared evenly between the government airline and the private companies. So in internal civil aviation the state competed with private enterprise to the advantage of the consumer and the material profit of the private investor.

By contrast, the tendency in Australian international civil aviation was towards government ownership and control. In 1931 Qantas Empire Airways, a private company registered in Queensland, carried air mail and passengers between Darwin and Sydney on the England to Australia route. In 1934 they took over the Darwin to Singapore section of the route. During the war Qantas kept the route to London open by flying from Perth to Colombo via the Cocos Islands, and in April 1946 re-opened the route through Singapore. In the following year the Commonwealth government acquired the remaining shares in Qantas. In December 1947 they began a service to Japan, in June 1948 to Hong Kong, and in November to South Africa. In 1945 Pan American World Airways began a service from San Francisco to Sydney, in 1946 British Commonwealth Pacific Airlines began a similar service, and in 1949 Canadian Pacific began flying from Vancouver to Sydney. Between 1951 and 1969 Air India, Air New Zealand, Alitalia, BOAC, Lufthansa, KLM, South African Airways, UTA and others began flights to Sydney.

At the same time the Labor government took steps to turn into reality those schemes, dating from the 1880s, for diverting the waters of the Snowy River to irrigate the plains of southern NSW, and generate electricity with the water that flows off the snow-capped mountains in the Australian Alps in the southeast corner of the State. In 1949 the government introduced into Parliament the Snowy Mountains Hydro-Electric Bill which outlined a project that would generate 1,720,000 kilowatts as against the 2,056,000 kilowatts of the Tennessee Valley scheme in the USA. This electric power was to be delivered to the cities of Melbourne and Sydney at about half the cost of production of electricity by thermal stations burning coal or oil. 'From the point of view of defence,' the minister introducing the bill added, 'those matters are of the greatest significance.' A bonus of the plan was that, after the water had passed through the turbines, it would be diverted through tunnels in the mountains to the inland, where the irrigation authorities could use it for food production on payment of a fee that would help to pay the cost of generating the electricity. The minister envisaged a future when the inland cities in the valleys of the Murrumbidgee and the Murray would carry a population of 1,000,000. This, he concluded, was an act of faith.

The first Qantas Empire Airways passenger plane, an Armstrong Whitworth, carried mail and passengers between Darwin and Sydney.

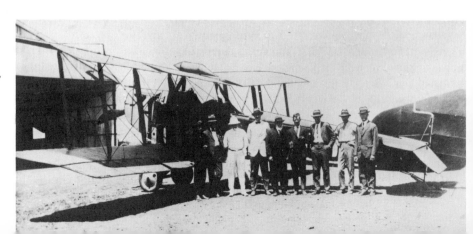

To carry out the master plan, engineering, electrical, tunnelling and dam-building firms from America, Italy, France, Norway, and Japan were given contracts. The manual labour and the driving of the trucks and the huge machines were done in the main by migrant labour. So Europe, with its great civilization, its joys, and its anguish, as well as its sense of the tragic fate of a man, moved into a part of the country where hitherto only Stone-Age men, men steeped in the wrongs of Ireland, and the English and the Scots, had barely scratched a sign to show those who came after them that they had been there.

In 1946 the government created the Australian National University in Canberra. The intention of the government was that the university should specialize in research in physics, medicine, the social sciences, and Pacific studies. Again, as in so much of what the Labor government did, the note on survival was tucked away amidst the idealism. We Australians, the minister argued, must do research in the Pacific 'if our future is to be safeguarded, and if we are to make our full contribution in the Councils of the Nations'. For Labor was just as preoccupied with the old nationalist aim of what the minister called 'our proper place in world affairs' as with the advancement of learning.

This sense of Australia as a social laboratory, as a pathfinder in humanity's march towards brotherhood and peace, as well as the conviction that the horrors and degradation of the depression must never return, lived side by side in Labor's post-war social welfare legislation with the motives of defence and national aggrandizement. From 1946 to 1949 the government extended and improved its welfare coverage. The victims of chance, economic vicissitudes, or other human misfortunes were protected. Humpty Dumpty could still fall, but this time on to the cotton wool of the welfare state rather than the cold, hard bricks of a laissez-faire capitalist society.

But by 1949 the Labor government was presented with two questions to which it had no answer. Was it using economic planning as the prelude to the introduction of socialism? Or was it using a form of state capitalism to protect the weak against the rigours of uncontrolled capitalism? If it had no plans or intentions to move from a capitalist to a socialist society, then, it was argued, some of its controls imposed in the stress of war were impeding economic development. The bank nationalization proposals of 1947, the continuation of fuel rationing, and the increase in the number of public servants in Canberra, created the suspicion that these men had become planners without any coherent social ideology. At the same time a series of strikes on the coalfields, on the waterfront, and in the shipping industry presented the government with a terrible choice, as the conservatives pounded them to maintain law and order, and the radicals abused them as storm troopers and agents of monopoly capitalism when they disciplined strikers. When Chifley ordered the troops to work the mines during the coal strike of 1949, the right wing of the party and their supporters in the electorate became frightened, while the left wing became disillusioned or disgusted. By that time the front bench men were exhausted by eight years of office. The loss of men of the imaginative drive of Curtin or the administrative skill of Beasley depleted their ability as well as their power to judge those ground swells in the electorates that in time engulf every government with an achievement as great as theirs. The same dilemma confronted Labor in its foreign policy as the world for which the ANZAAC pact was designed melted away like a snow drift. When the Indonesians revolted against the Dutch in 1947, the anti-imperialist tradition of the party, together with the general left-wing enthusiasm of the post-war years, pushed the government towards support for the Indonesians. When the wharf labourers refused to load ships carrying supplies to the Dutch forces, the government refrained from coercing them. At the United Nations their public statements were anti-colonial, while their backstairs intrigues and formal notes were more cautious. The revolt raised awkward questions such as the future of White Australia, to which Labor was still passionately attached. Besides, how could anyone be sure that anti-colonialism in Indonesia would not move on to anti-capitalism and even to communism?

It was the success of communism in eastern Europe and China that exposed the divisions within Labor and its spiritual bankruptcy. By 1948 there were communist governments in Poland, Czechoslovakia, Hungary, East Germany, Bulgaria, Romania, and Yugoslavia. The communist parties were increasing in strength in Italy and France. On 1 October, 1949, the People's Republic was proclaimed at Peking. Was the Labor government to recognize it as the legal government of China? The communist world hastened to recognize it; America refused. What was the Labor government to do? The right wing of the Party and the Catholics said No; those who were vote-conscious in an election year urged recognition after the elections in December; the radicals and the left clamoured for recognition. The vote went for delay, and in December Labor was soundly defeated by a Liberal and Country Party coalition, which at least had no inhibitions or agonies of mind on the communist issue.

This revival of the fortunes of the Liberal Party was in part a triumph for the political skill and courage of Menzies, who successfully exploited the divisions within the Labor Party, and in part a symptom of the division of the world into communist and anti-communist camps. After the crushing defeat at the elections of 1943, the fortunes of the non-Labor parties were at their lowest ebb. Faction fighting within the United Australia Party, ill-feeling between the United Australia Party and the Country Party, the personal bitterness generated by the political assassination of Menzies in 1941, and electoral failure, had brought both groups close to public ridicule and disgrace. With the formation of the Liberal Party in 1944 under the leadership of Menzies some of these wounds were healed. From 1945 to 1948 a band of young idealists, supported by the manufacturers, the traders, and the pastoralists, painted a rosy picture of possibilities if Australia could rid itself of the economic planners and the menace of communism. At the elections of 1946 the new party won seventeen seats in the House of Representatives. At the elections of 1949 they won fifty-six seats, the Labor Party forty-seven, the Country Party nineteen, and one seat went to an independent in a House enlarged from seventy-five to one hundred and twenty-three.

World events seemed to be playing into the hands of the Liberal Party. Communist North Koreans invaded South Korea on 25 June, 1950, and on

Jewish migrants arriving. Between 1947 and 1959, more than 700,000 migrants settled in Australia.

26 June President Truman denounced the North Koreans for unprovoked aggression and said that in response to the call of the UN Security Council he had ordered United States air and sea forces to help the Korean government. On 29 June the Australian government announced that it had put a naval squadron at the disposal of the United States for use in Korean waters, and on the following day the RAAF fighter squadron stationed in Japan was also put at their disposal. On 6 July Prime Minister Menzies called on Australians to enlist in the army, navy, and air force for service in Korea: 'We are,' he said, 'with all our imperfections, a Christian nation, believing in man's brotherhood, anxious to live at peace with our neighbour, willing to go the second mile to help him if he is less fortunate than we are.' So once again Australians volunteered for service overseas—some in the belief that they were defending Christian civilization against atheistic communism, some for adventure, some to escape their wives, and some for something to do. Up to the time of the signing of the armistice at Panmunjom in July 1953, two hundred and eighty-one Australians were killed or missing in Korea.

The demand for Australian primary products, especially wool, increased so steeply during the war that the Australian economy was swept up to new heights of affluence. Woolgrowers who had slaved for years to reduce their overdrafts bought luxury cars, labour-saving devices for their wives, stuffed their cellars with magnums of champagne, and went for expensive journeys overseas. The Korean war also strengthened the hand of the Menzies government against communism.

While Australia moved into a new era of affluence, the Menzies government accepted the American view that the salvation of civilization lay in the containment of communism both abroad and at home. On 12 July, 1951, the United States, Australia, and New Zealand initialled the draft of a security treaty that was to be called the ANZUS pact. At Manila in October 1954 France, the United States, Australia, New Zealand, the United Kingdom, Pakistan, Thailand, and the Philippines signed a treaty that formed the basis of the South East Asia Treaty Organization, or SEATO, by which they agreed to take common action against what they believed to be the most pressing threat to their own security and progress—namely, communist expansionism. The treaty covered not only overt aggression, but also subversion—the hope being to ensure that what the communists could not get by armed attack, they could not get by less obvious means. So Australia committed herself to the United States policy to resist what the Australian government called 'the aggressive policies of international communism'. The free world, they argued, had an interest in checking the growth of communist tyranny.

The Australians also had a moral as well as a self-interested motive to reduce poverty, disease, and ignorance in Asia. On these questions, as the Menzies government saw it, the dictates of humanity and the desire to survive suggested some form of material aid to the countries of south-east Asia. So when ministers of the British Commonwealth countries met at Colombo in January 1950 the Australian delegation, ably led by Percy Spender, the Minister for External Affairs, put forward a plan to achieve both political stability and economic progress. This came to be called the Colombo Plan. At the next meeting in Sydney in May 1950 the governments of Australia, Canada, Ceylon, India, Pakistan, New Zealand, and the United Kingdom each agreed to subscribe eight million pounds over three years to train people from south-east Asia and to send instructors, expert missions, and equipment to countries needing them. In September the Australian government announced its intention to spend 31,250,000 pounds over six years.

The United States joined in 1951, and the Philippines and Japan in 1954.

By the end of that year over six hundred students from south-east Asia had received Colombo Plan grants to study at Australian universities, and seventy-nine Australian experts had served in the countries of south-east Asia. By 1968 Australia had sent more than 1,500 experts, and received 9,400 students or trainees from Africa, Asia, and the Pacific under the auspices of the Colombo Plan. By these methods the Australian government contributed a mite towards bridging the gap between the European and Asian standards of living that was, they believed, an ever-standing reason for the people of Asia to fall into the clutches of the communists. SEATO remained the final line of defence against the spread of communism in south-east Asia. So with one hand the Australian government offered welfare, and with the other a sword.

On the domestic front the Menzies government prepared for a war to the death against the Communist Party. On 27 April, 1950, Menzies introduced into the House of Representatives the Communist Party Dissolution Bill, which declared that since the Communist Party was seeking the violent overthrow of the established government of Australia, that Party was illegal and dissolved. On 19 October the Communist Party and ten unions brought an action before the High Court to declare the act illegal. When a majority of the judges declared the act invalid in March 1951, Menzies asked for a double dissolution, and, after the elections, introduced the Constitution Alteration Bill in July to amend the constitution to enable parliament to pass laws for the peace, order, and good government of the Commonwealth with respect to communism. Before the campaign got under way Chifley died suddenly on 13 June, and Evatt became the leader of the Australian Labor Party. To assurances from the Right that civilization was in danger, and warnings from the Left that liberty was in danger, the Australian people cast 2,317,927 votes for and 2,370,009 against the proposal at a referendum on 22 September 1951. The Left hailed the result as a victory for Australian democratic traditions: what the Right thought was not made clear, though some whispered they were relieved to find a constitutional pretext for the traditional conservative policy of masterly inactivity.

With the death of Stalin in 1953 and the end of the Korean war in the same year, the ashes of the cold war became less and less warm. In Australia they were suddenly fanned into rather sulphurous flames by the Petrov affair. On 3 April, 1954, Vladimir Mikhailovich Petrov, a third secretary in the Soviet Embassy in Canberra, asked for political asylum. On 20 April his wife also asked for political asylum after a melodramatic flight in an aeroplane from Sydney to Darwin during which an Australian security man and Soviet diplomats fought for the possession of her soul. In a dramatic episode in the House of Representatives Menzies announced the appointment of a royal commission

Indian Colombo Plan students in 1960.

to examine expionage in Australia. In the heat of the moment there were promises of revelations more damaging to the Soviet Union than those made by Kravchenko in Canada.

Dr Evatt announced that he would represent men denounced by Petrov before the royal commission. Evatt, the intelligentsia of the Left, and the Communist Party were quite convinced that the Petrov affair was a plot between the Australian security service and the Australian government to slander and defame the Labor opposition, and a desperate move to use the anti-communist bogy in the forthcoming elections. The commission began its hearings on 17 May, 1954, digressed briefly to consider and reject the Evatt charge that the Petrov case was a conspiracy and a forgery, and continued to hear evidence till March 1955, when the three commissioners began to work on the report that in its conclusions had little more to say than what the man in the street took for granted—namely, that Soviet representatives conducted espionage in Australia.

By then the heat was out of the Petrov affair. By an odd irony its most permanent effect was to bring to a head the faction fighting within the Labor Party. Ever since the disastrous defeat in the elections of 1949 the party had been licking its wounds. So long as Chifley lived, the charismatic powers he exercised and his own conviction that the unity of the Party was essential to the salvation of Labor prevented a split. But after he died in June 1951 the election of Evatt as leader aggravated the faction fighting. Then, Labor's crushing defeat in the elections of May 1954 caused both sides to look for a scapegoat. The left wing of the Party was not happy about Australia accepting the American thesis on foreign policy. As they saw it, this meant an alliance with corrupt, reactionary, and inefficient governments in Asia; it exposed Australia to the danger of being on the losing side in a world war; it aligned Australia with those who seemed to be attempting to delay the liberation of the peoples of Asia from centuries of poverty and oppression; it alienated India, whose leader, Pandit Nehru, symbolized the groping of this section of the Labor Party for a third force, midway between communist Russia and China on the one hand and reactionary capitalist America and Chiang Kai-Shek's army on the other. This group wanted to recognize Communist China, to withdraw from military alliances with the United States, and build up a neutral position that owed allegiance neither to Moscow nor to Washington. On the other hand the right wing of the Party was deeply committed to a crusade against communism, both in the international field and in the unions. In the early 1950s they had supported the Industrial Groups, a right-wing labour organization that aimed to free the unions from communist domination.

After Dr Evatt announced his intention to appear as counsel before the Petrov Commission, events moved swiftly. At an angry meeting of the Party in Canberra the right wing called Evatt 'a disgrace to the Labor Party'. The left wing retorted that if the right wing saw Evatt walk on the waters of Galilee they would swear that the communists were holding him up. Things had got out of hand. A few weeks later, on 6 October, 1954, Evatt, pushed further left by the savagery of the right-wing faction, announced in the press that a small group of Labor members, particularly in Victoria, had become increasingly disloyal to the labour movement. This group, he said, had adopted methods that resembled those of the communists and the fascists, and was deflecting the movement from established Labor objectives and ideals. It seemed certain, he concluded, that the activities of this small group were largely directed from outside the labour movement. The group to whom Evatt referred retorted that he was a millstone around the Labor Party's neck, and that his only friends were communists and ex-communists.

At the twenty-first conference of the Australian Labor Party in Hobart in March 1955 the centre group dominated proceedings. On the one hand they approved of an earlier decision of the federal executive to remove political recognition of the Industrial Groups. On the other hand they reaffirmed their complete opposition to communism and all forms of totalitarianism, and emphasized that only a strong, united labour movement could prevent the growth of those evils. On the one hand they affirmed their conviction that co-operation with the United States in the Pacific was of crucial importance and had to be maintained and extended. On the other hand they passed resolutions that were thinly veiled criticisms of United States policy in the Pacific. 'Indo-China,' they maintained, 'was typical of those cases where inexcusable delay in recognizing a genuinely nationalist anti-colonial movement in Asia resulted in communism gradually capturing the nationalist movement.' Labor wanted more of welfare for the people of Asia, more assistance to relieve those suffering from poverty, disease, and lack of educational facilities, and less of the mailed fist. Labor wanted SEATO to devote attention to the work of peace. Labor wanted Austria, Bulgaria, Ceylon, China, Finland, Hungary, Ireland, Italy, Jordan, Korea, Libya, Portugal and Romania admitted tò the United Nations to make it a genuine world organization, truly representative. But Labor still had no alternative to SEATO, nor could it sketch a society pitched midway between the ideologies of Moscow and Washington.

To the outsider it seemed that the compromisers had won yet another battle. After stormy scenes in Victoria, when the clash between the factions was exacerbated by the influence of two powerful Catholic personalities, Dr Mannix, Archbishop of Melbourne, and B. A. Santamaria, a leading Catholic layman, the Industrial Groupers in Victoria formed the Anti-Communist Labor Party in April 1955. In New South Wales one section of the Groupers formed the Democratic Labor Party in 1956, and in 1957 the Anti-Communist Labor Party and the Democratic Labor Party merged to form the Democratic Labor Party. As a party they were pledged to make Australia and the world safe from communism, to purify Labor from careerism, opportunism, and corruption, and to create industrial democracy. In fact they succeeded in making Australia safe for the Liberal-Country Party coalition. For by attracting 9.41 per cent of the vote in the Commonwealth elections of 1958, including 14.75 per cent in Victoria and 5.59 per cent in New South Wales, and by instructing their supporters to give their second preferences to the Liberal-Country Party coalition, they exposed themselves to the charge that, however high-minded their intentions, their political contribution was on the side of conservatism rather than the liberation from party tyranny to which they aspired.

Nor were the leaders of the Liberal and Country parties any more successful in affirming a faith for the future. All through the years after 1945 the faith of Prime Minister Menzies in British institutions and British civilization never wavered. When he announced the death of George VI in the House of Representatives on 6 February, 1952, he was so deeply moved that his voice broke, and he found it difficult to continue. After he had told the House with a becoming dignity that he was quite incapable of saying what ought to be said, he slumped into his chair, rested his elbows on the table, and pressed the knuckles of his clenched fingers into his mouth.

By 1962 the great gifts of the man, the eloquence, the wit and the urbanity, were being used to defend a world that was crumbling before his very eyes. When the government of the United Kingdom proposed to enter the European Common Market, his political allies, the Country Party, sensing adverse effects on their pocketbooks, shouted loudly of the material conditions under which they would be prepared to consent. But for Menzies—and, indeed, for all

Swagman Harry Myers in the south-west of New South Wales in the 1950s. The swag was the travelling kit of the bush.

Liberals who had some notion that the body was more than raiment—Britain's entry would mark the end of the great dream of the beneficent and civilizing effect of the British way of life. For here at the very beginning of a new decade those Australians who believed in the stand against communism had to face the prospect that the price of such loyalty might be the end of the British Commonwealth of Nations. So Menzies and his followers found to their disquiet that their loyalty was to a class, rather than to a country or an empire.

Over the same decade the intellectuals and artists were confronting this same choice between the two worlds. They, too, were confronted with a new world. That affluent society produced in part by the rapid industrialization during the Second World War, the technological changes in production and communication, and the sudden increase in demand for Australian primary products during the hysteria of the cold war, was producing a material standard of living comparable with that of the United States of America. Each year the factories turned out more and more of the creature comforts and means of mass entertainment. The number of motor cars, motor mowers, electric stoves, refrigerators, hot-water jugs, toasters, electric shavers, vacuum cleaners, washing machines, telephones, radio sets, and TV sets per head of population compared favourably with the United States and Sweden. With the increase in material well-being, and with the end of economic and cultural dependence on the British Isles, and to a lesser extent on Europe, there developed a new confidence—not that brash, boastful, cheeky and larrikin confidence of the 1890s, but the confidence of those who no longer needed to comfort themselves

'Collins Street 5 p.m.',
an oil painting by
John Brack.

with the delusion of being 'new world'. When Bertrand Russell left Australia after a short tour in 1950, he commented that Australians were pioneers 'not only in the development of Australia, but in pointing the way to a happier destiny for man throughout the centuries to come'.

The publicists then were preparing to celebrate a coming of age. But the grounds for this confidence escaped the poets, the novelists, and the painters, and some of them turned to those questions on the nature of man and his destiny that have been posed by all civilizations in their time of flower. They probed the origin of evil and the causes of human suffering. They asked whether God or man is responsible for human pain; they asked, too, whether human beings ever could communicate with each other; they wrote of the tenderness and compassion that flower in people who have the courage to face the horror and tragedy of human life. Others argued that this preoccupation with evil and the counselling of resignation symbolized the spiritual sickness of bourgeois civilization. For them, only the destruction of bourgeois society could liberate the creative gifts of the people and restore to their literature and their art the hope and confidence of men who knew the way forward for humanity. So once again in its history Australia stood between two worlds.

The war in Vietnam forced Australians to say where they stood between the capitalist world led by the United States of America and the communist world led by the Soviet Union and China. In 1954 the French and Chinese governments had agreed to divide Vietnam between North and South at the seventeenth parallel, the North being under the communist government of Ho Chi Minh and General Vo Nguyen Giap, and the South, after 1956, under the dictatorship of Ngo Dinh Diem. In May 1959, to a background of a clash between Catholic and Buddhist factions, the spread of terrorism, and the threat

of anarchy, the Central Committee of the Communist Party of North Vietnam called for the creation of a united Vietnam through all appropriate means. In July that Party announced its intention to liberate South Vietnam from its capitalist oppressors. By January 1961 a national liberation front, the Viet Cong, had been formed in the south to join forces with the communists of the North to destroy what they called the 'US-Diem clique'.

So in December 1961 President Kennedy, after referring to the 'communist program of assassination, kidnapping, and wanton violence in South Vietnam', went on to say that the United States was prepared to help the Republic of Vietnam 'to protect its people and to preserve its independence'. In the eyes of some, the United States was fighting to resist a communist attack on South Vietnam. In the eyes of others, the United States had come to the assistance of conservative, if not corrupt, reactionaries in a civil war.

At that time the case for Australia assisting to prevent the spread of communism to South Vietnam, Thailand, and the Malay Peninsula seemed overwhelming. The victory of the Communists in the Chinese civil war, the close relations between the Soviet Union and China, and the even more alarming talk of an understanding between Peking and Jakarta, pointed to the need for some military action to prevent the countries of south-east Asia falling under communist control one after another like dominoes once the defences of the opposition had been destroyed. In April 1955 Menzies had announced that Australia intended to send troops to Malaya as a contribution to the defence of the SEATO area. The following December he had announced that these troops could be available for use against communist terrorists. In 1964 he announced the introduction of a selective system (choice by ballot or lot) of conscription for military service in which those selected for two years' training could be sent for military service overseas.

Top left: Poet Kenneth Slessor.

Above: Artist Sir William Dobell.

Above left: Poet and critic James McAuley.

Then to a background of an atomic explosion by China in October 1964, rumours of military disasters in South Vietnam, and alarming reports of the imminent collapse of all government in that country, Menzies announced on 29 April, 1965, the government's decision to send a battalion of troops to South Vietnam as 'the most useful additional contribution which we can make to the defence of the region at this time'. In 1965, after an episode in the Gulf of Tonkin, about which eyewitness accounts varied, President Johnson announced the momentous decision to bomb military targets in North Vietnam. The Australian battalion of 1,500 men arrived in Vietnam in May and June of 1965 and was located at Bien Hoa as part of the United States 173rd Airborne Brigade. By June 1966 the battalion had been replaced by a task force. In the following year the air force and the twin jet Canberra bombers of No. 2 Squadron of the Royal Australian Navy guided-missile destroyer *Hobart* began to assist United States forces in South Vietnam and in the demilitarized zone. By 1967 the strength of the Australian force was 6,300, of whom 40 per cent were national servicemen and the rest volunteers.

When the decision to send troops to Vietnam was first announced in April 1965, the leader of the Australian Labor Party, Arthur Calwell, opposed it bitterly, partly because that decision was based, he believed, on the erroneous view that the war had been begun by a communist invasion from North Vietnam. Calwell insisted it was a civil war. He also believed the government had misunderstood the nature of the communist challenge and was dangerously denuding Australia of her pitiful supply of troops by sending some of them out of the country. By tradition Labor was suspicious of expeditionary forces, even when dressed up in the modern language of 'forward defence'. Labor believed in a policy of welfare rather than guns for south-east Asia, though it was hard put to it to say just what it would do to stop the spread of communism in that area.

Outside the Labor Party, the Communist Party, some committed radicals, and high-minded improvers of mankind, the warnings of Calwell had fallen on deaf ears. Down to 1966 the Australian electorate returned to power the Liberal-Country Party coalition which was committed to the small expeditionary force, as the simple remedy against communist aggression, and to the promise of greater wealth by free enterprise. As the goods rolled off the production line, as metal mines were opened in the great Australian desert, as machines ripped the iron ore out of the earth, or plunged into the bowels of that earth and even into the mighty deep in search of oil, and as trade with Japan, the United States, West Germany, and the United Kingdom boomed, it seemed as though the whole continent was to be brought under the influence of bourgeois civilization.

A demonstration in 1966 against the Vietnam war, during President Lyndon Johnson's visit to Australia.

It seemed as though from Darwin to Hobart and from Broome to Brisbane suburbia was to be the last fate of a country which in previous generations had produced a William Charles Wentworth with his dream of a new Britannia rising beside the majestic waters of Sydney Harbour; a Ned Kelly with his dream of a life that was fearless, free, and bold; and a Robert O'Hara Burke with his sense of all the tragic grandeur in the human situation. For there had been giants in the land before the levelling and conformist flood of industrial society ushered in the age of the neon sign and the contraceptive pill. Material well-being for all was stripping away even the need for the great comforters of the past—the promise of happiness in the life of the world to come, or the promise of happiness on earth, or the poetry and music which had ministered in the past not just to delight but also to give the strength and the courage to endure. It looked as though the government had understood the spirit of the age: to provide all the creature comforts of suburbia and to foster the values of a people aiming for two cars in a family, a thirty-hour week, never-ending titillations on the television screen, and the opportunity to ride the boards at Bondi Beach in return for a token force in Vietnam.

By 1967 the voices of disquiet again began to be heard. The new Labor Party leader, Gough Whitlam, speaking like one of those prophets of old who had been nurtured in a harsh, dry land, warned that Australia had ceased to be an English farm and was now a Japanese quarry. Some were disturbed by the quantity of Japanese and American investment in Australia. Some were disturbed by what they called the corrupting and degrading influence of the American mass civilization—the pornography in the magazines and the violence in the television serials. Some were disturbed by the blank cheque the government seemed to have handed to Washington. In January 1966 Menzies in his own season of the sere, the yellow leaf, had retired full of honours. The development of Canberra and the expansion of the universities were the lasting monuments he handed on to posterity.

He had been replaced by Harold Holt as Prime Minister. Holt who was sustained in his private life by a commendable vision of all men being brothers, and in his public life by the dream of educating Australians to the need for closer association with the peoples of south-east Asia, was driven by an odd quirk of fate not only to announce during that year an increase in the Australian force in Vietnam but to put forward as a slogan expressing his government's enthusiasm for the American alliance the words 'All the way with L.B.J.' (President Lyndon B. Johnson).

Events in 1967 caused many of the articulate members of the community to question the wisdom of such a policy. The overthrow of Sukarno in Indonesia, the end of the Peking-Jakarta axis, and the ever-sharpening tension between China and the Soviet Union, seemed to provide a pause during which the question of Australia's security came up for review. Two events quickened the need for such a review. One was the announcement by the British government of their intention to withdraw their military forces from south-east Asia at an unspecified date in the early 1970s. The other was increasing disquiet at the drift of events in Vietnam.

Some argued that with isolationism bound to grow in strength in America after the terrible experiences in Vietnam, and with the British out of south-east Asia, Australia should emulate the example of Israel or Sweden and pursue a policy of armed neutrality. Some who were nauseated by the spectacle of a huge military machine pounding to dust large areas of a small nation took up the words of the Holy Father —'I beg of you in the name of Christ to stop.' Some were nauseated by the ghastly, hideous emptiness of what the Americans and Australians were offering as an alternative to communist conformism and greyness of spirit in Vietnam. Some were alarmed lest Australia be on the losing side in Vietnam. The Australian Labor Party reminded the electors that civilized values were being destroyed by western forces attacking jungle villages with napalm, phosphorus bombs and fragmentation bombs. Some, influenced by past traditions and political creeds which had denounced all wars as products of class hatred or imperialist ambitions, and mindful of the old radical tradition in Australia of championing the underdog, found to their undying pain that this great Australian myth of mateship and social equality was in danger of being laid to rest on the battlefields of Vietnam.

The decade drew to a close on a note of anxiety. On 17 December, 1967, Prime Minister Holt, who had lived through that terrible anguish of wanting men to be nice to each other only to find that he had come into his own in a time of hardening of hearts, was reported missing, believed drowned. When world leaders gathered in Melbourne to pay their last respects to him—for as a man he was much loved—the prophets of impending doom for Australia noted that, except for the President of the United States, Australia was host to those forces in Asia and Europe which belonged to the dustbin of history rather than to those shaping the future of mankind. When President Johnson announced in December 1968 that peace talks on Vietnam would begin in Paris, the relief was tempered by that undying source of disquiet: what was the future of the 'dinkum Aussie'? Would the price of survival as a people be the shedding of that attempt to preserve a European society? Was this that fourth or fifth generation which would be 'visited' for the racial insolence and pride of their forefathers?

It seemed, too, as though the age of the kings of the human spirit was drawing to a close, to be replaced by that age of courtiers in which the courtiers consume their substance looking for kings. It had been a decade of strange paradoxes. There had been at long last some great achievements of the human spirit in Australia. Patrick White wrote his novels; Alec Hope wrote his *Ode on the Death of Pius the Twelfth;* Douglas Stewart and Judith Wright sang in their poems a

Below: Welcoming placards for President Lyndon Johnson during his Sydney visit in 1966.

Below right: Harold Holt, Prime Minister from 1966 to 1967.

great hymn of praise to life; Sidney Nolan painted his *Riverbend* in celebration of the golden tree of life. The tinsel of opulence glittered more brightly than ever in city, town and country. The moral authority of religious and political creeds declined apace. The decade drew to a close with at least one great question left unanswered: how long could this affluence be enjoyed before Australia was swept by the great storm raging to her north? There was perhaps another question: just as Samson after being shorn of his hair was left eyeless in Gaza, was this generation, stripped bare of all faith, to be left comfortless on Bondi Beach?

Clockwise from top left:
Arthur Boyd,
Patrick White,
David Campbell,
Douglas Stewart,
Judith Wright,
Alec Derwent Hope.

CHAPTER THIRTEEN

AN AGE OF RUINS
1969—1986

ON 18 SEPTEMBER, 1890, the Cardinal Archbishop of Sydney, Patrick Francis Moran, had warned Australians to beware of worshipping those false idols which corrupt hearts, lest by so doing they usher in an age of ruins as the fruit of all the greed and striving and hopes and ideals of the white man since European civilization had first been planted at Sydney on 26 January, 1788. The cardinal had in mind the twin idols of materialism and atheistic communism. Nearly a century later, on the surface not even the sufferings endured in the two world wars of 1914-19 and 1939-45, the dropping of the atomic bomb at Hiroshima in August 1945, the depth of the crisis in capitalist society during the great depression, or the loosening of the conventions of previous decades, seemed to have shaken the faith of the average Australian in the capacity of both the land and the society to provide every adult with the opportunity to become an owner of property: a house, a plot of land, a car, and all the gadgets deemed essential for the gratification of the senses in an age given over to surface delights and titillations.

The many interests fighting for Australia

Superficially it was an age of growth and affluence. Population increased from 7.43 million in 1945 to 10.40 million in 1960 and 14.418 million in June 1979. The composition of the population also underwent a significant change. In 1939, on the eve of World War II, publicist after publicist boasted that 98 per cent of the Australian population was either born in the British Isles or descended from families in the British Isles. Australia, it was said at that time, with New Zealand, was the prime exemplar of British or Anglo-Saxon philistinism in the New World. By 1979 the immigration to Australia of refugees from the pre-war Baltic States of Estonia, Latvia, and Lithuania (known in Australia as 'Balts'), from the Soviet Union, Poland, the two Germanies, Holland, Yugoslavia, Italy, Greece, and Turkey, had so changed the composition of the population that 11.8 per cent had no connection by either birth or descent with the inhabitants of the British Isles. Melbourne, for example, previously pre-eminently a British city with an upper class which fawned on and imitated the English country gentry, became after Athens and New York the third largest Greek city in the world. Anglo-Saxon Australia had been changed into ethnic Australia.

In trade with overseas countries a similar revolution occurred. In 1939, 41.64 per cent of Australian trade was conducted with the United Kingdom and 4.22 per cent with Japan. By December 1979 exports to the United Kingdom had shrunk to 4 per cent while exports to Japan had risen to 28.8 per cent. Imports showed a similar trend—10.9 per cent from the United Kingdom and 17.6 per cent from Japan. The car market provided an accurate barometer of the great change which came over Australia with the decline of the United Kingdom as a world industrial power. In 1939, 64 per cent of all imported passenger cars on Australian roads had been either manufactured in the United Kingdom or assembled in Australia from parts made in the United Kingdom. By December 1979 that figure had dwindled to 8.5 per cent. Over the same years the proportion of Japanese cars increased from less than 1 per cent to 60.1 per cent.

Over the same period of time Asian goods became more and more prominent in the shops and in all public places where goods were on display. In the field of electronics—especially television, transistor radios, and electrical fittings—the products of National and Sanyo from Japan quickly occupied the place of prominence previously reserved for British and European firms such as His Master's Voice and Philips. In sporting goods the same shift in the source of supply occurred. The prestige and virtual monopoly in fishing equipment previously enjoyed by the British and the French was rapidly captured by the Japanese. Whereas previous generations had heard and heeded the advice to 'buy British and be proud of it', a new generation was growing up dressed in clothes manufactured in Asia, driving to work or to play in a Japanese car, and titillating their senses with entertainment conveyed to them by a Japanese viewer, receiver, or sound reproducer.

Once again a cry of protest against Japanese economic imperialism was heard in the land. Japan, it was said, was winning by economic imperialism that contest for the markets of the south-west Pacific which she had failed to acquire by the use of force during World War II. At the same time, American capital investment in Australia continued to grow. During the economic bonanza stimulated by American stock-piling during the Korean war, and re-kindled by the increase in demand for consumer goods during the long-drawn-out civil war in Vietnam, a new form of economic imperialism began to operate in Australia and in other parts of the world: Australia became a market for the multinational company, with headquarters overseas. In the metals industry, in the motor car industry and its ancillary, oil and petrol, in air transport and machine tools, companies such as CRA, IBM, Shell Oil, STC—to mention some of the more prominent in the public eye—revealed that they were exporting millions of dollars each year back to the parent company.

This left Australians on the horns of a dilemma. The United States of America and Japan were the principal disseminators throughout the world of the products of the technological revolution, which was supplying the consumers in the advanced countries of the world such as Australia with those products they required for a great wallow in that greed and titillation culture to which they were seemingly enslaved. World capital, know-how, and organizational skill had used inventions such as the jet engine to build aeroplanes capable of flying at over one thousand kilometres an hour. This finally removed one great source of Australian inferiority in the world—her isolation from the great centres of world culture such as London, New York, Moscow, Paris, Tokyo, and Peking, an isolation already eroded by radio, the overseas telephone, and the communications satellites. The other potent source of a sense of inferiority, the material backwardness, had also been largely removed by the creature comforts made available by those very multinational companies about which both radicals and nationalists had such grave misgivings. The opening of the Sydney Opera House on 20 October, 1973, symbolized that in things of the mind and the spirit Australia was beginning again to make its own distinctive contribution.

The radicals and the nationalists had misgivings about the moral effects of some of the goods transported to Australia by the multinationals. In addition to all those material goods which had poured into Australia from overseas

during the past three or four decades, Australians became more and more the
receivers of and participants in American cultural imperialism. American week-
lies such as *Time* and *Newsweek*, newspapers, gramophone records, musicals for
the stage, films and books, poured into Australia. In the eyes of the radicals
and nationalists in Australia, American economic imperialists had become most
powerful opinion-formers in Australia. American pop culture, with its money
values, its emphasis on sex, and its presentation of material well-being and
creature comforts as the greatest good in human life, were corrupting Australians, calling on them to worship false idols. Some radicals also argued that
American finance capital had become so powerful in Australia that it was
threatening the political independence of Australian governments—that hav-

*The dramatic and
formerly controversial
Sydney Opera House,
designed by Danish
architect Joern Utzon,
built between 1959
and 1973.*

ing almost acquired the power to decide many of the material conditions under which people lived, it would inevitably attempt to manipulate and influence Australian opinion in the direction of electing a government favourable to the interests of American big business.

By the end of the decade of the 1960s Australia was a deeply divided society. The fundamental issue had remained the same ever since the Great Strikes and the capitalist crisis of 1890-94, that issue being who should own the means of production, distribution, and exchange, and what principles should determine how wealth should be divided amongst the members of society. The conservative forces, the Australian Liberal Party and the Australian Country Party (known after May 1975 as the National-Country Party), believed that society was best served by private ownership of property, the profit motive, and material rewards to men and women of industry and skill. The Australian Labor Party believed in the socialization of the means of production, distribution, and exchange, having adopted that as their aim at the Brisbane Conference of the Australian Labor Party in 1922. This did not commit them to change either by force or by any other revolutionary means. Rejecting the Eureka principle that 'a lick on the lug' was the only way to achieve a change in the foundations of society, the Australian Labor Party was deeply committed to the use of the ballot-box as the means of making and unmaking social conditions. They remained a party of social democrats, a party committed to evolution, to moderation, to the use of the existing political institutions to achieve genuine equality of opportunity in such decisive areas of life as education, medical care, and careers.

Committed since 1905 to the aim of cultivating an Australian national sentiment, they were stronger advocates than the members of the conservative groups of such policies as an Australian national anthem and an Australian national flag. Unlike the conservatives, they did not stress their loyalty to the British monarchy or to any imperial ties or sentiment. In general they were committed to such slogans as 'Australia for the Australians' and to the defence of Australia on Australian soil. By contrast their opponents saw themselves as both Australian and British, as Australian Britons; as such they believed the first line of defence for Australia was on the battlefields of Europe or in the jungles of south-east Asia.

There was fundamental disagreement on the nature of the good society: Labor vaguely advocated a society free both of the moral infamies of the free

Defying the laws of gravity.

enterprise societies of the United States of America, Japan, and the Federal Republic of Germany, and of the greyness of spirit, the conformism, and the spiritual popery of the societies of eastern Europe and China; the Liberal and National-Country Party coalition pursued their faith in free enterprise and British political institutions. This fundamental disagreement introduced an era of political excitement and turbulence in the 1970s. This turbulence was probably aggravated by the numerically small but influential communist parties—the Australian Communist Party, which was critical of both Moscow and Peking; the Socialist Party of Australia, which supported Soviet policies; and the Australian Communist Party (Marxist-Leninist), which supported Peking. There were other small splinter groups on the left such as the Socialist Workers Party and the Students for a Democratic Society. Ever since the first dispatch of Australian advisers to Saigon in 1963, the parties to the left of the Australian Labor Party had been demanding the end of all aid to the Republic of South Vietnam. With the growing reports of the horrors of American bombing and the corruption of the morale of the fighting forces in the jungles and cities of Vietnam, one section of the Australian Labor Party, led by James Ford Cairns, appealed to the masses to force the Australian government to withdraw all forces.

After the death of Harold Holt on 17 December, 1967, the Liberal and Country Party coalition government behaved as men who had no answers to the great issues of their day, save dependence on the Americans. For six years they were convulsed by a leadership crisis. As a successor to Prime Minister Holt the Liberal wing of the coalition elected John Grey Gorton. He had much to commend him. Nature had endowed him with a warmth of heart and a generosity of spirit which distinguished him from the heart-dimmers and straiteners in the ranks of the conservatives. He had that friendly manner—that tendency to judge another man not by his rank or his standing in society but by whether he liked him as a man—which endeared him to the people at large rather than to the members of the Melbourne Club. Indeed he showed many of the qualities which seemed likely to mark him as a friend of the people, a people's man in an age of the masses, having by nature the mannerisms of a believer in material and social equality, despite the attempts of his teachers at Geelong Grammar School and Oxford University to bind him to the way of life of the exclusives. In politics he seemed to belong to the centre, being a supporter of the Commonwealth against the States, in favour of no further

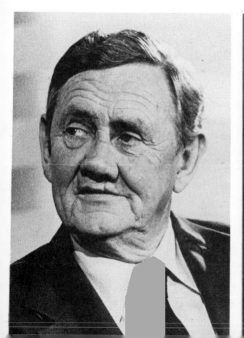

Far left: John Gorton, Prime Minister from 1969 to 1971.

Left: William McMahon, Prime Minister from 1971 to 1972.

commitments to the armed forces in Vietnam, and a strong believer in financial assistance by the Commonwealth to both education and the arts.

By his generous vision of the role of government both in politics and culture he offended the most conservative members of his own party. By his open pursuit of pleasure—he was known affectionately as 'Jolly John'—he angered those conservatives who believed it was the role of the politician to be aloof from those who amused themselves in traditional Australian ways. Through a series of misunderstandings, he quarrelled with and received the resignation of one senior minister of his government who already had a reputation for cutting down those who stood in his way. His name was John Malcolm Fraser. Within months of the resignation of Fraser as Minister for Defence, the political know-alls prophesied somewhat recklessly the end of a promising political career, and one half of Gorton's colleagues within the Liberal Party voted in favour of William McMahon as their leader. To his great credit, Gorton had the magnanimity to confer his casting vote on McMahon; but then, rather characteristically, he stood for and was elected as deputy leader. That was on 10 March, 1971.

William McMahon had some of the qualities which Australians associated with conservative leaders. He was reputed to be wealthy; he was well steeped in all those arguments in favour of rejecting any request for financial assistance from a government; he had never been known to utter one sentiment in public which might have caused any gentleman or gentlewoman to retrench a dish from the dinner table or, indeed, to curb any of their extravagance as major performers in a world where conspicuous waste was held to be a virtue. But McMahon had some of the gifts which might have helped capitalist society to work in more normal times. He was industrious; he knew his public finance; he knew from years of experience how government worked in Australia; he was prepared to spend hours on the telephone winning support for the decisions of his government. But nothing he did arrested the loss of support for conservatism in the electorate at large. The mass movement of dissent, the back-biting and character assassination within the Liberal Party, continued to be front page news in the press; the feverish scramble for shares in the booming metals industry disgusted many of the serious-minded. Above all, the ridicule of McMahon and his government by the new leader of the Labor Party, Edward Gough Whitlam, created the illusion that conservatism was so hopelessly corrupt and effete that Australia was about to be taken over by the social democrats.

Whitlam had been elected leader of the Labor Party in place of Arthur Calwell on 8 February, 1967. His whole public career had been dedicated to the proposition that reform and change must be achieved through democratic parliamentary methods. Whitlam had the charisma and the gifts with which to become a great reformer. He was born in Melbourne on 11 July, 1916, into a legal-cum-public service family. From his father, a gentle, hard-working, and high-minded member of the Crown Solicitor's Office, first in Melbourne and later in Canberra, he had learnt to cultivate 'excellence'; from his mother he had learnt to cultivate wisdom and understanding. From a boyhood in the pioneering days in Canberra he had built up a vision of an independent Australia. From his study of the literature of Greece and Rome during his years at the University of Sydney he had learnt to temper the enthusiasm he felt for the causes of reform and social justice with the Greek view that in life only young men believe the crown of life to be happiness—that old men who have seen the stricken heart of a proud man brought down know what life is really like. Experiences during the referendum campaign of 1944, especially the specious arguments advanced at that time by the conservatives, convinced him that the Labor Party was the one chance of steering Australia between the

*Gough Whitlam,
Prime Minister from
1972 to 1975.*

moral infamies of a capitalist society and the conformism of the communist societies. On 17 February, 1953, he took his seat in the House of Representatives in Canberra as member for Werriwa. On 7 March, 1960, he was elected deputy-leader of the Labor Party.

By the time he was elected leader of the Labor Party on 8 February, 1967, he had crystallized his opinion of how Labor should use its power when returned to government. Despairing of persuading the Australian people to engage in a large-scale reform of the constitution, he persuaded the members of the Labor Party and the electorate at large that it would be possible to introduce policies of social reform within the existing constitution. Believing, in the traditional Labor way, that public enterprise was the best way of counteracting or staving off the evils of monopoly capitalism in Australia, he persuaded his followers that much of what they all stood for could be achieved by the democratic process of victory at the ballot-box followed by the passing of legislation through the Commonwealth Parliament. He was assuming that Labor could also win a majority in the Senate, enjoy a measure of co-operation from the State governments, and count on at least the neutrality of the Governor-General.

With the zeal of a missionary, the wit of the very sophisticated, and the gift of being able to present his aims in memorable language, he began his campaign to teach Australians—including all Aboriginal Australians—that they could achieve a measure of equality of opportunity in education, health care, and in careers; he also began to teach Australians that they could pursue an independent foreign policy and reach standards in the world of art and letters which would once and for all rid them of the vestiges of their one-time colonial status, with its attendant sense of inferiority and the tendency to grovel and

'Irrigation Lake, Wimmera' by Arthur Boyd.

cringe in the presence of men and women from older civilizations. He proposed to end the disgrace of a rich and skilled country such as Australia producing so much inequality, so much poverty, and so much that was shoddy and sub-standard.

On the night of 2 December, 1972, it looked as though he would have such a chance. For at the election for the House of Representatives and one half of the Senate on that day, the Labor Party was returned with a majority of nine members in the House of Representatives. He had said that Labor had three great aims: to promote equality, to involve the Australian people in the decision-making processes, and to liberate the talents and uplift the horizons of the Australian people. Labor, he had said, proposed 'to give a new life and a new meaning in this new nation to the touchstone of modern democracy—to liberty, equality, fraternity'. In the excitement of the first victory at the polls since 1946, and of 'the vision splendid' which Whitlam had presented in his brilliant electoral campaign, few paused to ask whether the conservatives, in collaboration with the Democratic Labor Party, would not use their majority in the Senate to defeat the high-minded aims of the Whitlam government.

With a wild ecstasy and relish, Whitlam plunged into the task of proving that a social-democratic government could achieve equality without promoting either servitude or mediocrity and that a majority in Parliament was sufficient to carry out such reforms. In that first month of office his government rec-ognized the government of the People's Republic as the sole legal government of China, ended the military intervention of Australia in the war in Vietnam, announced a more independent stance for Australia in foreign affairs, and abolished compulsory military service. He also announced his intention to introduce as soon as practicable those reforms in education and health care which were, in his mind, the cornerstone in the building of a genuine equality in Australia. Pre-school education was to be made available to every Australian child, Commonwealth spending on schools and teacher training was to be the fastest expanding sector of budget expenditure, fees at universities were to be abolished, a universal health insurance system was to be introduced, a prices justification tribunal was to be established, and land rights were to be granted to Aborigines—not just because their case was beyond argument but because all Australians were diminished so long as Aborigines were denied their rightful place in the community. The Labor government proposed to make some atonement for that wrong committed against the original tenants of the Australian wilderness. The Labor government would remove the vestiges of British colonialism in Australia and end once and for all the role of Australia as a colonial power in the south-west Pacific by granting independence to New Guinea. The Labor government would never support or even be indifferent to the shameful policies of the government of South Africa or the illegal *de facto* white government of Rhodesia. Labor in foreign policy, as in domestic affairs, would steer a course halfway between the American, Japanese, and West German camp for believers in free enterprise, and the Soviet camp for the engineers of human souls.

Within a year of winning the election of December 1972, that shadow all too familiar to social-democratic governments, whether in Australia, the United Kingdom, Germany, Sweden, Norway, France or New Zealand—the shadow between their conception and their performance—began to loom. The media, after welcoming the change of government rather as the citizens of Melbourne rejoice and are exceeding glad when a cool southerly wind blows through their city after days of a hot northerly, began to reflect the alarm of the conservative forces in society that Labor represented a threat to the established order. Labor, it was whispered, had already used the institutions of the state to effect a minor redistribution of wealth. The press, commercial radio, and television, ably assisted by the skilled dispensers of abuse, character assassination, and motive-questioning amongst the conservative politicians, portrayed a government of visionaries, idealists and reformers as at best inept administrators and at worst men who were not free from the odour of corruption.

The appointment of Senator Vincent Gair, of the Democratic Labor Party, on 14 March, 1974, as ambassador to the Republic of Ireland seemed to lend weight to those who had quite different motives for blackening the reputation of the Labor government. On 5 March Gair had intimated to Senator O'Byrne, the President of the Senate, that he would be interested in a diplomatic post. Whitlam, believing that this was the chance to obtain a majority in the Senate, jumped at the suggestion. But the opposition bent political technicalities to their purpose and the scheme misfired. Gair got his diplomatic post, but Labor did not get their majority in the Senate. Whitlam was left looking like a man who had muddied his high reputation in the waters of political expediency.

Sniffing a great change in the political wind, the leaders of the Liberal party in the House of Representatives and the Senate believed it might be possible to use their numbers in the Senate to force the Labor government to an early election. The new leader of the Liberal party in the House of Representatives, Billy Mackie Snedden, knew that an early success at the polls was the only sure way to protect himself against the back-stabbers in his own party. Snedden had much to commend him to the people of Australia. Born on 31 December 1926, into a working-class family in Perth, Western Australia, he had risen from the occupation of newspaper boy to the Leader of Her Majesty's Opposition in the Parliament of the Commonwealth of Australia. He had achieved this without losing touch with the people from whom he sprang, or prostituting his talents to the bitch goddess of greatness. Nature had not endowed him with the intellectual power or the charisma of a Whitlam. Nature had given him kindness and a generosity of spirit which ensured him a warm place in the hearts of both supporters and opponents, but this probably robbed him of the ruthlessness essential to survival in the bear-pit of political life in contemporary Australia.

By April 1974 the Senate had ceased to act as a house of review and had taken on the role of the defender of the established order of society against the Labor government. They had twice rejected ten bills passed by the House of Representatives, all of which Whitlam claimed his government had a clear mandate from the people to bring into law. The Senate also rejected nine other bills, including the national health insurance plan (known as Medibank), which was one of the foundation stones of Labor's grand design to introduce a genuine equality in Australia. Senator Reginald Withers, whose face betrayed his own fascination with the numbers game rather than any interest in using political devices to make life easier or happier for the great mass of the people, had announced as long ago as April 1973 that his party in the Senate had 'embarked on a course to bring about a House of Representatives election'. He moved in the Senate on 10 April that because of maladministration the Senate would not grant this government funds until it agreed to submit itself to the people. From that time Withers and his supporters were to hammer relentlessly this theme of maladministration.

Whitlam and his colleagues, deeming the obstruction by the Senate amounted to a 'failure to pass' bills, asked Governor-General Sir Paul Hasluck for a double dissolution on 10 April, 1974. This was granted. In the campaign for the election on 18 May, 1974, Whitlam made moving appeals to the intelligence and idealism of the Australian people as well as to their sense of fair play. Snedden concentrated on Labor's failure to halt inflation and on the charge of inept administration. The power men in the Liberal party hinted at a decline in public and private morality under Labor, as though the hand-out programs of Labor in health, education, and Aboriginal affairs, and the more vulgar manifestations of the age of greed and titillation, were the fruits of an extravagant program of government spending. Labor was returned to power with a majority of five in the House of Representatives, but still with a minority in the Senate.

For a few months after the election Whitlam and his ministers had a brief respite from the campaign of vilification while the leader of the Liberal party engaged in an unseemly fight over the leadership. Ever since his failure in the May election, Snedden had been walking round like a man wondering whether he still had the numbers to survive another challenge to his position. Senator Withers was prepared to wait until such time as the Whitlam Government presented him with an opportunity to make a more effective use of his numbers in the Senate to destroy a government with a majority in the lower house.

In the deceptive calm which followed the storms of the electoral campaign, Whitlam offered the position of Governor-General to Sir John Kerr, the Chief Justice of New South Wales, who accepted. As the son of a boilermaker in Balmain and as a man who was said to be in sympathy with the aims of the Whitlam government to bring more abundant life to the great mass of people in Australia, Sir John could be trusted, it was believed, not to allow the office of Governor-General to be used as another source of power for the conservatives in Australia.

By the end of 1974 the men who exercised power in the Liberal Party had reluctantly come to the conclusion that Snedden lacked the capacity to handle Whitlam in the House of Representatives. The problem was to find a man who could both match Whitlam in the House and win votes in the electorate. In the eyes of many, John Malcolm Fraser seemed to be that man. Yet whenever a move was made, Fraser was quick to profess his support for the leader of the parliamentary Liberal Party. As late as 6 February, 1975, Fraser told the *Financial Review:* 'Bill Snedden has my full support.' Yet in the middle of March, when Andrew Peacock at last succeeded in bringing the issue out into the public gaze, Fraser declared his candidacy, giving as his justification his aim of restoring the chances of toppling the Labor government. At a meeting of the parliamentary members of the Liberal Party on 21 March, Fraser was elected as the new leader. Snedden seemed to be walking into the night. No one knew then quite what use Fraser would make of the position he had coveted for such a long time.

Fraser was an enigma; he had never worn his heart on his sleeve. Endowed by nature with much greater ability than his enemies conceded to him, he seemed to be one of those tormented men who had dedicated their lives to greatness, only to find that such greatness was as rare as catching the huge fish he dreamt would come one day into his net. Greatness warred eternally with the power to win the other things he craved. He was born on 21 May, 1930, into a family which belonged to the country gentry in Australia. He was educated at Melbourne Grammar School and Magdalen College, Oxford, at both of which institutions he was instructed in the arguments and steeped in the values of the class into which he was born. From his experience in England he picked up the conviction that it was meet and right to impose the morality of his own class on every member of society, as well as the belief that the members of his own class had an inherent right to rule.

Like most politicians with a taste and a great natural talent for leadership, he was a bundle of contradictions. Sincerely believing in the right of every man to decide for himself, he nevertheless required every member of his team to consult him before making a statement in public. His attitude to the Soviet Union would have won the approval of every right-wing political group in the western world; his attitude to China was indistinguishable from that of his sworn enemies in the Australian Labor movement. In many areas of public policy he spoke like a man determined to put the clock back. In Commonwealth-State relations he promised, if in office, to introduce 'a new federalism', which seemed to portend a return to the days before 1941. Yet on the question of South Africa and Rhodesia his opposition to apartheid and white minority rule was as uncompromising as any propounded by his Labor opponents. All in all he seemed most at ease when restating the slogans of conservatives about efficient administration and pruning government expenditure. The words which came most easily to his mouth were the time-honoured themes of con-

Prime Minister Malcolm Fraser campaigning at the December 1975 elections.

servatives—words such as 'decency', 'proper', 'good government', and 'the public interest'. Like all his predecessors in the conservative party, he thought that what he believed to be true and right for his own class coincided with the best interests of Australia.

Not long after becoming the leader of the Liberal Party, and therefore leader of the opposition in the Commonwealth Parliament, Fraser came to believe that the behaviour of some members of the Labor government was providing him with just that sense of moral indignation which he required to justify his own ambition and desire for power. He was able to convince first himself and then a very large number of Australians that the behaviour of certain members of the Labor government amounted to a scandal. In an attempt to raise standards within the public service, Whitlam appointed John Menadue to be Secretary of the Department of Prime Minister and Cabinet, and his own secretary, Dr Peter Wilenski, as Secretary of the Department of Labour and Immigration. Fraser and his men began to talk of 'favouritism', of 'jobs for the boys', and of the 'politicization of the public service'. There was worse to follow.

In November 1974 Dr Cairns, the deputy leader of the Labor Party, appointed Mrs David Ditchburn, known to the Australian public as Junie Morosi, as his office co-ordinator. Fraser and his men hinted that no man should use a high public office to promote the career of anyone with whom he enjoyed a very close friendship. By the use of the well-known methods of repetition and innuendo, Fraser and his men converted public opinion from one of admiration for a giant in the campaign against involvement in Vietnam into anger against a man whose conduct would not bear examination.

At the same time the Minister for Minerals and Energy, Reginald Francis Xavier Connor, put forward a plan to enable the Australian government to buy back much of the mineral wealth their predecessors had bartered to American and Japanese companies in exchange for flooding the Australian market with those consumer goods young and old alike deemed to be essential ingre-

A section of the trans-Australian railway across the Nullarbor Plain.

dients for a happy life. He wanted to stop foreigners from grabbing the mineral resources of Australia. He believed in the words of the old Australian poem:

> Give me men to match my mountains
> Give me men to match my plains
> Men with freedom in their vision
> And creation in their brains.

Connor was a man with a vision of the greatness of Australia and Australians when they would be liberated from the moral infamies of capitalist society—when they would have ceased to be the victims of the economic imperialism of the Americans and the Japanese.

The Connor plan was to raise a loan in the Arab world. This meant three things: the Australian government going outside the traditional sources of supply of loan moneys; the Australian government obtaining the approval of the Loan Council to raise such a loan, unless it was for some temporary purpose; the Australian government establishing relations with a financier who enjoyed the confidence of the men with money to lend in the Arab world.

In November 1974 the head of the Department of Minerals and Energy, Lenox Hewitt, authorized Tirath Khemlani, a financier with his headquarters in London, to act as an intermediary in the raising of money in the Arab world. Khemlani promised to get results 'in a few days'. Carried away by the enthusiasm aroused by such a promise and the vision splendid of Australia once again belonging to the Australians, on 14 December, 1974, the Executive Council authorized Connor to raise a 4,000 million US dollar loan 'for temporary purposes'. On 6 March, 1975, the Executive Council authorized J. F. Cairns to borrow 500 million US dollars overseas. On the following day he signed a letter to a Melbourne financier, G. Harris, who was also president of the Carlton Football Club, authorizing him to raise money overseas and offering him a once-only brokerage of one and a half per cent.

In June 1975, Philip Lynch, deputy leader of the opposition, who had been sniffing around the corridors of power for months for evidence of indecency, impropriety, or even corruption in the transaction of these loans, asked Cairns in the House of Representatives if he had given Harris such a letter. Cairns, in good faith, at first denied but later had to acknowledge there was such a letter. The opposition, sensing a chance to compound the rumours current about the private life of Cairns with corruption in financial matters, mounted a campaign of vilification and abuse in the press, radio, television, and parliament. Their aim was to convince the Australian people that the government of reformers and visionaries which they had elected in December 1972 and re-elected in May 1974 had degenerated into a band of inept administrators, financial bunglers, and men who had prostituted their high office for the indulgence of their private passions.

As though to provide evidence for this vilification, which had been conceived in the minds of men who believed in their self-appointed mission to govern Australia, the Australian economy, like the economies of other capitalist societies, had slumped into a grave crisis. The inflation rate, which had stood at 4.5 per cent in December 1972 in that halcyon moment when Whitlam seemed about to end the years of unleavened bread, had grown to 14.4 per cent by June 1974, and 16.9 per cent by June 1975. Unemployment had increased from 100,000 in December 1972 to 270,400 in June 1975. It seemed that Labor could not make capitalist society work. With a fanaticism which endeared him to his supporters, and branded him for ever in the eyes of Labor as a man interested only in power, Fraser kept up day after day, week after week, and month after month his attack on Whitlam as the head of the worst government since federation.

To the dismay of those who had believed that the Whitlam government possibly offered the final chance for Australia to show the world that it was capable of building a society free of the evils or errors in both capitalist and communist societies, the Labor leaders stopped referring to the vision which had sustained them and brought them victory in 1972 and stooped to debate the issues at the low level chosen by the opposition. So a moment of hope and promise in the brief history of European civilization in the ancient, uncouth continent seemed in danger of disappearing, as the conservatives and Labor engaged in an exchange of abuse about which party was the more competent in making capitalist society work.

In October 1975, just as the Whitlam government seemed to be recovering from the nadir in public esteem brought about by all the public abuse of their methods of handling the loans proposal, and by the behaviour of some of their ministers, the opposition again succeeded in proving that Connor had continued to conduct negotiations with Tirath Khemlani after his authority to do so had been revoked. Believing victory at the polls to be what Australians call a 'dead cert.', Fraser and his colleagues in the Liberal Party decided to advise the Liberal and Country Party senators to defer consideration of the Supply bill. This would force Whitlam to advise the Governor-General to dissolve the House of Representatives. Whitlam decided to tough it out in the belief that some Liberal Party senators would not use their constitutional power to defer a Supply bill and so starve the government into forcing an election for the lower house. When, after weeks of tension, neither government nor opposition showed any desire to compromise, Governor-General Sir John Kerr used his power under the Federal Constitution to appoint and dismiss ministers, and summarily dismissed the Whitlam Government on 11 November, 1975.

In the eyes of most conservatives the Governor-General had courageously saved Australian society from a government which seemed, in their eyes, to be bent on the destruction of the very foundations of civilized behaviour in the community. In the eyes of the supporters of Labor, the Governor-General was and always would be guilty of an act of treachery against the friends of a lifetime; he had also used the powers of his high office to serve the interests of a political party. Whatever the verdict of the electors on the policies and behaviour of the Whitlam government, nothing could ever atone for such treachery; nor would it protect the Governor-General from the undying hostility of Labor. The conservatives, in their lust for power, had connived at ripping the mask off the neutrality of the Crown.

To the anger of those who had seen the Labor government as possibly being the last hope for Australia to take a step forward by the method of the ballot-box rather than the use of force, Fraser and his followers in the Liberal-Country Party coalition spoke as though when in office they would find themselves like receivers in bankruptcy rather than inheritors of the great creative work of the Labor government. They spoke of their intention to slash government expenditure, to reduce inflation as a prelude to a consequential decline in unemployment, to restore the powers of the States to control their own affairs, to deprive all 'bludgers' of the opportunity of receiving unemployment benefits, and, in general, to act in what they called the 'national interest'. The appeal did not fall on deaf ears. At the election on 13 December, 1975, the Liberal-Country Party coalition was returned with a record majority in the House of Representatives and a working majority in the Senate. Once again the Australian electorate had demonstrated the truth that their history had fashioned them as sound conservatives: in a choice between the *status quo* and a mild change, they had opted very clearly for a conservative way of life.

In the years after the dramatic events of November 1975 the temper of public life did not change. Governor-General Sir John Kerr was hounded unmercifully by his opponents until it was clear that whatever the merits or demerits of his public actions he would never again enjoy the confidence of that 40 per cent of the population which was committed permanently to the Labor side. In December 1977 he resigned from his high office, still defended by the conservatives as a saviour of much they believed to be worthwhile, and vilified by Labor as a man who had betrayed the cause of the people. He was replaced as Governor-General by Sir Zelman Cowen, who immediately set about the Sisyphean task of restoring the reputation of the Crown for neutrality which Sir John's actions and subsequent behaviour had so gravely damaged.

In the meantime the Fraser government set about the task of fulfilling their election promise to restore sanity and probity to public life. They cut expenditure in the public sector of the economy. They carried out a major reform in the taxation system. They created an industrial relations bureau in an endeavour to improve the relations between capital and labour. They managed slowly to reduce the rate of inflation to just below double figures. With unemployment they were not so successful. The number rose from 278,400 in December 1975 to 439,200 in January 1980. They also had ideas of reducing the number of people dependent on government for their means of existence. Fraser himself stuck to his point that a 'hand-out culture' was both degrading and corrupting.

To test the response of the electorate to the government's attempts to dismantle some of what Labor had built, and to their efforts to restore stability to government finance, Fraser decided to call an election in December 1977. This time the electorate heard only a muted voice from the Labor leader, Gough Whitlam. The man who in November 1972 had electrified his followers with slogans about liberty, equality, and fraternity had been reduced by the never-ceasing abuse from his opponents, and the back-stabbing from within his own Party, to a man who was promising that this time he would be as efficient as Fraser. Once again the electorate chose the conservatives to govern Australia. Once again, when confronted with a choice between the old way of life and a step forward, a majority of Australians opted for the established order. With that dignity and majesty which had helped him to tower over supporters and opponents alike in his great creative years, Whitlam resigned from the position of leader of the Australian Labor Party. In his place his colleagues elected William Hayden, who promptly used his skill as a debater to restore the image of Labor with the electorate as a Party which could manage efficiently and justly the affairs of a modern bourgeois state.

Nothing Fraser and his government could do could stem the erosion of the old way of life. Consumerism had already corrupted the work ethic in which he believed. The sickness of society at large was too profound to be cured by or even glossed over by old-fashioned and anachronistic conservative talk about hard work and discipline. As the conservatives went on repeating the slogans of yesteryear, while the moneychangers again reaped their harvest, the serious-minded began to call in question the future of civilization in the ancient continent. Ever since the beginning of European civilization in January 1788, Australia had been fashioned to be a pioneer in the period of bourgeois democracy, and a conservative in the era of the people's democracies. In Australia power belonged neither to visionaries nor to women, but to ruthless and tough men. Throughout its history its people had been taught to equate material success with happiness, and material achievement with public virtue.

Ever since he had come to power in November 1975 Fraser had used his vast political talents and prodigious industry in an attempt to reduce inflation.

By the middle of 1982 it was clear that these efforts had not achieved the results the Prime Minister and his coalition colleagues had hoped for. The inflation rate was again in double figures, the number of the unemployed rose from 334,800 in 1975 to 674,000 at the end of 1982, and the interest rate had risen to 14.5 per cent.

The sickness of society had not been cured by the Fraser prescription: persuading or cajoling the working classes to emulate the ancient virtues of the yeomanry. Seemingly unaware of or uninterested in the warning of the prophet that 'Where goods abound parasites abound', more and more Australians surrendered to consumerism. The Mr Bigs in the drug world erected their 'grass castles', the finance companies and the multinationals erected more and more skyscrapers in Melbourne and Sydney; the old dignified city of Perth was almost lost to sight in the new concrete jungle; fun parlours multiplied and the breathtaking beauty of the southern Queensland coast was swallowed up in the tinsel consumerism of the moneychangers. At the same time the number of people living in real poverty increased year by year. By the end of 1982 in a population of 15.28 million, over two million were below the poverty line. The condition of the Aborigines underlined the contradiction between the affluence of some and the squalor and degradation of the ones for whom capitalist society had no role.

As the economic and moral crisis of society deepened, Fraser seemed to lose his great gift for sniffing the direction of the political wind. Frustrated by his

Robert Hawke, elected Prime Minister of Australia 5 March, 1983.

lack of a majority in the Senate, on 3 February 1983 he asked the Governor-General for a double dissolution. From that moment things went wrong for Fraser. With that dignity and magnanimity which had characterized his creative contribution to public life, Hayden announced his resignation from the leadership of the Australian Labor Party. He had put loyalty to the party above personal ambition. On the same day Robert James Lee Hawke announced that he would be a candidate for the leadership of the Labor Party, and that he understood that he would be the only candidate. By late afternoon on that day Fraser had his double dissolution; he also had to fight a most formidable opponent.

Hawke was already widely known as Australia's most charismatic politician. From the moment he was confirmed as leader of the Labor Party excitement and hope were revived amongst those who for years had fretted at the spread of dullness and despair in Australia. Hawke was an enigma. At times he spoke and behaved like an Ishmael: a wild man who raised his hand against every man because, he believed, every man's hand was raised against him. At other times he spoke like a populist, a people's man who wanted everyone to take a seat at the great banquet of life. He was both a power man and a people's prophet, a pragmatist and a missionary. He was born on 9 December 1929, the second son of a clergyman, and educated at state schools and the universities of Western Australia and Oxford. He had learnt his politics in the rough-and-tumble of the Australian Council of Trade Unions where he had a meteoric rise to power as President in 1970. Some believed that the experience had typecast him as a brash local boy who had made good but had nothing else to commend him except the charismatic smile, overweening ambition and his success as a 'fixer'. But by 1982 the suffering he had endured as the reward for the wild years seemed to have increased both his wisdom and his understanding.

During the election campaign he rose to great heights. He spoke of his aim of 'bringing Australians together'. He spoke about 'the kids of despair', of kids using drugs, and of the break-up of family life in Australia. He talked of his hope of creating a better Australia, a country in which there was genuine equality of opportunity. Women wept when they heard him, old men began again to dream dreams, and the young, if not to see visions, then at least to entertain hope again. By contrast Malcolm Fraser played on the fears of those who had a financial stake in society and asked Australians to give a vote of confidence in the record of his government.

On 5 March 1983 the Australian Labor Party won a resounding victory, having a majority of twenty-five in the House of Representatives. Once again in the history of Australia a Labor government had an opportunity to prove that a majority of Australians had a capacity for better things. In the moment of victory Hawke was magnanimous; in the moment of defeat Fraser was dignified. For a moment that face, which had always been presented as the external sign of an inner courage and resource, cracked. For the man also had a private face which he rarely risked allowing others to see. Hawke talked of consensus; Hawke spoke as a believer and a lover. The people had accepted the message. By contrast, the intellectuals and the prophets of doom went on lamenting that, as in other western countries, there was now no one to listen to, no one with anything to say.

Hawke believed he had something to say. He believed Labor could give capitalist society a human face; he believed Labor could administer the affairs of the bourgeois state more efficiently than the Liberal and the National (formerly the Country Party) Parties; he believed Labor's policies of modest social reform would not necessarily be accompanied by the uproar, excitement and enthusiasm of the Whitlam years. Whitlam had dreamt a great dream: Hawke believed Labor could reduce unemployment, inflation, and the number of industrial disputes.

Hawke also believed in consensus between the government, the trade unions, and the employers on a prices and incomes policy. In April 1983 he presided over a meeting in Parliament House of representatives of the Commonwealth, the States, the trade unions and the employers' and professional groups. Those present — save Joh Bjelke Petersen, the National Party Premier of Queensland — endorsed a 53-clause communiqué which outlined the principles to be observed by the parties in the implementation of the government's economic and social program. This covered wage fixation, budgetary and marketing policy, taxation policy, industry protection, overseas borrowing, and the recognition of the need for business profitability. It also acknowledged the need for government programs to help disadvantaged groups such as the unemployed, women, and Aborigines.

Within six months Hawke's policies began to bear fruit: the rise in the numbers of unemployed was halted, the rate of inflation declined, and the number of industrial disputes diminished. Labor had at last proved that it could give capitalist society a human face while administering efficiently and economically the affairs of the bourgeois state.

With the confidence of a man who had succeeded where his predecessors such as Scullin and Whitlam had failed, Hawke again appealed to the electors for their approval on 1 December, 1984. The government was returned with a reduced majority. Some attributed his success to luck. He had, it was said, the luck of a batsman in cricket who is dropped before he has scored and then goes on to make a century. Some said the end of the drought and the world economic revival played a more decisive part than the policies, industry and panache of Hawke and the members of his government. Some said the divisions in the ranks of his opponents, the feuding between the 'wets' and the 'dries' on fiscal policy, and the unseemly struggles for the leadership of the opposition prepared the ground for the second Labor victory. Whatever the causes, Hawke had shown that Labor had become a successful machine for the capture of political power. So far Labor had not shown that it was in origin a band of 'inspired idealists' who believed in the capacity of the Australian people to 'steal fire from heaven'.

The revolution in the Australian way of life has occurred outside politics. The revolutions in transport and communications, and the booms in minerals, have ended the material backwardness and isolation — the prime cause of the inferiority complex, and the grovelling to the English. Being mistaken for an Englishman or an Englishwoman has gradually ceased to be the ambition of even the 'comfortable classes' in Australia.

After the disappearance of God, Australians had clung all the more firmly to the Judaic-Christian morality. For decades Australians had had a morality without a faith. By the 1960s the horrors of the First World War, compounded by the holocaust of the Jewish people during the Second World War, and the dropping of atomic bombs on Hiroshima and Nagasaki in August 1945, had weakened belief in either a benevolent, caring God, or the capacity of human beings to build a better society. This time the puritan morality was gradually dropped. In the 1960s a revolution occurred in the way of life. Nude bathing, nudity on stage and screen, the use of four letter words on stage, screen, radio, television and the printed page, the contraceptive pill, and the demand for the repeal of laws making homosexual behaviour between adults a criminal offence, were all part of this revolution.

The decline of faith begat nihilism, and nihilism begat hedonism. It looked as though in the contest between Mammon and 'millennial Eden' Mammon had won. The dreams of all those who had migrated to the great south land had evaporated. The Aborigine had been corrupted and debased by contact with the white man. The voices of the Catholic who had spoken of a land dedicated to the Holy Spirit, the Dutch Protestants who had called for the discovery of a land that would yield 'uncommonly large profit', and the pleas of the followers of the Enlightenment with their faith in human perfectibility, had all dropped from a roar to a whisper. Mammon had won: Mammon had infected the ancient continent of Australia. The dreams of humanity had ended in an age of ruins.

But there are signs that the children of this generation may prove wiser either than the children of God or the children of light. The Aborigines have called on the white people to redress an ancient wrong: the Aborigines have rediscovered the source of their strength in their relationship with the land and the spirit of the place. Some of the young people, inspired by the wisdom of the old, have combined to protect the fragile beauty and the resources of the ancient continent against the bulldozer of the developers and the beneficiaries of the prevailing greed and titillation culture. The giant of British philistinism in Australia has received a mortal blow. The shackles of the old puritan morality have been loosened.

Australians have liberated themselves from the fate of being second-rate Europeans. Australians have begun to contribute to the never-ending conversation of humanity on the meaning of life, and the means of wisdom and understanding. So far no one has described the phoenix bird which will arise from the ashes of an age of ruins. No one has risked prophesying whether an age of ruins will be the prelude to the coming of the barbarians or to taking a seat at the great banquet of life. The life-deniers and the straiteners have been swept into the dustbin of human history. Now is the time for the life affirmers and the enlargers to show whether they have anything to say, whether they have any food for the great hungers of humanity.

A NOTE ON SOURCES

1. GENERAL REFERENCE

D. H. Pike, ed., *Australian Dictionary of Biography,* 10 vols. Melbourne, Melbourne University Press, 1966—86.

Australian Encyclopedia, 6 vols. Sydney, Grolier Society of Australia, 1977.

Percival Serle, *Dictionary of Australian Biography,* 2 vols. Sydney, Angus and Robertson, 1949.

2. DOCUMENTS

Manning Clark, *Sources of Australian History.* London and New York, Oxford University Press, 1957.

Frank Crowley, *Modern Australia in Documents, 1901—70,* 2 vols. Melbourne, Wren Publishing Pty Ltd, 1973.

Kathleen Fitzpatrick, *Australian Explorers.* London and New York, Oxford University Press, 1958.

3. GENERAL HISTORIES

Manning Clark, *A History of Australia* (5 vols. to date). Melbourne, Melbourne University Press; London and New York, Cambridge University Press, 1962—81.

R. Maxwell Crawford, *Australia.* London, Hutchinson and Co.; New York, Longmans Green, 1952.

Frank Crowley, ed., *A New History of Australia.* Melbourne, W. Heinemann, 1974.

Gordon Greenwood, ed., *Australia: A Social and Political History.* Sydney, Angus & Robertson; New York, Frederick Praeger, 1955.

W. K. Hancock, *Australia.* London, Ernest Benn, 1930; New York, Charles Scribner's Sons, 1931.

Humphrey McQueen, *A New Britannia.* Melbourne, Pelican Books, 1970.

D. H. Pike, *Australia: The Quiet Continent.* London, Cambridge University Press, 1962.

Geoffrey Sawer, *Australian Federal Politics and Law.* Melbourne, Melbourne University Press, 1956; London and New York, Cambridge University Press, 1957.

Alan G. L. Shaw, *The Story of Australia.* London, Faber & Faber; New York, Roy Publishers, 1955.

Russel Ward, *Australia*. Englewood Cliffs, New Jersey, Prentice Hall, 1965.

——, *A Nation for a Continent*. Melbourne, Heinemann Educational Books, 1977.

Alan Watt, *The Evolution of Australian Foreign Policy, 1938—1965*. London and New York, Cambridge University Press, 1968.

4. ECONOMIC HISTORY
N. G. Butlin, *Investment in Australian Economic Growth, 1861—1900*. London and New York, Cambridge University Press, 1963.

Brian Fitzpatrick, *The British Empire in Australia*. Melbourne, Melbourne University Press, 1940; London and New York, Oxford University Press, 1941.

——, *British Imperialism and Australia*. London, Geo. Allen & Unwin, 1939.

Edward O. C. Shann, *An Economic History of Australia*. London, Cambridge University Press; New York, The Macmillan Company, 1930.

5. SOCIAL HISTORY
Margaret Kiddle, *Men of Yesterday*. Melbourne, Melbourne University Press, 1961; London and New York, Cambridge University Press, 1962.

Russel B. Ward, *The Australian Legend*. London and New York, Oxford University Press, 1958.

6. THE ARTS
Robert Boyd, *Australia's Home: Its Origins, Builders and Occupiers*. Melbourne, Melbourne University Press; London and New York, Cambridge University Press, 1952.

Henry M. Green, *A History of Australian Literature*, 2 vols.   Sydney, Angus & Robertson, 1961.

Cecil Hadgraft, *Australian Literature*. London, William Heinemann, 1960.

Geoffrey Serle, *From Deserts the Prophets Come*. Melbourne, Heinemann, 1973.

Bernard Smith, *Australian Painting, 1788—1960*. Melbourne, Melbourne University Press, 1962.

A view of the Parramatta River from Windmill Hill, Sydney.

SOURCES OF ILLUSTRATIONS

The Age Page 236.

Australian Information Service Page 227 and page 241.

Australian National Gallery and Sidney Nolan Page 6: Burning at Glenrowan, 1946-47, by S. Nolan, an enamel on composition board.

Australian National University and Sidney Nolan Back endpaper: Riverbend, by S. Nolan, oil on hardboard, 1966.

Australian War Memorial Page 170: H11577; page 182: A3825; and page 185: E833.

Canberra Times Page 231 (centre right): 6 Jan. 1976.

Cinema International Corporation Page 203.

Cinesound Productions Page 204.

Dixson Library Page 122: The colonized, by S. T. Gill.

Max Dupain Back jacket; page 36; page 39; page 46; page 190; and page 235.

John Fairfax and Sons Ltd Page 228; page 230 (bottom left); page 231 (top right); page 231 (bottom centre); page 231 (bottom right) and page 248.

The Herald, Melbourne Page 218: 4 Dec. 1980; page 222; and page 230 (bottom right).

Mitchell Library Page 38 (top right); and page 42.

Museums and Art Galleries of the Northern Territory Pages 13 and 34.

David Moore Front endpaper.

National Gallery of Victoria Page 226: Collins Street 5pm, by J. Brack, oil on canvas, 1955; and page 240: Irrigation Lake, Wimmera, by A. Boyd, resin and tempera on masonite.

National Library of Australia (RNK   Rex Nan Kivell Collection) Page 2: Nouvelle-Hollande: Nelle Galles du Sud — Vue d'une Ville de Sydney, Capitale de Colonies Anglaises aux Terres Australes . . . (1803), drawn by C. A. Lesueur, copper engraving in Peron, F. A., *Voyage de decouvertes aux Terres Australes* . . ., Paris, 1807, RNK; page 8: Arthur Phillip Esq., by F. Wheatley, engraved by W. Sherwin, in *The Voyage of Governor Phillip* . . .; page 10: A canoe and natives of Mulgrave's range, by R. Cleveley, engraved by T. Medland, in *The Voyage of Governor Phillip to Botany Bay*, London, 1790; page 14: Captain James Cook FRS, by J. Webber, mezzotint; page 15: Native sepulchre; page 18: Hump back'd Maria, a female native well known about Sydney, by T. R. Browne, watercolour, RNK; page 20: Scene in a Sydney street, *c.* 1828, by C. Rodius, lithograph in his *Natives of NSW*, Sydney, 1834, RNK; page 21: E. Searle Coll.; page 22: A view of the governor's house at Rose Hill, in the township of Parramatta, by E. Dayes, engraved by J. Heath, RNK; page 24: Landing at Botany Bay, etching (hand-coloured), 1786, RNK; page 26: A view of Sydney cove, drawn by E. Dayes, engraved by F. Dukes, 1804, RNK; page 27: The residence of John McArthur Esqre near Parramatta, New South Wales, by

J. Lycett, aquatint in his *Views in Australia and Van Diemen's Land*, London, 1824; page 28: Parramatta, New South Wales, by J. Lycett, aquatint in his *Views in Australia and Van Diemen's Land*, RNK; page 29: Nouvelle-Hollande: Nouvelle Galles du Sud. Vue de la partie meridionale de la Ville de Sydney Capitale des Colonies Anglaises aux Terres Australes . . .(1803), drawn by C. A Lesueur, copper engraving in *Voyage de decouvertes aux Terres Australes* . . ., RNK; page 31: Major Johnston with Quarter Master Laycock, one sergeant and twenty five privates of ye New South Wales Corps defeats two hundred and sixty armed rebels, 5th March 1804, watercolour, RNK; page 33: A native family of New South Wales sitting down on an English settler's farm, watercolour, RNK; page 38 (top left): engraving in E. C. Booth, *Australia Illustrated*, London, 1873; page 39 (top): Military barracks, Sydney, drawn by C. S. Hext, engraved by C. Hutchins, hand-coloured lithograph, RNK; page 40: In W. Joy, *The Explorers*, Shakespeare Head Press, Sydney, 1964; page 41: John Oxley, by Lawson Balfour, oil, owned by Historic Memorials Committee; page 44: Governor Davey's proclamation to the Aborigines, 1816, coloured lithograph; page 48: View of Sydney, on the south side of Norfolk Island, drawn by E. Dayes, line engraving by W. Lowry, RNK; page 50: Mrs Macquarie's seat, Govent domain, Sydney, NS Wales, lithograph by A. Earle in his *Views of New South Wales and Van Diemen's Land*, vol. 2, London, 1830, RNK; page 52: Lady Darling with her daughter and son, 1825, by J. Linnell, oil, RNK; page 56: Two kangaroos in a landscape, 1819, by J. W. Lewin, watercolour, RNK; page 58: Florishing (sic) state of the Swan River thing, hand-coloured etching, RNK; page 61: William Charles Wentworth, by F. Rodway, oil, owned by Historic Memorials Committee; page 62: The entrance of Port Jackson, and part of the town of Sydney, New South Wales (detail), by J. Taylor, coloured aquatint, 1823, RNK; page 66: Skirmish between bush-rangers and constables, Illawarra, watercolour, RNK; page 70: *Illustrated London News*; page 72: Edward Gibbon Wakefield, drawn by A. Wivell, stipple engraving by B. Holl (sic), RNK; page 74: *Illustrated Australian News*, 24 March 1875; page 74: Leading from stocks to Paxton's lode, Burra Burra mine, April 12, 1847, by S. T. Gill, watercolour; page 75: The Kapunda copper mine, by B. T. Solly, in *South Australia and Its Mines*, 1846, RNK; page 76 (bottom): Caroline Chisholm, hand-coloured lithograph, RNK; page 77: E-migration or A flight of *fair* game, hand-coloured lithograph by A. Ducôtés, 1832, RNK; page 79: A government jail gang, Sydney, NS Wales, drawn by A. Earle, lithograph in his *Views of New South Wales and Van Diemen's Land* . . ., RNK; page 80: Vue Generale D'Hobart-Town, drawn by L. Lebreton, tinted lithograph in *Voyage au Pole Sud et dans l'Oceanie Sur les Corvettes l'Astrolabe* . . ., vol. 2, Paris, 1846, RNK; page 82: Bushmen watering horses in the desert of Australia, by G. Hamilton, hand-coloured etching, *c.* 1840, RNK; page 83: An exploring party looking for a sheep run, coloured lithograph, RNK; page 84: Dipping sheep, coloured lithograph, RNK; page 86; page 87; page 92: Aquatic fete on the Governor's domain, Sydney, 1840, by W. Gosford, oil, RNK; page 94: The old and new home stations, 1870, drawn by N. Chevalier, engraved by A. Wilmore, in E. C. Booth, *Australia Illustrated*, RNK; page 90: Panshanger near Longford, Tasmania, 1918, by W. Hardy Wilson, pencil drawing; page 95: Cottage in Davey Street [Hobart, Tasmania], by W. Hardy Wilson, pencil and French crayon drawing; page 96: *Van Diemen's Land Anniversary and Hobart Town Almanack for 1831*, Hobart, 1831; page 97: Attack on a settler's hut, possibly by J. Bonwick, watercolour, in his *Last of the Tasmanians*, London, 1870, RNK; page 103: From the verandah of an Australian station, showing river, watercolour, RNK; page 104: Gold buyer. The market price discussed. Eagle Hawk, by S. T. Gill, coloured lithograph, RNK; page 106; page 106: Mr E. H.

Hargraves, The gold discoverer of Australia, by T. T. Balcombe, hand-coloured lithograph, RNK; page 108: The invalid digger, in J. Sherer, *The Gold Finder of Australia*, London, 1853; page 110: The Government escort and mail containing the gold, arrival at the Treasury, Sydney, by M. Claxton, pen and wash drawing, RNK; page 112: My new chum mate, watercolour, RNK; page 113: *Illustrated Australian News*; page 114: in W. B. Withers, *The History of Ballarat*, Ballarat, 1887, RNK; page 116: Forest Creek, Mount Alexander diggings, by S. T. Gill, coloured lithograph, RNK; page 120: Return of Burke and Wills to Cooper's Creek, drawn by N. Chevalier, engraved by J. C. Armytage, in E. C. Booth, *Australia Illustrated*, RNK; page 124: *Australasian Sketcher*, 25 Dec. 1875; page 125: A primrose from England, drawn by E. W. J. Hopley, lithograph by J. R. Dickens, 1856, RNK; page 125: *Australasian Sketcher*; page 126: A bush race in Darling Downs, Australia, by S. A. Lindsey, gouache wash drawing, RNK; page 128; page 129; page 129: *Australasian Sketcher*, 10 June 1876; page 131: Victoria Tannery, near Melbourne, by T. Ham, steel engraving, in his *Illustrated Australian Magazine*, Melbourne, Nov. 1850, RNK; page 131; page 132: *Illustrated Sydney News*, 15 June 1867; page 132: Claremont House, the residence of Mr George Bashford and family at Limestone, near Ipswich, Queensland, April 1881, by C. Hirst, pen, ink and watercolour; page 136: Natives stalking emus, by W. F. E. Liardet, watercolour, RNK; page 137: [Kangaroo hunt, on horseback], watercolour, RNK; page 142: [Street scene, 1879], by C. Marchard, oil on canvas, RNK; page 142: *Illustrated Australian News*, 7 June 1879; page 142: *Australasian Sketcher*, July 1883; page 143; page 143; page 143; page 144; page 146: *Australasian Sketcher*, 22 Jan. 1876; page 146; page 147; page 148: E. C. Booth, *Australia Illustrated*; page 150: *The Worker*, 30 Sept. 1893; page 150: Melbourne *Punch*, 2 June 1888; page 151: *Australasian Sketcher*, 4 June 1883; page 152; page 153; page 155: *Illustrated Australian News*, 1 May 1889; page 157: *Illustrated Australian News*, 21 Aug. 1886; page 159: G. Reid, *My Reminiscences*, London, 1917; page 161; page 164: *Australian Star*, 20 July 1895; page 169: *Illustrated Australian News*, Nov. 1888; page 169; page 172; page 172; page 173; page 174: Opening of Parliament, Melbourne (detail), engraved by C. Nuttal; page 176; page 180; page 180: *Bulletin*, 2 Ap. 1908; page 180; page 181; page 183; page 187: Melbourne *Punch*, 10 July 1919; page 189: *Australian*, 20 Sept. 1919; page 192; page 194; page 194; page 195; page 197; page 198; page 200; page 200; page 201; page 202; page 202; page 203; page 210; page 210; page 213; page 220; page 225; page 227; page 227; page 231 (top left); page 231 (bottom left); page 231; page 239; page 243; page 249: Parramatta River with a distant view of the western mountains, taken from Windmill Hill, Sydney, by E. Dayes (after a painting by T. Watling), watercolour; page 250: Part of Main Road 1859 [Ballarat], by F. Cógne, coloured lithograph, RNK.
Reno Simeoni Page 232.

State Library of Victoria Page 54: E. Delessert, *Voyages dans les deux Oceans*, Paris, 1848; and page 76 (top): Capt Lonsdale's house, by W. F. E. Liardet, watercolour.

INDEX